RECCE

RECCE

SMALL TEAM MISSIONS
BEHIND ENEMY LINES

KOOS STADLER

CASEMATE
Oxford & Philadelphia

Published in Great Britain and
the United States of America in 2016 by
CASEMATE PUBLISHERS
10 Hythe Bridge Street, Oxford OX1 2EW, UK
and

1950 Lawrence Road, Havertown, PA 19083, USA

© Koos Stadler 2015
Published by agreement with NB Publishers, a division of Media24 Boeke
(Pty) Ltd. Originally published by Tafelberg, an imprint of NB Publishers,
Cape Town, South Africa in 2015

Hardback Edition: 978-161200-404-4

A CIP record for this book is available from the British Library

Printed in the United Kingdom by TJ International Ltd

For a complete list of Casemate titles, please contact:

CASEMATE PUBLISHERS (UK)
Telephone (01865) 241249
Fax (01865) 794449
Email: casemate-uk@casematepublishers.co.uk
www.casematepublishers.co.uk

CASEMATE PUBLISHERS (US)
Telephone (610) 853-9131
Fax (610) 853-9146
Email: casemate@casematepublishing.com
www.casematepublishing.com

Dedicated to my father, Koos,
who kindled the spirit of adventure in me,
and my dearest wife, Karien,
who had no option but to scale every cliff with me.

Contents

I HAVE WRITTEN this book to share something of the world I lived in for more than ten years of my twenty-four-year Special Forces career – the little-known world of the Small Team operator. For those ten years I specialised in reconnaissance. I breathed, ate and slept reconnaissance. The experience I gained with the recce wing of 31 Battalion from November 1978 to December 1981 shaped my character and prepared me for life at 5 Reconnaissance Regiment, where I served as a Small Team operator from 1984 to 1989. My subsequent career, both in Special Forces and beyond, was based on the strict code of conduct and principles embedded during that period.

Over the years, the art of reconnaissance became a passion. After being exposed to the intricacies of tactical reconnaissance at 31 Battalion's recce wing in the Caprivi, I did Special Forces selection and finally fulfilled my dream of joining Small Teams, the strategic reconnaissance capability of the then Reconnaissance Regiments, commonly known as the Recces. There are many misconceptions – and often crazy, fabricated stories – out there about Special Forces. Few people perhaps know that there were different Recce units, each with a dedicated field of specialisation. Even fewer people are aware of the existence of the highly specialised Small Teams and the extraordinary role they played in the Border War (1966–1989).

This book was written over more than two decades. To paint as accurate a picture as possible, I had to rely on notes made over the years, on my memory, on the recollections of my colleagues and on limited documentation. By telling my story I hope to shed some light on the concept as well as the capabilities of the specialist reconnaissance teams of the South African Special Forces. However, I do not attempt to provide a comprehensive history of Small Teams or a detailed account of the stages through which the capability developed.

Since this is a personal account, I can only credit those individuals with whom I deployed. While it isn't possible to mention the names of all the operators who formed part of the specialist reconnaissance fraternity, I wish to acknowledge the pioneers of Small Teams in South Africa, individuals like Koos Moorcroft, Jack Greeff, Tony Vieira and Sam Fourie, and operators like Homen de Gouveia and Justin Vermaak, who did excellent work while with 1 Reconnaissance Regiment. If I omit from my story the names of Special Forces operators who participated in reconnaissance missions during their careers, it is simply because I did not have the privilege of working with them.

More importantly, since there has always been some rivalry between Small Teams and the regular Special Forces commandos, I wish to state that I never doubted their abilities. Neither do I dispute their superior fighting skills nor their excellence in combat. On the contrary, I have been impressed by the level of professionalism of numerous Special Forces soldiers.

Finally, I am happy to share the joys and sorrows I experienced with my comrades, and I proudly recall the unique code of conduct that we lived by, as well as the close bond and mutual respect we shared in both 31 Battalion's recce wing and 54 Commando.

KOOS STADLER

PART I

Courage and Action

"We fear naught but God"

motto of 5 Reconnaissance Regiment,
from the unit's Code of Honour

LIST OF ABBREVIATIONS

ALO	air liaison officer
CO	candidate officer
CSI	Chief of Staff Intelligence
DR	dead reckoning
DZ	drop zone
E&E	escape and evasion
ECCM	electronic counter-counter-measures
ECM	electronic counter-measures
EMLC	electrical, mechanical, agricultural and chemical engineering consultants
FAPLA	Forças Armadas Populares de Libertação Angola (People's Armed Forces for the Liberation of Angola)
FNLA	Frente Nacional de Libertação Angola (National Front for the Liberation of Angola)
HAG	helicopter administrative area
HF	high frequency
LP	listening post
LZ	landing zone
MK	Umkhonto we Sizwe
MPLA	Movimento Popular de Libertação de Angola (Popular Movement for the Liberation of Angola0
NCO	non-commissioned officer
OAU	Organization of African Unity
OC	officer commanding
OP	observation post
PLAN	People's Liberation Army of Namibia
PT	physical training
RPG	rocket-propelled grenade
RSM	regimental sergeant major
RV	rendezvous
SADF	South African Defence Force
SAM	surface-to-air missile
SOPs	standard operating procedures
SWAPO	South West Africa People's Organisation
TB	temporary base
UN	United Nations
UNITA	União Nacional para a Independência Total de Angola (Union for the Total Independence of Angola)
UNTAG	United Nations Transition Assistance Group
VHF	very high frequency
ZNDF	Zambia National Defence Force

1

Target

SILENTLY and with slow, deliberate movements, I slide my pack off. I reach for the first charge and a set of glue tubes. With practised fingers I undo the straps of the pouches and arrange the rest of the charges so I can reach them easily. I feel strangely calm and ready for the task at hand.

The fear I used to experience is absent. Instead, sheer determination has taken over. Deep inside I know that I am well prepared to get the job done and that the stakes are too high for me to fail.

I slip the pack back on and drape my AMD rifle[1] in a fireman's sling down the centre of my back to allow freedom of movement. Then I start the stalk towards the MiG-21 fighter jet, silenced pistol cocked and ready in the right hand, charge in the left and night-vision goggles on my chest.

Ten metres from the aircraft, I stop to observe with the night-vision goggles. The darkness of the night is absolute, as we hoped, but it also means that I cannot see below the fuselage of the aircraft. Not even with the beam of the

infrared torch can my goggles penetrate the complete blackness under the belly of the huge aircraft crouched on the
tarmac.

The night is dead silent. There is no sound from beneath the
plane, nor can I make out any shape under the belly. I realise
I need to go low to observe better. Slowly and stealthily I
ease forward to move into the blackness under the fuselage
so I can look up against the ambient light of the sky. I crouch
to move in under the wing.

Then suddenly, without warning, a voice pierces the
silence of the night from the darkness underneath the plane.
My worst fear has just come true.

"Who are you . . .?"

The voice is hesitant, restrained by fear. Then stronger,
more demanding:

"*Who* are you?"

The all-too-familiar cocking of a Kalashnikov shatters
the fragile night air. Barely three metres away, it cracks
invisibly like a rifle shot in the quiet night.

For many years of my adult life I lived in a small world, a
world where two people operated in a hostile environment
that in a split second could erupt in violence – a world of perpetual vigilance. Sometimes we were hundreds of
kilometres into enemy territory, miles away from the comforts of suburban life and the reassuring presence of other
people. It was a realm far removed from the normal world,

one filled with nagging fear and uncertainty, with hunger and thirst.

Then there was the silence. For long stretches of time I would work in absolute quiet, while communication with my single team member was limited to hand signals or the occasional whisper.

This was the world of the specialist reconnaissance teams, or Small Teams.

For most of my adult life I have been a soldier. Looking back today, I realise I was destined to join the South African Special Forces, or Recces, as they were commonly known, and eventually to become a member of the elite Small Teams. From my early childhood, stalking small game in the dunes of the Kalahari, to my first taste of tactical reconnaissance during a three-year stint at the reconnaissance wing of 31 Battalion (a Bushman unit in the Caprivi), I knew that reconnaissance was what I really wanted to do.

During those three years I spent most of my time on tactical reconnaissance missions behind enemy lines in the southern parts of Zambia and Angola, patrolling for enemy presence and stalking guerrilla bases, honing my skills until they became second nature. Then I did Special Forces selection and fulfilled a lifelong dream: to become part of this elite group. However, this was not my ultimate destination. For a year I battled with the authorities to let me join the specialist reconnaissance teams, at that time stationed at 5 Reconnaissance Regiment at Phalaborwa. Finally, even the system could not hold me back any longer and I walked through 5 Recce's gates to join Small Teams.

Yet, despite the Honoris Crux on my chest and a whole stack of certificates and commendations, I have been the antithesis of the Special Forces hero. I have been scared – to death. I have had to run away from life-threatening situations more times than I can remember, and certainly more than I would care to acknowledge. At one point, running away became my full-time hobby. I excelled at it. But, with God's grace, I have never shown my fear, and have always crawled back, often in a literal sense, to complete my mission.

2

Boy Adventurer

I WAS BORN in Upington as the son of a teacher but then became the son of a preacher. At the age of 44 my father enrolled for a seven-year Theology degree at Stellenbosch University and became a minister in the Dutch Reformed Church. My twin sister and I, the youngest of six children, were still very young when our family temporarily relocated to Stellenbosch.

I had a fantastic, joyous youth for which I mostly have my parents to thank. Both of them left immeasurable and unforgettable impressions. At heart my dad was a hunter and adventurer. Although I easily call up a picture of him in the pulpit wearing his *toga*, the cassock worn by Dutch Reformed ministers in those days, I will always remember him as a man of the bush.

He had an intimate love and passion for the southern African veld, particularly the Kalahari (or Kgalagadi), and had a keen interest in its fauna and flora. He loved the outdoors and was a hunter of the old school. He despised hunting from vehicles, which became popular in the Kalahari in those days, and would sit for hours in the shade of an n'xoi bush, patiently outwaiting and outwitting the game. And he loved his God. Often I stumbled across him earnestly praying behind a bush in the veld.

My mom was a beautiful, soft-spoken and very loyal minister's wife. In her quiet way she was the bedrock of our family life, providing inspiration to my dad, routine and discipline to her children and solace to everyone even faintly in need of support. I owe to her my aversion to large groups of people and rowdy parties, and I have her to thank for giving me the specific temperament required of a Small Teams operator.

As a boy I used to go with my dad, then minister of the Dutch Reformed congregation at Ariamsvlei in South West Africa (now Namibia) to prayer meetings on the farms. These trips always brought excitement. Often we'd go hunting or camping on one of the farms, and invariably there would be something challenging to make the trip memorable. Once, while driving the International – the eight-cylinder pick-up provided by the congregation – in the rugged area north of the Orange River in South West Africa, the vehicle broke down on a deserted farm road high up in the rocky hills. A prayer meeting on the farm was about to commence and there was no way for our hosts to know that we were stuck.

As my mother and sister were also present, there was only one option: I had to travel the remaining distance on foot, while my dad stayed with them at the vehicle. He explained the route to me: it was a short-cut through the hills and valleys. Then he sent me off, with a reminder to conserve my precious water and maintain my direction with the help of the sun.

After walking for four hours I found the farmhouse. A vehicle was dispatched and the farmers from the surrounding farms quickly put together a salvage team and had the International back at the farmhouse in a matter of hours. I was tired but happy, because I knew it would earn me some respect among the farm boys of the community.

The year was 1972 and I was twelve years old.

Those years at Ariamsvlei offered everything and more a young boy could hope for. We ventured out to the farms bordering the town, swimming in the cement dams and stalking small game. I learned to shoot at an early age and almost every day I used to walk around with my pellet gun, hunting pigeons or shooting at targets. Life was bliss.

In many respects my upbringing was strict, but it taught me valuable lessons. Late one evening, the local police sergeant knocked on the door of the parsonage. Two young men from the community had been in a head-on collision on a secondary road not far from town. It turned out that one of them had overtaken a truck without seeing the oncoming vehicle in the dust column. When my parents arrived at the scene in the International, both men were dying, trapped in their vehicles, but there was time to pray for them.

The community was shocked by the news that two of their promising sons had lost their lives. One young man was buried on his parents' farm, while the other was to be buried in the local cemetery a few kilometres out of town. Whether my dad felt that we as a family had to display our sympathy by preparing the gravesite, or whether he deliberately wanted to teach me a lesson, I could never figure out, but digging the grave became my responsibility. I did not object, since subconsciously I probably shared my dad's sentiments and, in any event, I loved the challenge of physical exertion. Armed with pick, shovel and a bottle of water, I was dropped off by my dad. After instructing me on the location and the measurements of the grave, he left.

Within an hour or two my hands were blistered and the grave was barely two feet deep. The rocky earth and the blazing sun of arid South West Africa had taken their toll. Dad arrived with more water and some of my mom's home-made ginger beer. After seeing my hands he left to fetch some Ballistol, a gun oil that was used as an ointment for just about anything. The Ballistol turned everything into a slippery mess – not only the blisters and boils on my hands but also the pick, the shovel and my face as I tried to wipe off the sweat.

That night every muscle in my body ached. I was sunburnt red like a tomato. My hands were a mess. I was dead tired, but determined to go the full six feet the next day. However, my swollen and blistered hands wouldn't let me touch a breakfast spoon in the morning, let alone a shovel. Mom objected to me doing any further digging, threatening Dad with all kinds of punishment if he dared take me to the gravesite again. But once she realised that I had no intention of giving up, she wrapped my hands in bandages and covered them with a pair of gloves. Out at the gravesite I managed another few hours of digging. By that afternoon I was at four feet, but then my hands wouldn't grip any more.

But I simply had to finish, since the funeral was in two days' time. I decided to take one tiny patch at a time and go the full depth, then move on to the next, steadily working to dig the rest of the grave piece by piece.

This experience taught me that where I had a clear and worthy goal, I needed to apply every ounce of energy to reach it, regardless of the cost. My father arrived that afternoon with a seasoned labourer, who dug the remaining two feet in less than two hours. But that didn't bother me. I knew that, given time, I would have managed it. My sore body and blistered hands were a kind of reward – and a silent tribute to the two guys who had died.

In 1973 my twin sister and I were sent to boarding school in Upington to start high school. As the only minister's son among the farm boys from the Kalahari I was an easy target and soon baptised *Dominee* (reverend), or sometimes even called *Dissipel* (disciple) or *Priester* (priest). But I also made good friends and survived fairly easily.

Long weekends and holidays were spent with my folks in South West Africa. Having turned fifteen in March 1974, I would take up my favourite pursuit of stalking small game in the veld, roaming my old haunts outside Ariamsvlei and often hunting with my dad during hunting season. I also started hiking long distances with a crude backpack on the dirt roads leading from the farms, often sleeping over at the houses of my parents' friends.

The year 1974 also saw change coming to our otherwise quiet town. Large convoys of military vehicles would pass through, often stopping over to refuel or to overnight on the large square next to the BSB (Boere Saamwerk Beperk), the cooperative serving the district's stock farmers.

Scores of army trucks and armoured cars would be parked in long queues along the square, while hundreds of troops would all of a sudden be walking about, playing ball next to their encampment or just hanging around and chatting with the few curious locals.

I soon learned that there was a war on in Ovamboland along the northern border of South West Africa. Since 1966 insurgents from the South West Africa People's Organisation (SWAPO) had been infiltrating from neighbouring Angola into the farming areas, killing civilians on the farms and planting landmines on the roads in the northern border areas in their bid for an independent Namibia.

In 1974 the South African Defence Force (SADF) took over the responsibility from the South African Police for guarding the 1 680-km border between South West Africa and its northern neighbours, Angola and Zambia. Although I didn't take note of it then, in June of that year 22-year-old Lieutenant Fred Zeelie became the first South African soldier to be killed in the Border War. Zeelie was also the first Special Forces soldier to lose his life in the war.

What I also did not know in 1974 was that a massive – and eventually long drawn-out – civil war was looming in Angola. In April of that year, following the so-called Carnation Revolution in Lisbon, Portugal indicated its intention to give up its colonial rule of the country. The three main Angolan liberation movements – Holden Roberto's FNLA, Jonas Savimbi's UNITA and the Marxist MPLA of Dr Agostinho Neto – started competing for control. Fighting broke out in November 1974, starting in the capital city, Luanda, and spreading to the rest of the country.

Angola was soon divided between the three groups. The FNLA occupied northern Angola and UNITA the central south, while the MPLA mostly occupied the coastline, the far southeast and, after capturing it in November, the oil-rich enclave of Cabinda. Negotiations between the parties and the colonial power led to the signing of the Alvor Agreement on 15 January 1975, naming the date for independence as 11 November 1975 and setting up a transitional government. The agreement ended the war for independence but marked the escalation of the civil war. Fighting between the three liberation forces resumed in Luanda hardly a day after the transitional government took office. The coalition established by the Alvor Agreement soon came to an end.

I became aware of these events only when convoys of white Portuguese-speaking refugees started passing through Upington, their cars loaded to capacity with all their worldly belongings. The MPLA, backed by the Soviet Union and Fidel Castro's Cuba, gained control of Luanda on 9 July 1975. Many white Portuguese, having supported the colonial regime, felt threatened and fled the country in great haste, leaving most of their possessions behind. I also could not have known then that within a few years I would be taking part in the Border War, fighting shoulder to shoulder with many ex-Angolans.

In late 1975 the SADF launched Operation Savannah, a large-scale offensive deep into Angola. The operation was initiated in secret on 14 October, when Task Force Zulu, the first of several SADF columns, crossed from South West Africa into Cuando Cubango province. The operation was aimed at eliminating the MPLA in the southern border area, then in southwestern Angola, moving up into the central regions, and finally capturing Luanda.

With the Angolan liberation forces busy fighting each other, the SADF advanced rapidly. Task Force Foxbat joined the invasion in mid-October. The territory the MPLA had gained in the south was quickly lost to the South African advances. In early October South African advisors and anti-tank weapons helped to stop an MPLA advance on Nova Lisboa (later Huambo). Task Force Zulu captured Villa Roçadas (later Xangongo) then Sa da Bandeira (Lubango) and finally Moçamedes (Namibe) before the end of October.

The South African advance was halted just short of Luanda, and the forces started withdrawing late in January 1976. Many reasons were given for the termination of the operation, but in essence South Africa at that time stood alone in its quest to oppose communist expansionism in southern Africa. Moderate African countries like Zambia and Côte d'Ivoire, which had originally requested South Africa to intervene, could not provide any assistance themselves.

Western countries like the United States (US) and France had promised support but never committed. US support of both the FNLA and UNITA was sporadic and inconsistent, and finally came to an end at the critical moment when South Africa was poised to take Luanda. Neither UNITA nor the FNLA was politically strong enough to sustain a take-over of Luanda.[2]

3

The Seed is Sown

DESPITE the new visitors to our town, the Border War was not at the top of my mind. I was fighting another war – my own battle for survival at boarding school, where things had become rather challenging for me.

I became a prefect at the too young age of sixteen, when I was in standard 9 (grade 11). As the only school prefect residing in the boys' boarding house, I often had to stand my ground against the toughest of the district.

Surrounding the front yard of the boys' hostel were lush green mulberry trees that bore juicy fruit in summer, naturally serving as a welcome supplement to the monotony of hostel food. However, the mulberries also held an attraction for the coloured boys of the neighbourhood, mostly the kids of maids working in our whites-only suburbs. For a number of junior boys in the hostel it became a pastime to ambush the coloured boys, isolate one or two of them, and then beat them to a pulp.

Soon the coloured kids, realising the dangers of picking fruit from the trees, started taking only the ripe fruit that had fallen to the ground, thinking this would be seen as a lesser transgression. But to the hostel boys the fruit was "theirs", whether it was still on the tree or lying on the ground, so the practice endured. At the same time, a group of senior boys would sit on the steps in front of the main entrance and direct the youngsters, shouting encouragement once the boys had launched an attack.

I didn't think much of it until one day when I was passing the outer perimeter on my way from the shop. A young coloured boy was lying on the ground, sobbing and bleeding from the face, and unable to get up. A number of his attackers were still hanging around, shouting abuse at him and telling him to clear off. On the steps in front of the building a number of seniors were watching the show, shouting an occasional encouragement.

I walked over to the boy and helped him up, and then tried to wipe the blood from his face with my handkerchief. But he was too frightened and shied away, protecting his face with his arms. Eventually he limped off.

Turning back to the hostel, I faced the group of attackers. There was defiance in their gaze; how could I betray them by caring for their prey? I chastened them for abusing one small boy while they were many. I ordered them to go back to the hostel and made my way to the entrance where the spectators were still sitting. As I walked past them, they cursed me under their breaths for befriending their enemy. No one challenged me openly, but from then on I had to deal with being called all sorts of names behind my back.

From ensuing discussions about the attacks on the coloured boys, I realised the majority of the boys in the hostel did not support the wilful abuse, but neither did they challenge the hardliners on the issue. For a small minority the abuse was just "innocent fun".

During that time I also had an unfortunate run-in with one of the resident teachers. He was the staff member on duty one Monday morning when I reported that two guys had laid their hands on some alcohol and got terribly drunk over the weekend. The two culprits were serial offenders, and everyone in the boarding house was aware of their antics.

Later he called me in and confronted me in the presence of the two perpetrators. He said that if I declared there and then that the two pupils had been drunk, he would expel them immediately. The catch was that I knew both boys' parents were personal friends of the teacher, and that there was no way this kind of harsh action would be taken against them based only on my word.

I left the office biting my lip, after the teacher had forced me to admit that I had made it all up. After that, a number of guys had it in for me, and the teacher — who taught agriculture — was watching me for anything that went faintly wrong at the hostel. On top of that, some hostel kids started calling me "Dropper", for "dropping" the two innocent drinkers in their time of trouble.

By the end of my third year at boarding school my dad accepted a call to become a minister of the Dutch Reformed Church in Africa, the black arm of our denomination in Upington. Although we lived in a white suburb, my father's church was in Paballelo, the mainly black township outside town, from where he would serve both the black and coloured congregations. I was rather relieved to leave boarding school and move back in with my folks.

I took every opportunity to accompany my dad to church services and meetings, and so got to know the coloured and black communities around town rather well. At the time the political situation in South Africa was highly volatile and any kind of mixing between the different race groups was unthinkable. This kind of exposure to people of other races was uncommon for most children my age.

It was expected that I would pay the same respects to the *moruti*, the African minister and my father's colleague at the church, as to any white minister who visited our home. The principal of Paballelo High School, a Mr Xaba, was an elder in the church and a personal friend of my father's. The black people I met as a teenager, those I learned to love and respect, were no less intelligent, human or sincere than any white person. In retrospect, I realise that this experience played a major role in shaping my outlook, and especially my attitude when dealing with individuals and colleagues from other races, later in my life.

At school the teachers must have realised early on that I was not a rocket scientist in the making. Neither was I a superhero on the sports field. Since I had less ball sense than a farm gate in the Kalahari, I was no good at cricket or rugby (although there were a few flashes of brilliance on the rugby field, provided I did not have to touch the ball). But in due course I discovered my forte. On the longer distances I could outrun anyone in the district. At the age of seventeen I did the 80-km Karoo marathon in 7 hours 19 minutes and 48 seconds, a record time for my age group, and it made me a hero at school.

It was in a school classroom that I would learn about the Recces for the first time. I guess it was a matter of fate that I found myself standing in the agriculture class one morning early in 1976. Agriculture was not one of my subjects, and it was also taught by my least favourite teacher – the one who was a resident at the hostel and had it in for me. I had gone to fetch a book from one of my mates, who was in the class, and came upon a group of boys listening intently as Piet Paxton, a fellow pupil, told them about the Recces, the elite of the country's armed forces. Piet explained how they were selected and then trained to operate on land, from the air and at sea. I was transfixed. I often wonder whether, subconsciously, I did not already make up my mind that day to become a Recce.

In the mid-1970s the military conscription period in South Africa was increased from one to two years, mostly as a result of the intensifying Border War and the subsequent demand for troops in the operational area. Every white male would be called up for service and I was no exception.

On 2 January 1978 I boarded the troop train at Upington station and bade my family goodbye. My destination was the 4th South African Infantry Battalion (4 SAI) at Middelburg. A new adventure had begun.

In those days a standard joke was that the boys from Upington joined the Army to sport long hair and boots. For me, basic training was a complete culture shock. I could never have imagined having so many English-speaking guys in my platoon. The swearing and cursing were unbearable and I could scarcely believe the explicit pictures and graffiti behind the toilet doors. Drinking was totally foreign to me.

But boy, was I fit! And I could shoot. Out in the veld I turned out to be a natural. Soon I could not bear the insubordination of some of the conscripts or their lack of commitment to our training. Deep inside me this thing started growing – the urge to rise above the normal ill-discipline, no-care attitude and incompetence of the average conscript.

The prospect of becoming an officer was tempting. One weekend during my basics at Middelburg, I had to clean the officers' mess of the unit as part of extra duties. I was astonished; people merely a year older than me had all this luxury! They were served by waiters and treated like kings! In those years, junior leaders were selected during their first year of national service to do the junior leader's course at the Infantry School and became corporals or lieutenants; they would then be sent to infantry units as platoon and section leaders during their second year of service.

In March 1978 I was transferred to the Infantry School in the town of Oudtshoorn. I was a shy and somewhat bewildered nineteen-year-old. The Infantry School was not easy, but I thoroughly enjoyed the training, especially when our platoon lived out in the veld and the instructors seemed to soften their approach slightly. The crisp, ice-cold mornings in winter, with the snow thick on the Swartberg, brought out the best in everyone, and our platoon soon shaped up to be a close-knit bunch.

During that year at Oudtshoorn I learned a lot about myself, especially about my own strengths and weaknesses. I realised that, compared with most of the young servicemen around me, I started functioning well once the pressure was on and the going got really tough. I learned to keep my mouth shut and laugh inwardly at the way the instructors created artificial pressure to test us.

Towards the end of the year, the time came for the dreaded Vasbyt 5, a route march and series of tests through the Swartberg mountain range over a five-day period. It was designed to test our endurance and was quite tough. The second evening of the exercise, the whole company got together and established a temporary base (TB) in a pine forest, the purpose of which was to show us a new recruiting film for the Recces, entitled *Durf en Daad* (Courage and Action). I was hooked. That night it became my ultimate, and this time expressed, goal to be a Recce.

On the evening of day three, as we topped a rise high up in the mountains, it started snowing. The instructors panicked, because we did not have the gear for surviving subzero temperatures at night, so they called all the platoons together and moved us by truck down into Die Hel, a remote and secluded valley in the Swartberg range.

Everyone was fairly drained on the last day of the march. No one wanted to carry the Bren (machine gun) and the high-frequency (HF) radio any more. At one of the rest breaks that last evening, the guy who had been carrying the Bren just left it lying, not bothering to hand it over to anyone. A strapping farm boy in my section just looked at me, picked up the radio he had been carrying, and said, "Tough shit, Jakes, jy wil mos Recces toe gaan [Tough shit, Jakes, you're the one wanting to join the Recces]," and started slogging on.

Between the two of us we carried the Bren and the radio throughout that night to the final destination, a farmhouse in a beautiful valley deep in the mountains. Late in the night, as we walked in the darkness under a lane of trees, the smell of fresh oranges suddenly filled the air. As I reached up, my fingers touched the fruit. Without even taking our kit off, we picked some of the oranges, which turned out to be ripe, and ate them – peel and all – as we continued on our way. The fruit invigorated us and we finished the last few kilometres refreshed and in good spirits. A few years later, under vastly different circumstances, I would have a similar experience during an extremely sensitive Small Team operation near the town of Lubango in Angola.

When the different Army units started recruiting among the junior leader candidates at Oudtshoorn in October of 1978, I carefully considered my options. I was told outright by my colleagues that joining the Recces was not an option. They were the real killing machines – professional soldiers who had a different attitude to life. Back then I was skinny, with a pimpled baby-face, and looked much younger than I was. I wouldn't fit, they told me.

A wonderful opportunity, which turned out to be my greatest break in life, presented itself when a recruitment team from 31 Battalion, a Bushman unit based in the Western Caprivi, visited the Infantry School. The unit also happened to have a very successful reconnaissance wing that was responsible for tactical reconnaissance in small groups, while the regular companies would deploy in the offensive search-and-destroy mode.

Frannie du Toit, the fierce-looking lieutenant from the recruiting team, made up my mind for me when he said that I would have it all in one – reconnaissance operations with the Bushmen and living right there in the Caprivi bush. The next three years at 31 Battalion would be the finest time of my career.

While the operations might have been of a tactical nature and not conducted at the professional level I later got to know as a Special Forces operator, that period was formative in many respects. I had to dodge some bullets, and I saw death for the first time. I saw people not capable of handling the pressures of combat, but I also met many who were. I worked with a number of outstanding soldiers who made a lasting impression on me. And, most importantly, I was exposed to numerous missions and, albeit by trial and error, developed a unique concept for conducting reconnaissance operations.

PART 2
The Bushmen

"You can do anything with enthusiasm. Enthusiasm is the sparkle in your eyes, the swing in your gait. It is the grip of your hand, the irresistible surge of your will, the energy to execute your ideas. Enthusiasts are fighters. They have fortitude. They have staying qualities. Enthusiasm is at the bottom of all progress. With it there is accomplishment. Without it there are only alibis . . ."

– Henry Ford (1863-1947)

Operational area

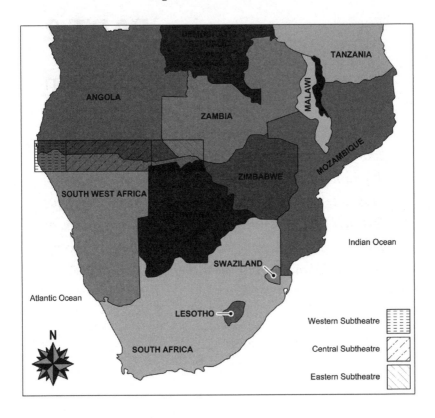

1

Into the Unknown

IN NOVEMBER 1978 a C-130 military transport aircraft carried two groups of adventurous youngsters to the theatre of war. One group had volunteered for 32 Battalion, a unit of ex-FNLA soldiers founded by Colonel Jan Breytenbach and moulded into an all-black South African combat unit; and then there was my group, which was headed for 31 Battalion at the military town of Omega in the Caprivi.

Led by white officers and a mix of white and Bushman non-commissioned officers (NCOs), 31 Battalion had been formed by Colonel Delville Linford, one of those rare characters who did things in an utterly unorthodox style – and got away with it. Although I never met him, since he had already left the unit when I arrived, his photos were everywhere and his influence was still tangible.

We were a mixed group of candidate officers (COs) and lance corporals fresh from the Infantry School. Upon arrival at Rundu we boarded a Kwêvoël (a 10-ton truck with a mine-protected cab) for the journey to Omega. It turned out to be an unforgettable experience. Everyone was somewhat scared of what lay ahead. We sat on top of our kit and watched the bush rushing past. Piled up against the cab were bags of maize. From the rush of air a fine maize dust constantly sifted down on us. Suddenly a thunderstorm broke – typical summer weather in the Caprivi, as we were soon to discover during operations in the bush. But it was not long before the sun broke through the clouds and our clothes started to dry on our bodies – with the maize still sticking to our clothes and faces. We were delivered to Omega as a Kwêvoël-load of freshly baked bread – walking rather stiffly and smelling like a bakery!

Captain Frans "Gor-Gor" Gunther introduced us to 31 Battalion and put us through a brief initiation. He was an impressive character with an overpowering personality and an equally dominating moustache. Rumour had it that the sides of his moustache would droop if he was in a bad mood but stand out firmly if he was happy with your performance. I had the good fortune never to see the great moustache drooping. Over the next three years I would have the pleasure of deploying with my recce team along with Frans Gunther's C Company.

After the weeklong introduction to the base, candidates for the reconnaissance wing were separated from those who would join the regular companies. While the latter attended an induction course to learn how to handle their Bushman platoons in counterinsurgency warfare, eighteen of us went on selection for the recce wing.

In the mid-1970s the need for a tactical reconnaissance capability led to the formation of reconnaissance platoons at the infantry units permanently based in the operational area of the Border War. At the time, 31 and 32 battalions were the first to deploy tactical recce teams into Zambia and Angola, with the aim of locating SWAPO bases situated across the border in what were believed by SWAPO to be "safe" areas.

Initially, the tactical recce wings were trained in minor tactics by instructors from the Reconnaissance Regiments, and conducted recce missions in the tactical sphere of operations, many of them prior to attacks or raids against enemy bases and infrastructure. Over a ten-year period, roughly from 1976 to 1986, the reconnaissance wings took a lot of weight off the Reconnaissance Commandos by conducting special operations for sectors 10, 20 and 70 in the operational area.[3] This allowed Special Forces the freedom to operate in the strategic environment.

Although there was never a clear-cut distinction between tactical and strategic deployments, it was generally accepted that the tactical recce wings would operate in the direct areas of responsibility of the sectoral commands, at the time stretching as far as 60 km into Angola and Zambia. Yet there were numerous exceptions to this general rule. Many Special Forces missions were in fact conducted in what was considered the tactical sphere, as was the case with pseudo-guerrilla operations carried out by 51 Reconnaissance Commando on both sides of the South West Africa–Angola border.

Textbook definitions of the time described strategic reconnaissance as operations in which a team operated independently, with no direct support from air or land resources. The information gained from the mission would also not automatically lead to a follow-up action by own forces, but would have an effect on the strategic outcome of the war. Tactical reconnaissance missions were, however, seen to be conducted in the tactical sphere of operations, within range of air- or land-based support, while the outcome would always be an immediate action by own forces.

The modus operandi of the tactical reconnaissance platoons varied from unit to unit. A recce patrol leading the advance in front of a fighting force would often be armed and ready for combat, thus a sizable number of four or six operators would be the order of the day. For a recce on a SWAPO base, a patrol would consist of no more than four men. This number was reduced to two if penetration of the facility was required. Often, even in the early days, the sparse undergrowth and the nature of the terrain would preclude the use of bigger teams, so by the late 1970s the concept of small teams had already been tentatively applied by the tactical recce wings.

The selection for the recce wing turned out to be the toughest experience of my life so far. Selection started with a week's PT course at the base, from 05:00 in the morning until late at night. The idea of the PT sessions was supposedly to get us fit and ready for the bush phase, but it just managed to make us dog-tired, as we were still adjusting to the hot and humid weather of the Caprivi. Then we were taken out into the bush for the real selection, which turned out to be a never-ending slog through the bush, naturally with full kit, from one rendezvous (RV) to the next. At each RV, the instructors would meet us with a new little surprise, either a stiff PT session in the sand or leopard-crawling for what felt like miles. Then we would be given a new compass bearing to the next RV some impossible distance away, where they would meet us the following day.

For the first leg of our adventure we were given a grid reference on the Angolan cutline – the border between the Caprivi and Angola – to be reached by the next morning. Carrying packs weighing in the order of 30 kg, we walked through the night and were in time for a PT session right there in the Caprivi sand on the Angolan border. At 09:00 we got our next RV – another grid reference approximately 30 km further east down the Caprivi Strip. We had to report there by the following morning at 08:00, which I thought was impossible, given the thick vegetation and the state we were in.

Once they had given us our orders, the instructors departed. We had no food, and only the water left in our packs. Just us and the endless savanna of the Caprivi. Fortunately the bush was lush and green after the splendid summer rains. There was water in abundance in the omurambas (open stretches of grass-covered plain, generally running parallel between the dunes). I decided that there was no better time to cover the next leg than now. The less we needed to walk during the night, the better.

Easier said than done, as there and then I was confronted with a situation I regard as my first real test of wills with another adult. A fellow candidate officer, a character I did not have much time for, took the role of leader upon himself and declared that we would rest over the heat of the day and start that afternoon at 15:00, giving us enough time, he reckoned, to cover the 30 km before 08:00 the next morning. We argued. Everyone was tired and he won the day.

I decided that they could rest; I was leaving. Quietly, I turned around, put my pack on, found my bearing on the compass and started moving out. Only one other guy realised the stupidity of the group's decision to wait out the day while being on recce wing selection. He shouted, "CO, wait, I'm coming with you", shouldered his pack and fell in behind me.

For the two of us the experience turned out to be an excellent introduction to the realities of the bush. We encountered lots of elephant and other game. We soon learned where to find water in the omurambas, and how to avoid the elephant herds by circling downwind, and also how to watch each other's back.

Once, while filling our water bottles at a water hole, we had a seriously close shave with an elephant bull. My buddy was sitting opposite me at the water's edge, watching my back from the other side of the water hole, when I suddenly saw an elephant emerging from the brush right behind him. I didn't even have time to shout. But he saw my frightened face and jumped. At that point the elephant still hadn't seen him. His startled shout and quick reaction probably saved his life, as the elephant got as much of a fright as he did and charged away into the bush.

In the end, we were well in time for the RV. The rest of the selection group was found a day later, after they had started discharging flares and generally making themselves noticed by firing into the air. They had run out of water on the first day and got lost, as they did not keep count of the minor cutlines they had to cross during the night. To give them a reasonable chance (as the instructors did not really know what had happened), they were put back on the course. They were moved by vehicle to an RV further along the route the selection course would cover, and in the process did a much shorter selection than us.

The selection continued for another week. I lost count of the days and of how many candidates were left. To this day I do not know what distance we covered during the course. I also did not care how many guys properly passed the selection, because, as it soon turned out, after our selection and the Minor Tactics course, the first operational deployment sorted out the ones that were not cut out for the job.

I learned two critically important things during that week. The first was something I had already started to understand the day I had to dig the grave in the cemetery outside Ariams-vlei: never even think of giving up, because then you will. The second was: do what you believe is right, without compromise, and never blindly follow the crowd. These truths became my guiding principles during my Special Forces operational career.

I did three selection courses in my life: the first at 31 Battalion, the second at the Parachute Battalion – the infamous PT (physical training) course – and finally the Special Forces selection course. Looking back, I can honestly say that the first one was the toughest, by far. I can also declare that never on one of them did I even consider quitting. And I also know that, in a certain sense, there was an element of fun to all of them.

After a week of fattening up at Omega, our training started in earnest. During our recuperation week, we were issued with "special ops" kit – old alpine rucksacks, SWAPO webbing and an assortment of foreign weapons – AK-47s, RPDs, RPGs and some Eastern Bloc pistols.

The Monday morning after the rest week, we reported to the recce wing HQ and loaded our kit on the Unimog trucks lined up on the road. We drove out to Fort Vreeslik (Fort Terrible), the recce wing's training base hidden in the lush Caprivi bush some fourteen kilometres south of Omega. Three highly experienced and tough-looking instructors from the (then) Reconnaissance Commandos had arrived from Fort Doppies, the Special Forces training base on the banks of the Kwando River (Cuando in Angola), to present our Minor Tactics training.

The training turned out to be an experience in itself. I had always marvelled at the term "tactics", unsure of what it really meant, and what people could actually teach me about tactics. The course leader and his two instructors finally enlightened me. For four weeks we were drilled in the finer techniques of patrolling, anti-tracking, approaching and penetrating a target, contact drills, ambushing, evasion and reconnaissance. Finally, a week before the course was supposed to end, we terminated it ourselves.

One morning at 02:00 I was rudely awakened by AK-47 shots and some fierce shouting and swearing. When I tried to get out of my self-built lean-to shelter, frightened out of my wits, I found it blocked by the instructors. The next moment a smoke grenade was lobbed into the confined space, and I had no option but to evacuate the shelter, taking a thatched wall and some of the instructor's T-shirt with me. By this time the entire base seemed to have erupted in chaos. Apparently, the instructors were not happy with our performance and had decided to show us some real action. The "action" was of course induced by a healthy dose of Red Heart rum – at the time the standard Recce beverage. Earlier that night we had watched as the three instructors steadily downed two bottles between them.

Smoke from the grenades filled the air, an RPG launcher went off and the rocket exploded in the branches of a tree some distance from the base. Everyone was shooting everywhere. I decided to put our recently acquired evacuation drills to the test, and ran blindly into the bush. Most of the guys were already there, having fled the base and reorganised in an open area to the west. Since there was still a lot of random shooting, we withdrew into the thick bush and bedded down for the rest of the night. By early morning we had made up our minds; as some of the guys were still missing, we would

walk back to Omega and just call it quits, as everyone had
had enough of the real-action treatment.

The officer commanding (OC) of the unit was not entirely
happy with the turn of events. The instructors were called
in to base and requested to return to Fort Doppies. Before
they left, the course leader, a battle-hardened young officer
from 1 Recce approached me and said, "Stadler, I expected
more from you. I am really disappointed."

Unfortunately I was too young and inexperienced to challenge him. I turned away and left it at that. But at least I
knew that I wouldn't be deterred from joining the recce wing
by a pack of drunkards chasing me around.

Our unit commander reported the incident to the OC 1 Recce,
who did not take kindly to it. Sadly, it created a lot of animosity
between 31 Battalion and Special Forces, and led to a mutual
distrust that lasted as long as the Bushman unit existed.

However, the whole affair did have a positive outcome.
All the students returned to Fort Vreeslik and did a second
Minor Tactics course under the capable leadership of Lieutenant
Frannie du Toit (who had recruited me for 31 Battalion) and
his team of operators running the recce wing. This time we
did the Minor Tactics course with the very same Bushmen
who would deploy with us. We slept, ate and trained with
them for another four weeks, absorbing everything they
could teach us about bush warfare.

In Angola, many of these Bushman soldiers had been
"Fletchas" while the majority of us were still at school. The
Fletchas, or *Flechas* (arrows), were Portuguese Special Forces

units created during the colonial war. They operated as platoon-sized subunits consisting of local tribesmen and rebel defectors who specialised in tracking, reconnaissance and pseudo-terrorist operations. Many of them joined the SADF after Angolan independence.

There was a wealth of information to be gained from them. Their extraordinary knowledge of the bush was especially helpful, as we soon discovered during the training and subsequently during operations. I used every opportunity to learn from the Bushmen. Our instructors' considerable knowledge and dedication were also an inspiration. Frannie and his team were mature and professional, and guided us with great patience through the intricate paces of the course.

To this day I maintain that the minor tactics training I received during those few weeks in the remote areas of the Western Caprivi ranked among the highest-quality training ever presented in our defence force. I absorbed every single bit of information and made an effort to become one with the bush.

Frannie, in my eyes a military scholar of the first order, believed the bush provided you with everything you needed to gain the tactical advantage against an adversary – provided your eyes were open to the opportunities it offered. He encouraged me to read all the classic works of irregular warfare, including F Spencer Chapman's *The Jungle is Neutral*, a book that would guide our thinking and in a certain sense become the recce wing's doctrine for the years that I served at 31 Battalion.

Operational sectors

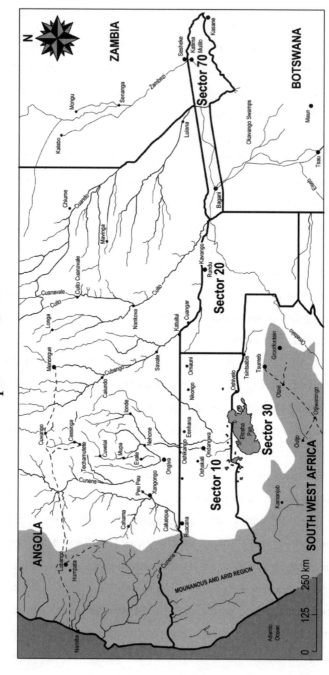

2

Bush Baptism

IN SEPTEMBER 1978 the United Nations (UN) Security Council approved Resolution 435, which provided for a cessation of hostilities on South West Africa's borders with Angola and Zambia. The South African forces in the area had to be reduced to 1 500 over a period of three months, and elections would be held, overseen by the United Nations Transition Assistance Group, or UNTAG. A demilitarised zone was to be introduced, but this never transpired because SWAPO continued its incursions into South West Africa.

As a young candidate officer fresh from Infantry School, I was oblivious to all of this. My focus was strictly on proving myself capable of leading a reconnaissance team into the bush.

An attack by SWAPO on Katima Mulilo on 23 August 1978 began a new phase in the conflict, this time between South Africa and Zambia. Katima Mulilo was the headquarters of Sector 70, which was in charge of operations in Eastern Caprivi. In a standoff bombardment using 122 mm rockets, ten South African soldiers were killed when a rocket penetrated a barrack room.

The South African forces reacted swiftly with cross-border raids by three combat teams. By the time the South Africans arrived at their targets, SWAPO had already vacated the guerrilla camps and no significant military successes could be claimed. But the message to Zambian president Kenneth Kaunda and SWAPO was clear and simple: don't mess with us.

During 1979, a series of well-planned cross-border operations into southwestern Zambia proved more successful. The reconnaissance wing of 31 Battalion played a prominent role in locating enemy bases and leading forces in to their targets.

At the time, the National Party government considered Zambia as a communist ally in the so-called total onslaught against South Africa. While the country maintained reasonably good trade relations with South Africa, it was under pressure from the Organization of African Unity (OAU) to support the liberation movements, including SWAPO and the ANC.

South Africa put much pressure on Zambia, via the UN, not to support SWAPO or provide a safe haven for its cadres. Consequently, the frequency and intensity of SADF operations against SWAPO into Zambia increased. The Zambian National Defence Force (ZNDF) inadvertently became involved, since SWAPO utilised the ZNDF's logistical supply lines and often established their bases close to ZNDF deployments. The result was that the Zambian government began to pressure SWAPO to stop its activities in the southwestern parts of the country, since the South African Defence Force was causing a lot of trouble for them. The Zambian government also increased its pressure on South Africa, via the UN, to conclude peace talks with SWAPO.

My first deployment with the 31 Battalion recce wing was meant to be a daring little venture into southwestern Zambia to try and capture a SWAPO official on the road between Sesheke and Luso along the Zambezi River. This was early in February 1979. At the time, SWAPO was very active between the Kwando and Zambezi rivers in this corner of Zambia, and the area served as a transition and staging point for cadres moving to the front in Angola. It was an excellent training area for a guerrilla force. The terrain was quite similar to that of the operational areas in southern Angola and northern Namibia (Ovamboland). Up to that point the southwestern corner of Zambia was considered safe by SWAPO, since regular South African forces had not been operating across the border into Zambia.

Our mission was to ambush a SWAPO vehicle along the road and bring back a senior cadre alive for questioning. The ultimate purpose would be to determine the position of SWAPO deployments in the Zambian theatre of operations. Three of us were to form one early-warning group further north along the road, while another group of three would deploy south of the ambush site. The main force, the ambush party, consisting of Frannie du Toit and eleven guys, Bushmen and white operators paired off, deployed at a tactically suitable position between the two early-warning groups. They would be ready to spring the ambush once either group reported the approach of the SWAPO vehicle.

One thing stands out from those few days: I have never been so wet and so miserable for such a long time. We were using mostly SWAPO equipment, because the deployment was meant to be non-traceable, and of course the SWAPO kit would provide a measure of deception if we were spotted by an adversary. We only had ponchos that barely covered our bodies. From day one I was soaking wet – and stayed like that for the rest of the time. We could not move an inch in the early-warning position and could only shiver to stay warm. Making coffee or warming up food wasn't an option, as our hide was literally two metres from the road.

The operation was terminated because the ambush party was compromised by a member of the local population (or LP, as they were referred to) who stumbled onto their position and ran away before anyone could react. We had to rush back to a predetermined RV and anti-track to ensure that our tracks were not discovered and followed back to the border. It was quite a relief when the deployment was called off. I would certainly be better prepared next time!

Once the team had regrouped at the RV, Frannie called me and asked whether I could lead the team back to the exfiltration point. I was eager to prove myself in the bush and I didn't hesitate a moment. Through the lush vegetation of the African bush and over a distance of 30 km, I managed to navigate to the exact point where we needed to cross the border to re-enter the Caprivi. Although this was a small feat, it gave me great confidence in my abilities, and it convinced Frannie that I was capable enough to be deployed with him.

Of the many valuable lessons learned during this operation, one was that the success of counterinsurgency operations had to be measured in relative terms. An operation could seldom be labelled an outright failure if the stated objective was not in fact reached (as it was in this case), because it very often led to additional operational benefits, such as intelligence gained. The mere presence of South African forces in an area where they had not been expected also had an impact, and often intelligence gained on a "failed" mission would lead to the successful execution of a future operation.

A second key lesson was this: the bigger the force, the greater the chances of being detected. Over the next three years I discovered this to be a fundamental truth.

In 31 Battalion recce wing the norm at the time was to deploy in six-man patrols on reconnaissance missions. Since these jobs were of a tactical nature (as opposed to strategic), and contact with the enemy therefore almost inevitable, the reasoning was that the team should be strong enough to handle itself in a punch-up. During many of those deployments the team used to have a company from 31 Battalion right behind it, not more than a few hundred metres away.

The whole purpose, I discovered, was in fact to find the enemy, get them tied up in a fight so that they wouldn't run away, and then have the company move in for the kill. It never worked, as the SWAPO detachments always followed the classic Mao Zedong tactics of "running away today to fight another day". They never got tied up in a firefight unless they had chosen the killing field. They knew the lay of the land and were highly flexible in the bush. Contrary to what we were led to believe – that the SWAPO cadres were scared of the South African forces and chose to run away during any encounter – I learned that they were shrewd tacticians and often fierce fighters, most probably because they were fighting for a cause they were willing to die for.

Incidentally, during my years at 31 Battalion, but especially later during small team operations with Special Forces, several nerve-racking experiences taught me that running away was a valid technique that should be part of your arsenal of tactics, and that it did not necessarily mean defeat. The guerrilla mantra became a way of living, and so we adopted guerrilla tactics for the same reason SWAPO did – to survive! Among the special operations fraternity at Katima Mulilo I became known as a "fast runner", as in most of my operations hasty not-so-tactical withdrawals were required to save our skins.

After this initial deployment, a series of reconnaissance tasks came our way. Frannie du Toit was an expert and I was lucky to be picked for a number of jobs with him. With his forceful personality and uncanny knack for reconnaissance, he was considered a bit of a maverick. Since he had selected and trained the Bushmen in the early days of the recce wing, he had the choice of some of the best men.

Our first deployment after the initial ambush attempt was a reconnaissance mission to locate a SWAPO forward detachment in the area of Kalabolelwa, also situated along the Zambezi River. Tango Naca and Dumba Katombela, two seasoned members of the recce wing, who formed part of Frannie's regular team, were picked for the task.

Tango was one of the old-style, fierce Bushman soldiers who seemed to possess a sixth sense that made him almost supernaturally good in the bush. He could read a track like a storybook. He knew the bush intimately, understood the habits of the birds and animals, and had a natural, inbuilt sense for danger. Never while operating with Tango would we encounter enemy or local population without us knowing about them first. On numerous occasions we would locate them before they could become aware of us, allowing us to take evasive action or merge with the undergrowth.

One week before the infiltration we were airlifted to Katima Mulilo for final preparations and briefings. We spent most of our time in the ops room at Katima, planning routes and emergency procedures, and preparing maps for the deployment. We deployed from Mpacha Air Force Base before last light one day late in February 1979.

The Super Frelon dropped us in an omuramba 30 km southwest of our target area. It was a strange feeling, just the four of us in the belly of the huge helicopter, flying into the unknown. The adrenaline was pumping, as I had no idea what to expect. After twenty minutes we reached the landing zone (LZ). As we ran down the ramp into the field of small mopane trees outside, I was half expecting the enemy to be waiting to mow us down, but nothing happened.

The bush was quiet. And hot. And as the sound of the helicopter faded in the distance, an utter loneliness engulfed me – as if I was left alone in a noiseless world.

But I had no time to ponder this feeling, at least not right there. It would become a familiar sensation that I would experience a thousand times over, often in situations much more threatening than this. We waited until after last light to ensure that there was no immediate reaction, and then started moving in the direction of the target.

The operation would last for two weeks, as we had quite a large area to cover. Frannie's plan was to look immediately for signs of the enemy along the main road curving along the Zambezi River; he reasoned that any sizable force needed to be supplied, and would therefore require some form of logistics. The local population was spread along the Zambezi, while the only road negotiable by vehicle was the one running parallel to the river on its western bank. Once we had located signs of enemy presence, we would turn our focus on them to locate the base.

We circled the area from the north, first moving along the slopes of an omuramba leading east towards the river, then cutting in along the road moving south. After seven days, having covered a 30-km stretch along the river, we still hadn't found any sign. Either the information was wrong or the base was further south. Frannie called for a pick-up, which was pointedly denied, as we were supposed to deploy for fourteen days.

An argument ensued, as the Tactical HQ (commonly referred to as Tac HQ) demanded to know whether we had actually covered the whole forest area away from the river. The more Frannie tried to explain that it wasn't necessary, since we had covered all the possible entrances, the more they insisted that we patrol the actual bush.

To me it seemed ridiculous to stay for another seven days if we knew the base wasn't there. It would make more sense to go back, reassess where the enemy could be and deploy again. Little did I know that this would be only the first of many similar situations. In fact, it was quite common for the bosses at headquarters to think they knew better than the guy on the ground risking his life.

During the two days we waited in the lush green bush for a decision on whether our job was done or not, I had another unique experience with the Bushmen. Tango Naca had kept a close eye on a little bird from the moment we moved into our hide. The bird twittered and darted around us, and then flew off, only to come back after a while and frantically flap its wings. At first I thought Tango was irritated by the little bugger, as it could give our position away.

But then he approached Frannie and whispered something to him, to which Frannie nodded his head and gave him a thumbs up. Tango indicated to me to follow him and Dumba as they set off after the excited bird. After about a kilometre the bird started going mad, circling us and constantly going back to a fallen tree we had passed. Tango's face lit up and a huge smile spread across his wrinkled features as he formed the word, "Honey!"

The Bushmen had a fire going in no time, and then made a crude smoke generator with green leaves wrapped around a burning branch. While I kept a lookout, the two Bushmen went about with their hunting knives, cutting away at the branches and then digging into the tree trunk that concealed the golden combs of honey.

Finally they managed to pull some of the combs from the tree trunk, stacking them on a large piece of fresh bark that served as a tray. We carried the honey back to the hide, and soon feasted on the pure golden sweetness from the bush. The syrup and large chunks of honey that we could not finish were stored in water bottles and taken back to base the following day – once the Tac HQ had finally agreed to extract us.

My first real contact with an enemy force took place during a deployment just north of the Matabele Plains in southern Zambia. SWAPO had established a number of training bases and transit camps in the relatively safe area of Ngwezi Pools. Our deployment formed part of a much bigger operation conducted by Sector 70 from its headquarters at Katima Mulilo.

Operation Saffraan was launched on 7 March 1979, concurrent with Operation Rekstok into Angola. The operation was partially in retaliation for the SWAPO attack on Katima Mulilo the year before, as well as for the frequent incursions into the eastern parts of the Caprivi at the time. As one of the main actors taking part in the offensive, 31 Battalion was tasked to deploy its companies in a wide-sweeping area operation against SWAPO bases between the Kwando and Zambezi rivers, while the recce teams were to act as cut-off groups north of the Matabele Plains.

With three teams of six each, we formed a fighting patrol of eighteen guys geared up for serious fighting. We knew that there was an elite SWAPO unit called Typhoon rehearsing in that area. Typhoon specialised in deep infiltrations into the farmlands of South West Africa, where they would attack farmsteads and harass local communities.

Our mission was to find elements of this group and hunt them down. We infiltrated by helicopter and, over the following week, did a wide sweep of the bush from where the group allegedly operated. On the third day we started picking up signs of guerrilla activity. Tracks of SWAPO soldiers often led into and out of the local kraals, although we could never pinpoint the guerrillas.

Towards the end of the first week we decided to use our resupply as a ruse to make the enemy believe we had left the area. At a cluster of kraals, in broad daylight and in full view of the population, we started moving south. We left a clear track and made it quite obvious that we were leaving. That afternoon, about ten kilometres further south, we called in the helicopters for a resupply. Afterwards, we meticulously wiped out all signs of our presence. We split up into teams again and decided on an RV where we would meet the following day. Each team then applied anti-tracking techniques and circled back to the predetermined RV.

After stealthily joining up at the RV, we decided to keep a low profile and not make our presence known. We sent out small patrols to locate signs of enemy presence, and were soon rewarded when a team reported fresh tracks going into a kraal complex. We circled the kraal to the opposite side from which the enemy patrol had entered. Frannie then deliberately exposed two of the Bushmen, dressed up in SWAPO attire, to the inhabitants of the kraal, whereafter we pretended to withdraw, and then moved into a thicket not far from the kraal complex.

The SWAPO patrol, not knowing whom they were dealing with so far from the South West African border, took the bait – hook, line and sinker. They aggressively pursued us into the bush. And we were ready. The patrol approached us in line-abreast formation, so by the time Frannie initiated fire we had the nearest ones covered. The one I had in my sights was barely 20 m away. Along with four others he went down under the initial high volume of fire, while the rest started scrambling in all directions.

By now most of the guys in our formation had broken cover and were rushing forward in an uncoordinated fire-and-movement attempt. Halfway through the contact I recall Frannie running forward, shouting at the top of his voice to the Bushmen: "Don't shoot, don't shoot. That's a bicycle!"

Afterwards we had a laugh when we heard what it was all about: The OC Sector 70 at Katima Mulilo had promised the Bushmen a bicycle as a reward for each SWAPO cadre brought back alive. While we didn't get any bicycles, since none of the enemy was taken alive, we were nonetheless elated about the way the contact had turned out, especially because we had not lost anyone in the firefight.

We set up a temporary base (TB) with proper all-round defensive positions in case of a retaliatory attack. Once we had reported the contact to the Tac HQ, we started collecting evidence. Five SWAPO cadres had been killed, but it was clear from the blood spoor that at least three more were seriously wounded. Since the contact had been too far into enemy country, it was decided not to launch a follow-up due to the lack of dedicated air support.

The Tac HQ also informed us that the intelligence guys wanted all the bodies to be brought out, as they considered the collection of weapons, equipment and documentation, along with the actual faces, fingerprints and personal belongings of the cadres, as critically important. So we set about collecting weapons and kit, and started dragging the bodies to an area that we had prepared as an LZ for pick-up.

Two helicopters were dispatched to airlift the teams and the dead cadres to the operational HQ in the area of Ngwezi Pools. After we had been dropped off for debriefing, the bodies were taken to Katima Mulilo for intelligence processing. Our teams conducted two more recce missions to try to locate SWAPO deployments, but by that time all the enemy bases had been abandoned. Operation Saffraan was called off and the unit returned to Omega.

At the time I didn't give the piled-up bodies at the LZ much thought. The rush of adrenaline and the physical exertion of collecting the bodies and equipment in the heat of the day didn't allow much time for reflection. But later on I would often think of the people who died at our hands. How did they end up wasted, far from their loved ones, under the harsh African sun? And would their families ever know where they were and how they had died?

3

Brothers in Arms

FOR A YOUNGSTER of twenty, those years at Omega in the Caprivi were pure bliss. As a second lieutenant leading a reconnaissance team of six, consisting of two whites and four Bushmen, I had just enough freedom to mostly do my own thing without having the responsibilities of a more senior rank. We lived for the day – and for the operations that followed in quick succession.

By this time I had signed up for "short service", which involved an additional two-year contract to the compulsory two years of national service. It also meant a healthy salary package, considering that I was also earning "danger pay" during the three years I served on the border.

At the time, more than 4 000 Bushmen lived at Omega. Of this number about 800 were soldiers, and the rest consisted of their families. The soldiers were divided into four companies: A Company (composed of Baraquenas, an indigenous tribe from the Cuando-Cubango region), B and C companies (Vasquelas, Bushmen formerly scattered across the southern regions of

Angola and northeastern South West Africa) and D Company (a mix of Baraquenas and Vasquelas). Each company had its own HQ in front of its living quarters.

Omega was like a fair-sized town and indeed had to be managed like one, as all the essential services had to be maintained. The school used to have in excess of 300 pupils, who were mostly taught by national servicemen. There were about 250 whites, the majority of whom were single men who lived in prefabricated wooden huts (called "kimbos") at the centre of the base. Three or four of us used to share a hut. For the married officers, warrant officers and NCOs, there were about fifteen "married quarters", either wooden houses or caravans.

Daily life at the base revolved around the officers' bars and messes. We were a close-knit community, and an exceptionally healthy spirit reigned. On Sundays the OC would close the bars and the whole unit went to church, after which the bars would reopen and everyone, married couples included, came together for a magnificent brunch. Occasionally we held concerts, with virtually everyone participating, and performing artists also visited the unit.

The recce wing's training base, Fort Vreeslik, was built in a secluded spot about 14 km south of Omega where few people ever visited. When not on operations, we spent most of our weekdays there. The base was situated in the pristine and unspoilt bush of the Western Caprivi. The huts were built of poles and thatch that we collected from the bush ourselves.

In the centre was a fairly large "lecture hut", where classes were presented. Since we built the camp ourselves, there was a sense of ownership among the recce wing guys. Every time we visited Fort Vreeslik, we would add a new hut or do maintenance on the structures. It was our pride and joy, and we considered it a special place.

The Bushman soldiers I used to work with in the recce wing were extraordinarily well adapted to the environment. They knew the uses of each plant, recognised every track in the wild and understood the habits of each animal. They were invaluable when it came to making deductions from any disturbance in nature, and they could predict enemy actions from the most imperceptible signs left by an adversary. While the older men were admittedly more experienced in the ways of the bush, the younger ones were equally at home.

In my experience, the Bushmen were hunters rather than fighters. A Bushman soldier's value, at least from the reconnaissance perspective, lay in his ability to track, stalk and outwit the enemy. Combined with his uncanny knowledge of the bush and his ability to survive, a Bushman made the best of partners in a reconnaissance team.

While there wasn't much we could teach the Bushmen about the bush, their tactical skills were not well developed. Training therefore centred on tactics and weapon handling. A typical Minor Tactics course would include tactical movement in different patrol formations, ambush techniques, contact drills based on the fire-and-movement principle, and of course reconnaissance skills such as observation posts (OPs), listening posts (LPs) and stalking techniques.

Once we decided to play a trick on the Bushmen while I was presenting a lecture to them. A loudspeaker system was set up on the other side of the base, playing a recording of lions roaring and other game sounds. At some point during the lecture I heard the faint but distinct sound of young lions panting. A visible question mark formed on the faces in front of me and I could hear whispers of "lion, lion". "No," I pretended to put them at ease, "you know there are no lions here . . ."

But I hadn't even finished speaking when a deafening roar suddenly sheared the afternoon air. They were up like one man, diving for their weapons, which had been left outside the lecture hut. Rifles cocked and ready, they lined up to face the lions, but no one dared go forward. Every time the lion roared, they jumped back into line. By this time I could barely keep a straight face. When an elephant trumpeting followed another round of roaring, they realised that they had been had. Some of them were so angry with us that they dropped their weapons and refused to continue with the day's training.

Tango Naca was hand-picked for the recce wing long before my arrival at the unit, and he had numerous specialised missions to his credit. As he was highly respected by both Vasquela and Baraquena, the white leader group relied heavily on his wisdom not only in training and combat but also to help resolve domestic problems at the base. With Dumba Katombela he formed part of a formidable team, and during those first deployments I tried to absorb every little thing they could teach me.

Later on, after I had selected and trained the first group of Baraquenas from A Company, Xivatcha Shekamba and

Chimango Kanyeti became my permanent team buddies. I soon realised that the Baraquenas were equally well adapted for reconnaissance work, having been exposed to the same hostile conditions as the Vasquelas in Angola. I deployed on a series of reconnaissance missions with them, and today I have to admit that I owe my survival to both of them.

A buddy pair typically consisted of one Bushman and one white operator, as the natural skills and instincts of the Bushmen were considered critical for our survival. However, most of the Bushmen soldiers were still illiterate, and their level of both English and Afrikaans left much to be desired. While they could set up a radio and convey elementary messages, they could not draft reports or encode and transmit messages. It was therefore essential to have a combination of Bushman and white buddy pairs in the team.

Back then, the size of a team was determined by practical considerations. We wanted the team to be as small as possible, as the conventional six-man team was considered cumbersome and left far too many tracks. The four-man team appeared to be the best size for tactical reconnaissance.

Buddy pairs could also act independently when required. For the final approach to a target, for example, one buddy pair could stay behind in a hide, set up the HF radio and act as both relay station and emergency rendezvous point (better known as a crash RV) for the recce team. The recce team, in turn, could leave their packs in the hide and do their final approach in light order. Very high-frequency (VHF) radio communications would be maintained between the two groups. If the recce team could not locate the target, they would return to the hide and the whole team would move further into the suspect area. This procedure, called "caterpillaring", would be repeated until confirmation could be obtained that the enemy was either present or not.

Over the years that I served with 31 Battalion recce wing, I steadily built up my knowledge of guerrilla operations. The tactics and skills required for reconnaissance missions became second nature, and I would eventually develop my own philosophy and create a unique concept for these missions. This tactical foundation served me in good stead in my later career in Special Forces, and would eventually form the basis for doctrine we conveyed during training.

It remained a challenge to infiltrate undetected through hostile and often populated areas towards a target, and we constantly tested new ideas and developed techniques to try to outwit the enemy. Consequently, the means of infiltration towards a target area was subject to much deliberation. While parachute infiltration had always been considered, it had never actually been done, because the Bushmen had never been exposed to airborne operations and had not done the training.

That was why, at the end of 1979, I was sent to Bloemfontein to do the basic parachute course at 1 Parachute Battalion – with six Bushmen. We prepared ourselves well, and by the time the course started we were super-fit. The time in South Africa turned out to be an astonishing experience, as the men from the bush had never even seen a high-rise building, nor a lift or an escalator. For most of them, a tar road was a novelty, while the many shops and businesses were almost too much to comprehend. Whenever I took them to town, the seven of us had to hold hands to stay together, especially when crossing roads.

As it was the height of the apartheid era, I tried to prepare them beforehand for what was to come. But even I was shocked by the way African people were treated, whether by shopkeepers, train conductors or simply people on the street. More than once I had to intervene in a shop and tell a clerk that the Bushmen were with me and that I wanted to buy the items for them. It was embarrassing in the extreme, as racism was completely foreign at Omega, and I had difficulty in making them understand how a system like that could rule our society.

The parachute course did not go down well with the Bushmen. Although they were exceptionally fit, they could not pass the heavy lifting and power exercises of the PT course – the two-week physical training programme that served as selection for parabats. I was disappointed, as we had all trained together at Omega, and I found the PT course a breeze. I even had the time and energy to spend my evenings with the pretty girls of Bloemfontein!

Four of the Bushmen eventually went on to do the actual jumping phase, but again, to my disappointment, they could not master the landing drills. Only one of them qualified, though we often let the rest of the group jump once back in the Caprivi.

At the end of the course, we made our way back to Pretoria by train. At Germiston station we had to transfer to another train, and I warned them beforehand that the train, an urban commuter-type, would stop for only a few seconds. We had to get on as quickly as possible and there would be no time to waste with our luggage. When the train approached, we were standing at the ready on the platform. As the door opened, I threw in my luggage and some of the Bushmen's and then stepped on board. Two of them followed me, but when the train suddenly started to pull away they decided to stick with their buddies on the platform and jumped off before the doors could close, leaving me with half the luggage on the train. As I looked out of the window, they were clutching each other in a pathetic huddle on the platform.

Since all of my luggage was on the train, I had no option but to stay. I was really worried, as I knew the Bushmen had no clue about where to go, and we hadn't agreed on an emergency RV beforehand, as we always used to do. I only managed to get off about four stations later. I left the luggage with another soldier going to Pretoria and took the next train back to Germiston. But there was no sign of my comrades, and apparently no one had seen them.

In low spirits, I took the next train to Pretoria. But, lo and behold, as the train pulled in to the station that evening, there they were – standing by their luggage, smiling and waving at me. They even made fun of me for arriving so late.

Back at the unit, we soon settled into the normal routine of training, waiting for deployment orders for the next mission, and then preparing and rehearsing for the job. The road construction base at Chetto, about 60 km from Omega, was the ideal venue for many of our rehearsals, as it provided a real-life target in a thickly vegetated area.

During one such rehearsal at Chetto, with Xivatcha Shekamba, I got a nasty wake-up call and was taught a lesson I would not soon forget. After observing the "enemy" for some time, we infiltrated the base by crawling under the double fencing during the small hours of the night, leaving a trail as prominent as a bulldozer's. We settled down under an upturned engineer's boat right in the centre of the camp, from where we watched the base awakening and even had a giggle as we observed their morning parade from our snug little hide.

Our happy state was not to last for long, because soon after the parade the security section of the base discovered our entry point and followed our tracks. With shouts of "AWOL!" and "Lazy bastards!" the trackers challenged us to vacate our position. Soon the whole engineer community had gathered around us, and it was rather embarrassing to crawl out and face the daylight. The base commander pretended that he was not aware of the exercise. He alleged that he thought we were real enemy and consequently permitted a fair measure of "manhandling" by his troops. However, he ensured a happy ending to our misfortune by taking us for some refreshments in the camp bar, and then giving us a free ride back to Omega.

As a tactical reconnaissance capability, the 31 Battalion recces were in high demand for intelligence collection missions in the areas of responsibility of sectors 20 (Rundu) and 70 (Katima Mulilo). Our mission was to locate enemy bases and installations in the "near" areas, up to a distance of roughly 60 km across the border, while the Reconnaissance Commandos were supposed to perform strategic missions. However, this rule was only loosely applied, as the Reconnaissance Commandos operated wherever there was a demand.

I was once told outright by the OC that they preferred the 31 Battalion recce wing to the teams from Reconnaissance Commandos, as we were constantly exposed to tactical deployments and virtually lived in the bush. Intelligence reports from a reconnaissance by the 31 Battalion teams were detailed and to the point. We were prepared to deploy at any time and at short notice. No fuss was made about support and we never had outrageous demands about rations, resupply or assistance from other support services. If there was a job to be done, we'd simply get on and do it.

In the early days of the war, a typical deployment into Zambia would normally be conducted from Katima Mulilo, which was situated on the banks of the Zambezi River opposite the Zambian town of Sesheke. At that point, in early 1980, President Kenneth Kaunda still vehemently denied the presence of freedom fighter training camps in Zambia. Consequently, whenever South African forces ventured into Zambia the rest of the world was led to believe that we were targeting Zambian soldiers and civilians. Zambia was in a precarious position: as a member of the Commonwealth it had to manage its relationship with the West but it also wanted to remain faithful to the independence movements.

The recce wing therefore did not deploy overtly into Zambia.[4] Since most deployments were of a clandestine nature, our modus operandi, including tactics and equipment, was adapted to ensure that deployments and equipment could not be linked directly to South Africa. We wore nondescript olive-green uniforms that could be confused with those of SWAPO, indistinct flat-soled boots that made anti-tracking easier, and we applied stealth tactics to avoid detection by enemy forces and the local population.

At about this time, Commandant (the rank was later changed to lieutenant colonel) Gert Opperman took over command of Sector 70. His nickname was "Rooi Gert" (Red Gert), presumably not only for his ginger hair but also for his fiery temperament. His second-in-command, Major Fred Oelschig, was a seasoned soldier and a brilliant tactician. Both men were extraordinary leaders. They understood the necessity for reconnaissance and the importance of having a small group of specialised and motivated men to do demanding jobs – particularly those behind enemy lines that could not be done by regular soldiers.

Upon receiving the warning order at Omega, a brief appreciation would be done to determine essentials, such as the size of the team, weapons and equipment to be taken along and the duration of the deployment. An HQ element would then be despatched to the Sector HQ at Katima Mulilo, Rundu or Oshakati – depending on which sector was involved – to set up the Tac HQ, initiate the necessary liaison with the HQ, the Air Force and other support elements, and start collecting information.

For deployments into Zambia, the teams settled at a secluded location, normally a fenced-in old building close to the runway at Mpacha Air Force Base, which was about 20 km from Katima. The team leaders would typically do their appreciation and planning at the Sector HQ in Katima, while the rest of the team, under the leadership of the senior NCO, would start preparing radios, rations, water and whatever specialised equipment was needed.

The final briefing to the HQ was done by the senior team leader, always with the air liaison officer (ALO) and pilots in attendance.

Written orders and overlays with the emergency plan were handed in and the team then gathered at Mpacha for final preparations. Rucksacks were secretly loaded onto the helicopters by the support guys while the teams stayed out of sight. Our standard procedure was to wait, already blackened and kitted up and all nerves, at a small hut near the end of the runway. The choppers would taxi out, as if they were doing routine preflight checks, until they reached the exact spot where the teams would slip from the brush and jump on board.

On one such deployment, we were to fly out in two Alouette helicopters after following the same boarding procedure. The pilots were briefed that the team would consist of two whites and two Bushmen and that we would board each Alo as a black and white buddy pair. The other white guy in the second buddy team was a sturdy farm boy from Namibia. By the time we had to board, he had already covered his face with camouflage cream and wore an Afro wig to round off the picture. Once my buddy and I had boarded the first helicopter, the pilot took off. But the second Alo didn't move. We circled back and the flight engineer eventually handed me a headset. The pilot in the Alo on the ground wanted to know where the second white team member was, as only two Bushmen had boarded his helicopter. I cleared it up when I told him to look a bit closer at the second "Bushman".

Another one of these missions across the great Zambezi took us into an area east of Sesheke. The terrain was new to us and quite difficult to operate in. The Zambezi flood plain, which extends quite far north of the river, consists of open marshy areas inter-spersed with clusters of tropical forest barely 100 m wide. While under the cover of these clusters of bush, everything was fine – except for the squadrons of mosquitoes and battalions of ticks that pestered us. Once in the open, though, the team would be completely exposed. We also knew that should we be isolated inside one of these forest clusters, escape would be virtually impossible, as a mobile enemy force could easily encircle them.

The team once again comprised four members – two whites and the now trusted couple, Xivatcha and Chimango. We were in quite a predicament since we needed daylight to find signs of enemy presence, but moving in the day was risky. We therefore decided to move in the early morning and late afternoon to scan the area for tracks. We would adopt the typical casual style of patrolling that the SWAPO cadres used – single file and with weapons slung across our backs – in the hope that from a distance we would be mistaken for SWAPO should we be spot-ted. After dark, we took off our shoes and moved barefoot to find a hide far away from where we had been the previous day.

On the fourth afternoon we suddenly heard voices in front of us – in the same cluster of trees we had just entered. As we moved into cover we noticed boot tracks all around, and real-ised that we must have entered the lion's den. The next moment we saw soldiers leaving the thicket on the opposite side, but did not know whether they had seen us or not.

I decided to inform the Tac HQ immediately, as the terrain didn't allow too many manoeuvring options, and we had no idea of the enemy's position and strength. I didn't even encode a message, but hastily informed Major Oelschig what our position was and what we intended to do. I also told him that I would give them an update in thirty minutes. We took in a hide to make a map appreciation, and had just settled down when we heard vehicles coming our way. I prayed that they would pass the cluster of trees where we were hiding, but our luck had run out. Ural trucks came to a halt on the opposite side of the little forest, and we could distinctly hear shouted commands, doors banging and tailgates being flung open.

It was time for action. I kept Xivatcha close to me, as I had learned to rely on his instincts in situations like this. We went down and prepared for the worst, as a stealthy withdrawal was now out of the question.

There were four trucks, all loaded with soldiers who were now making a lot of noise and shouting obscenities in Kwanyama at us, their enemy, whom they suspected to be the "boers". After debussing from the vehicles, the soldiers formed up for a search. But for some strange reason – probably because they confused the tracks of the smaller group that we had initially encountered with our own – they formed up facing away from us.

As we watched this spectacle unfold, we realised that the enemy had no idea where we were, and were shouting and making a commotion in order to scare us out of our hiding place. It was only a matter of time, and sooner or later they would realise that we hadn't left the cover of the bush, so I decided that we had had enough excitement for one day. We picked up our kit and, with that very cluster of tropical bush to mask our retreat, bent down low and ran in the opposite direction.

After some time Xivatcha, who was running ahead of me, tilted his head and looked at me, his face lighting up: "Aeroplane . . ." he smiled. "Boer aeroplane."

I quickly switched on the UHF radio,[5] and straight away the reassuring voice of the pilot came across: "Kilo Sierra, this is Cheetah. Do you read me?"

"Cheetah, this is Kilo Sierra. Angels from heaven," I managed to get out. "You come as if you were sent!"

"We have indeed been sent. Thought you were in trouble. Where's the enemy?" the pilot asked.

The next moment two Impala jets thundered overhead, and we almost jumped with joy. I directed the pilots towards the area where the enemy had been, but either they had cleared out or were hiding their vehicles, because the Impalas could not pick up anything, and the pilots had to be content with delivering some speculative fire into the bush.

During the debriefing back at Katima, it transpired that Major Oelschig had dispatched the fighters directly after speaking to me on the radio, without waiting for my update thirty minutes later. He declared that he couldn't afford to have South Africans killed on the opposite side of the river, as "South Africa was not at war with Zambia". To the team it was reassuring to know that our ops commander was someone with vision and a gut feel.

On a practical level, I would learn many things during my years at Omega, not only about surviving in the bush but also about my brothers-in-arms. Our Bushman buddies were indispensable in most operations, but there was one thing you couldn't ask of them: to do a tactical river crossing.

I discovered this during a mission when we had to cross the Cuando River to reach our target. The Cuando flows from the central highlands of Angola in a southerly direction, forming the border between Zambia and Angola and eventually cutting through the Caprivi (where it is called the Kwando) to its marshy end in the Linyanti Swamp in Botswana. A fighting patrol from the recce wing was tasked to harass a major SWAPO supply line – a road stretching along the eastern shore of the Kwando River to SWAPO bases along the Caprivi border.

To ensure that the team reached the road undetected, it was decided to cross the Luiana and Kwando rivers on foot, a task that soon proved to be nearly impossible. Firstly, it transpired that few of the Bushmen in the team could swim. Therefore we had to take inflatable mattresses and ensure that every non-swimmer was assisted by a guy who could swim. The situation was complicated by the fact that the Kwando River was no less than five kilometres wide at our point of crossing.

Fast-flowing streams rushed past marshes covered in thick reeds. The many small islands meant the team could take breaks, even though we had to battle swarms of mosquitoes that vigorously attacked us throughout the crossing. We made the rucksacks float by wrapping them in groundsheets, after which the webbing and weapons were tied on top.

Around a bend in a particularly broad stretch of river, I came across Joao Antonio, a Bushman who carried the team's RPG-7. He looked at me with a guilt-ridden face that said it all: his equipment had capsized and the RPG launcher was at the bottom of the river, along with a set of three booster charges that formed part of the rocket. We dived after it and managed to retrieve the whole lot. After the crossing we let the boosters dry in the sun, hoping that they would do their job when we needed them.

The entire team finally made it across the river after 36 hours of painstaking work, and we reached the eastern shore exhausted but relieved. Approximately two kilometres from the intended ambush position we split the team in two; the team leader led the ambush party to the road and I stayed behind with a small reserve team, manning the radio.

Events at the ambush site turned out to be quite interesting, as I learned later. On the second day a SWAPO resupply truck came rushing down the road. Joao, the man with the previously submerged RPG-7 launcher, positioned himself squarely in the centre of the road, crouching down for a better shot. His first attempt was met by a disheartening "click" as the weapon failed to respond. No luck the second time either. The situation demanded desperate action. At this point Joao, fiercely aggressive and determined to stop the massive machine thundering down the narrow road, drew his alternative weapon, a 9 mm pistol, and started emptying it into the truck, which by this time was virtually on top of him.

Fortunately, the rest of the ambush party did not wait for Joao to bring the truck to a standstill and also opened up with every weapon they had. Joao cleared the road just in time before the truck crashed into the bush. Our team leader then made a sweep of the killing ground, took photos of the truck and the victims, and led his team back to our position. That same day, we were lifted by helicopter and flown back to Omega.

4

First Small Team Ventures

AT THIS TIME, although subconsciously, a new and more refined concept of tactical reconnaissance missions started taking shape in my mind. Conventional military doctrine dictating reconnaissance operations had proven itself flawed and ill-adapted for the kind of enemy, population and terrain that we encountered on a daily basis. Of course, there wasn't a blueprint for recce missions. It was something that had to be learned and developed slowly through trial and error.

The one aspect of doctrine that had not been decided on conclusively was the size of the team. Conventional wisdom prescribed that a team doing a recce at a tactical distance in front of a fighting force had to be strong enough to fend for itself in a punch-up. Also, in order to cover a larger area, more feet on the ground were required. Thus, a recce team consisting of six or eight members was not uncommon. In fact, having such numbers was often a saving grace since recce teams invariably had to switch to fighting mode.

Operations by 31 Batallion recce wing

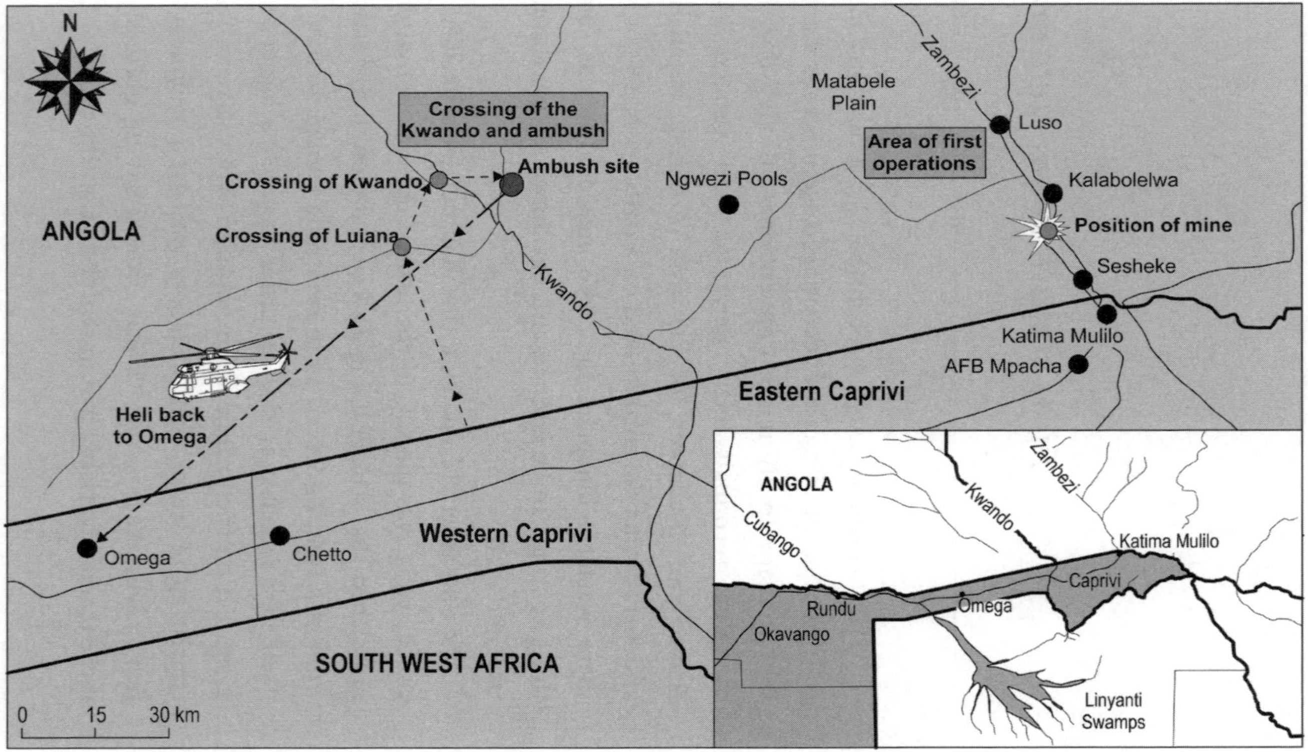

The downside of this modus operandi was that once you were on an independent mission without any immediate backup, you were fairly exposed as a big group. The more feet on the ground, the more footprints you'd leave and the more noise you'd make. In areas with soft sand and sparse under-growth, it would be impossible to hide a team of eight. Once you were on the run from a large enemy force, control over eight team members would also become challenging.

This was illustrated clearly by an incident when Sector 20 at Rundu requested a team to do a recce of a FAPLA[6] brigade HQ at Mpupa in southeastern Angola. It was to be a clandestine mission, and the aim was to locate the base and do a detailed close-in recce, with the eventual purpose of passing the infor-mation on to UNITA for a large-scale base attack. However, this information was never disclosed to us, probably because the planners thought we would be a security risk.

I picked an eight-man team, four whites and four Bushmen, to rehearse for the job, as I thought that such a large target would require more feet on the ground. The intention was to leave a two-man element outside the base, and let three two-man teams cover the three main target areas within the base. We were also told that, as the South Africans were not officially operating in the area and were supposedly not supporting UNITA at the time, the operation could not be compromised at any cost, hence the use of helicopters for insertion or extraction would not even be considered. All equipment needed to be non-traceable, and no sign whatsoever could be left to suggest that South Africans had been in the area.

This was the last point-target reconnaissance I would ever do with a recce team bigger than three. The operation almost turned into a major disaster, and was in many respects a turning point for me, mainly because of the lessons we learned from our mistakes.

We started rehearsing weeks ahead. We sat for hours in the ops room at Rundu studying aerial photographs of the base and surrounding areas. We spent many hours determining routes in and out, identifying hiding places and working out emergency procedures. The base, which consisted of an HQ and three large defensive systems occupied by two battalions, served as the main headquarters and forward airfield for FAPLA forces in the area. Guided by the intelligence officer from Chief of Staff Intelligence (CSI) dedicated to the deployment, we identified complex trench systems surrounding the base and worked out a tricky approach route through them.

As usual, we spent many hours on detailed rehearsals, practising every drill, every possible method of stealthy movement and various immediate-action drills in case things went wrong. By the time we deployed, we were confident that our plan would work. What we did not realise beforehand was that the vegetation surrounding the target was not dense enough to hide a team of eight, and the soft sand of the Angolan savanna would make effective anti-tracking almost impossible.

We infiltrated for five days, taking it slowly in order to leave no tracks and to ensure that we reached our target unobserved. A slight navigational error over a 40-km distance, with no landmarks to plot your position, could lead to disaster. At the time I had not fully mastered the art of multi-legged dead reckoning (DR) navigation, whereby the navigator, in the absence of recognisable terrain features, has to rely completely on maintaining his bearing and judging his distance. I realised too late that navigation should be planned in the same detail as the rest of the deployment.

On the night we finally had to penetrate, I came to the shocking realisation that we were about three kilometres south of the target, and were about to penetrate one of the forward early-warning posts, located in a deserted farmhouse. During the last three days of the infiltration we had rainy, overcast weather and absolutely no way of identifying a landmark to guide us.

We had to admit defeat and return to Rundu to work out a better route to the target. When we deployed again, we approached the target within four days. Using DR, I navigated to the last step, and found the target with relative ease. On the morning of the fourth day, the team was huddled together in a thicket that did not provide enough cover at all – and barely two kilometres from the target. To make matters worse, the hiding place was right next to a well-used pathway, frequented by both soldiers and civilians. We kept a low profile, sweating out the day.

By early evening we were up and about, relieved that we had not been seen and ready to penetrate the base. I established comms to brief the Tac HQ on our intentions, and then the team fell into formation and started the approach to the target area.

On the perimeter we left a two-man team with a radio, Tinus "Putty" van der Merwe and his buddy, to establish the crash RV (the point that would serve as rendezvous in case of emergency) and to guard the kit, while the three recce teams entered the dragon. The six of us stalked between two trench systems, where we could hear soldiers on both sides going about their business, and then made our way towards the centre of the target area. Once on the runway inside the base, we split up, one team going north, one south and my team, the indomitable Chimango Kanyeti and a somewhat self-assured me, moving eastward in the direction of the river.

For the first time in my operational career I had a peculiar experience that would often repeat itself later, but at the time was unique and quite inspiring. As we stalked towards our target, following the route I had painstakingly planned, experiencing the terrain and features as we had seen on the aerial photos, I had the distinct feeling that I had been there before. I experienced an eerie and very real sense of déjà vu. Because we knew every centimetre of the terrain, and because Chimango and I had rehearsed in similar conditions, we both had the feeling that we had done this before, on this exact stretch of earth!

Then I made the dumbest mistake of all. As we moved east, we also approached against the low moon. It was 02:00 and the quarter moon was rising above the treetops, providing just enough light to restrict our vision and cast dark shadows under the cluster of trees we were approaching – the exact position where we expected the enemy to be.

There is no sound as ominous as the cocking of an unfriendly AK-47 in the middle of the night – especially if you are at the wrong end, exposed and not sure where it's coming from. We were suddenly challenged from the shadows of the line of trees ahead of us. The first to gather his wits was Chimango. As the voice behind the AK-47 demanded to know who we were, Chimango answered in the local vernacular, which, fortunately, he understood. Pretending to be drunk, he mumbled something to the effect that we were on our way to our platoon. That gave us the split-second advantage we needed.

We did not wait for the man behind the voice to make up his mind as to whether we were friendly or not, but just gapped it out of there. This would not be the last time the cocking of an AK-47 in the dead of night would bring an operation to an abrupt end. And I can honestly say that I never grew to like that sound particularly.

Our next challenge was to get the teams together, because by that time we had run out of comms with them. At last we managed to raise the other two teams, one to the north and the other to the south, on the radio and call them back to the crash RV. By that time there was enough commotion around us to wake a sleeping dragon, so no one felt the need to hang around. We moved out along the same route by which we had entered, carefully avoiding the defensive positions where we could now hear the sounds of soldiers awakening and preparing for the day. On the outskirts of the base we met up with Putty, who was still manning the crash RV and guarding our kit.

There was barely an hour of darkness left, and we made good use of it. We ran west, away from the base, and then, in an attempt to deceive the enemy, turned north and started applying various anti-tracking techniques. Eventually we swung west, then turned south, thinning out, changing direction, walking backwards in our tracks and generally behaving frantically. By 09:00 we realised that the FAPLA guys had launched a massive follow-up. Behind us we could hear vehicles closing in, distinctly pushing over vegetation and revving up through the brush. Vehicles were also advancing on the road to our west, probably dropping off teams to cut in on our tracks. To the east, we were cut off by the Cuito River. To the south lay the Cubango (Kavango) River – still to be crossed once we got there.

It was up to me to make the call: we either had to compromise the mission by a helicopter pick-up or run the risk of a contact or one of our team members being caught. I opted for the easy ride home. The Puma picked us up about 15 km north of the border, literally grabbing us from under the noses of the follow-up force. It was quite a red-faced affair, as the South African forces were blamed for aggression against the MPLA and I was the one who had to answer for having caused an international incident. The South African government, of course, categorically and vehemently denied involvement and simply passed the blame to UNITA.

At least we didn't leave any equipment, wounded soldiers or dead bodies behind. That definitely would have won me the gold medal. But one good thing did come of it; I vowed that I would never again do a close-in reconnaissance with a team of eight, or approach the lion's den against the rising moon.

When the adrenaline started pumping, fear was a constant companion, and, like every young soldier, I had to learn to cope with it. My fellow soldiers used to handle their fears and uncertainties in different ways, often by excessive drinking. Since I didn't drink, I had to find other ways of letting off steam. Apart from my faith in God, as well as a strong tie with my parents, I developed my own techniques for managing my fear.

I realised firstly that I had to be completely at peace with the bush. While being alone in the veld had long ago become second nature to me, the added dimension of danger required an altogether different mindset. Danger came in all sorts of forms, whether from the wild game that frequented most of our areas of operation, or from the ever-present threat of a real and dangerous enemy. Even the threat of being detected by a member of the local population while lying up in a position close to the enemy would get the adrenaline pumping. So we trained at every opportunity. Whenever I had the chance, I would sleep in the veld – alone. During holidays in South Africa, I used to go hiking or camping by myself. And I kept myself fit, going on long, tiring runs to clear my mind.

The second technique was to plan operations in the finest detail, making a plan of action for every possible scenario that could go wrong, and then rehearsing each in the same minute detail. Thirdly, since I had developed a love of classical music, especially opera, during my formative years, I used to listen to music as a means of easing the tension and relaxing the nerves.

While a smaller team could move with stealth and hide away easily, it was limited in firepower and would only really act defensively. Marius Hibbers was a big-framed and stouthearted product of rural South Africa who had joined the recce wing at about the same time as I had. Together we had forged a solid four-man team along with two of the newly trained Vasquela Bushmen. The four of us did a series of recce missions into southwestern Zambia.

One pitch-dark night we were approaching a target area close to Kalabolelwa along the Zambezi River. SWAPO detachments had allegedly sent elements further south to set up early-warning posts along the Zambezi River. Our task was to confirm the existence of these forward posts and locate their exact position – a similar job to the one I had done with Frannie du Toit in the same area the previous year.

At the time there were large herds of elephant roaming southwestern Zambia between the Kwando and Zambezi rivers. The bush was lush and green. The team had been doing good time during the infiltration and bedded down at about 22:00 that night to get a good night's rest before closing in the following day. Although it was unwise to move closer to the river in daytime, as the shore was densely populated, we needed daylight to locate signs of enemy presence.

Around midnight I woke up with a start. Hibbers had one hand on my wrist, the other on my mouth. "Elephants," he whispered, pointing in the darkness towards where I could hear the snapping of branches and the grumbling of their stomachs.

"It's okay," I said, "it's only elephant," stating the obvious. Then I realised that he was already out of his sleeping bag, sitting at the ready with his weapon. Even the two

Bushmen, who would normally not be in the least bothered by the giants of the bush, were sitting up.

"They're too close," Hibbers said and pointed upwards. It was only then that I realised that one of the elephants was virtually looming over us. The black hole in the sky above me turned out to be the hulk of the animal's body. It was clearly time for a withdrawal.

Without thinking, I did something that almost led to disaster. I had often heard that the rhythmic beating of a stick against a tree, or even tapping the magazine of a rifle, would scare the beasts away (it presumably resembled the pounding of drums – supposedly ingrained in an elephant's mind as a sign of danger, since it indicated human presence). So I started hitting my magazine with a stick I managed to find in the dark.

But clearly this elephant had not read the manual on "rhythmic pounding of drums in the African bush", since it gave a frightened snort . . . and charged.

Fortunately, by this time I was out of my sleeping bag and ready for a hasty retreat. Our saving grace was the trunk of the large tree under which we had bedded down. Both Hibbers and I slipped behind the trunk and ran for a mopane silhouetted in the dark. The two Bushmen charged off into the night, followed by the angry elephant. I went up the mopane, with Hibbers following suit.

Once order had returned to the night around us, we found ourselves clutching the branches of a sapling, barely five feet above the ground. The elephant could have picked us off like ripe fruit.

After I had gathered everyone – and some of my lost dignity – we packed up and moved out onto our bearing, since the new day had already started to dawn.

That afternoon, we reached our target area in the vicinity of Kalabolelwa. Information indicated that the SWAPO elements would be on the eastern side of the road leading down to Sesheke, in the populated area between the road and the Zambezi. As we approached the road, we realised that the bush was too open to lie up in during the day, so we waited for last light.

The exact location of the enemy post was unknown to us, and to try to locate it in the dark would have been suicidal. We decided to establish a listening post close to the road for the night, knowing that we would have to move away from the inhabited area along the river before first light.

At about 22:00 automatic gunfire erupted to our east, followed by the fierce trumpeting of elephants. It seemed that SWAPO were facing a similar ordeal to ours the night before and were now obviously trying to scare the animals away.

Before long, we heard vehicles approaching on the road from the north, followed by the noise of some equipment being loaded onto a vehicle, accompanied by much talking and laughter. It then dawned on us why the cadres were so blasé about their position: they had clearly been expecting the vehicles and were preparing to move out of there.

Hibbers suddenly stood up next to me, pack on his back and rifle at the ready.

"Let's go!" he said.

"Go where?" I demanded.

"Attack them. They don't know we're here. Now's our chance."

The big man was serious, which presented me with a different kind of challenge, as he was adamant that we should launch an attack on the unsuspecting enemy. No matter how much I tried to explain this was not part of our mission and that we couldn't blindly attack an unknown number of enemy in the pitch dark, particularly since we were only four, Hibbers remained fiercely convinced that this was a golden opportunity. He was actually at the point of leaving us behind and charging in there by himself.

After some time, however, we could hear the vehicles departing to the south, and the bush around us became quiet again.

We spent a short while at first light investigating where the enemy had their temporary base close to the road, and where they had embarked on the vehicles. There was no sign of any further presence, and we concluded that the SWAPO element had been moved closer to the border. Over the next three days we made good our exfiltration by patrolling back to the cutline, and were picked up at the border by our own Tac HQ elements.

My first two-man team deployment brought home some of the most valuable lessons I ever learned. Tinus van der Merwe and I were tasked to do a recce of the ZNDF installations around Sesheke to determine if there were any SWAPO elements among them. The targets were all on the northern side of the tar road stretching east–west along the Zambezi River, which at this point forms the border between Zambia and the Caprivi.

The two of us, being new to the game of small team reconnaissance, rehearsed our actions extensively. We crawled around

Omega and the surrounding bases in the Caprivi in the small hours of the night. We practised our emergency procedures and RV drills over and over. When we were ready, we reported to the Sector HQ at Katima Mulilo and presented our plan. One dark night we were taken across the Zambezi by an engineer section, after carefully watching the opposite shore for two days.

For this deployment we thought it best to wear civilian clothing and Afro wigs that we had trimmed short to more or less resemble an African hairstyle. Putty bought a set of brand-new khaki longs, while I donned my soft grey flannels from school. As the khaki trousers only arrived at Omega on the day we deployed, we did not have time to rehearse with them. Mistake number one.

Putty's new khakis made their presence known whenever he moved, because the chafing of the material between his legs created a sweesh-sweesh sound. I was walking in front and had to listen for enemy activity and did not particularly welcome this addition to the audible night life. But the more I told him to keep quiet, the more irritated he got. That whole night we were accompanied by the nagging sweesh-sweesh of Putty's pants, which enticed every single dog in southern Zambia to join in the choir of barking dogs as we moved through the villages along the river's edge. Eventually my buddy was walking with his legs spread apart, which must have been uncomfortable and tiring.

During the deployment we mostly walked barefoot to mini-mise the number of boot prints left behind. On the second morning, after we had walked with our boots tied to our

Top: As a 17-year-old, in 1976 I completed the 80-km Karoo Marathon in the town of Laingsburg in 7 h 19 min 48 sec. Long-distance running has always been a favourite sport of mine.

Left: My father, Koos Stadler, was a minister of the church and a man of the veld.

Top: My father, Koos, and mother, Riegie, visited me at Omega in the Eastern Caprivi. At that time I was a lieutenant in 31 Battalion's reconnaissance wing.

Bottom: The headquarters of 31 Battalion's C Company.

Top: Xivatcha Shekambe, scout extraordinaire, on roll-call parade. Xivatcha taught me much about the bush during my time at Omega.

Bottom: Two senior Bushman soldiers of 31 Battalion's reconnaissance wing. On the left is Tango Naca, with whom I often deployed.

Top: Bushman soldiers on the basic parachute course at 1 Parachute Battalion in Bloemfontein. The course proved to be challenging for most members of the recce wing.

Bottom: 31 Battalion's recce wing on the runway at Omega prior to deployment. From left to right: Tinus "Putty" van der Merwe, Steven Steinhobel, Charles Henning, Jorrie Jordaan, Neil Reinolds, Gerhard Nel (behind), Frik Theron, me and Xivatcha Shekambe. Mark Templeton is seated in front.

Left: As a lieutenant with
31 Battalion. Even then I only
wanted to do one thing –
reconnaissance.

Below: A sketch of an
operator with Afro wig
and SWAPO hat as disguise.
SWAPO uniforms and black-
ened faces were standard
during clandestine missions.

Operator
with Afro wig
and SWAPO hat.

Koos Stadler

Left: Frans Gunther commanded 31 Battalion's C Company and was infamous for his drooping moustache when something wasn't to his liking.

Below: The lecture room at Fort Vreeslik near Omega where 31 Battalion's recce wing did their training and prepared for operations. This was where the "roaring lions" incident took place.

Left: In a playful tussle with Tinus "Putty" van der Merwe (right) at Omega.

Below: The bar at Fort Vreeslik.

MPUPA RECCE
EARLY WARNING POST

OLD PORTUGUESE FARMHOUSE

MAIN BUILDING
ANTENNA
FIRE PLACE
NO VEHICLE
6-8 SOLDIERS
NO WOMEN
NO DOGS OR OTHER ANIMALS

(OP)

My sketch of a FAPLA early warning post in an old farmhouse near Mpupa in southeastern Angola. Annotations were done in code and later (during the debriefing) drawn in on the sketch.

Candidates were tested on both a physical and psychological level during Special Forces selection. The image below shows two of the doctors on my selection course (the man in the middle and the one on his knees).

Top: Typical accommodation on the Special Forces' Bushcraft, Tracking and Survival course.

Bottom: Setting traps and snares was part of the daily routine on the survival course in the Caprivi.

Send ye men up in the land beyond Jordan to spy out the ways thereof, the goings and comings of the people, the wines and honeys of the land ...

MOSES

Visitors to the Small Team headquarters at 5 Reconnaissance Regiment at Phala-borwa were welcomed by this emblem at the entrance. Later the official badge depicted Joshua and Caleb (pictured below), two spies sent out by Moses, under a Southern Cross.

With members of 5 Recce during my first Small Teams exercise in the valleys of the Blyde River Canyon. From left to right are Corné Vermaak (intelligence officer), me, and operators José dos Santos (back), CC Victorino (front) and Jo-Jo Bruyns.

Opposite:
Top: The "mean team" from 5 Recce were, from left to right, CC Victorino, Neves Matias, Dave Scales, Boet Swart and André Diedericks.
Bottom: Small Team operators André Diedericks with his buddy Neves Matias and me with my buddy José da Costa, alias "Mr T".

Left: André Diedericks at Ondangwa prior to a deployment. His pack weighed in at 94 kg.

Below: The Small Team members during Operation Cerberus: from left to right are me, CC Victorino, Neves Matias and André Diedericks. Note the camouflaged BRDM-2 armoured vehicle with SA-9 missile system behind us.

Two sketches I made of the ingenious methods used by UNITA soldiers to get our vehicles up and running again. The top image illustrates how they recovered the BRDM/SAM-9 after a breakdown, while the bottom one is of the improvised jack they made when the vehicle had a flat tyre.

Right: My friend and legendary Small Team operator André "Diedies" Diedericks. Note the two Honoris Crux medals on his left chest.

Left: André Diedericks and Neves Matias after they were awarded the Honoris Crux silver and bronze respectively.

packs for most of the night, we moved into our hide just before first light. Suddenly I realised one of my boots was missing. It must have come undone during the night and fallen from my pack. I had to rush back in almost full daylight and was relieved to find the boot at the point where we had our last break. I made it back to Putty just as the first children started using the path on their way to school.

On the last night of the deployment we still had one more target to do – a platoon guard post and weapon position at the end of the Sesheke airfield runway, just north of the tar road. Not knowing any better, Putty and I stashed our packs and AK-47s a few hundred metres from the target. Clever and eager as we were, we decided to penetrate the base area with pistols only. I crawled in front, Putty following some distance behind. Then, out of nowhere, a guard appeared and started shining a weak torch all over me.

I froze, not knowing whether he had recognised this foreign crawling object as a human being or not. I watched him fumbling around in the dark, apparently uncertain and hesitant to open fire on something he could not identify. The next moment he let go, and a fair-sized stone, presumably from a catapult, hit me on the upper leg – not on the bum, as my Special Forces comrades have alleged for years!

We ran, trying to keep direction in order to find the weapons and packs in the dark. Eventually we sat down to decide on a plan of action, as the packs were now in the wrong direction, too close to the enemy base. Before we could manage to find any sensible solution, we realised that we were being cut off from the tar road and the river. Vehicles were moving down in our direction from the base area, while people were talking excitedly all along our escape route to the south. We ran for it, shooting wildly into the bush with our pistols, and broke through the line of soldiers that were encircling us.

In the chaos, Putty and I were separated and each of us had to make it to the river on our own. Eventually, however, as a result of the many hours of rehearsals, we managed to locate each other again in the darkness by means of a special whistling signal that we had perfected exactly for emergencies like this.

The boat was ready for the pick-up and we made the RV safely and in time, much relieved that we were unhurt. On the banks of the Zambezi, waiting for the boat to come, Putty, who had not been particularly religious at the time, pulled me by the shirt and said: "Let's say a prayer to thank the Boss . . ."

My second small team deployment followed not long after that. Kobus "Kloppies" Klopper and I moved to the area of my first deployment, the lush bush between the Zambezi and Kwando rivers. Our mission was to plant a mine on the road stretching north–south along the western bank of the Zambezi River. To avoid the mine detonating indiscriminately and injuring civilians, we had to master-detonate an explosive charge under a military vehicle, preferable one belonging to SWAPO.

We made our way across the border at night, and meticulously anti-tracked the roughly 30 km to the target area. Since it was winter and large areas of grassland had been burnt, the going was extremely slow. At the road, during the third night, Kloppies planted the mine while I kept a listening watch. To conceal his tracks and remove the soil from the hole he was digging, Kloppies used his sleeping bag, dragging it across the road surface as he moved along. Before first light I moved 100 m up the road to act as early warning for vehicles coming from the north, while he found a spot from where he could watch the road dipping through a valley to the south and wait for the right target.

Daylight found us dug in on the side of the road and covered with dry grass and leaves. I was lucky enough to have found an anteater's hole, into which I crawled, having to cover only my head and shoulders and my AK with the dry leaves lying around. Then the long wait began.

Throughout the day we had to remain vigilant, as people were constantly using the road and we were lying barely three metres away. At one point I thought my cover was blown when a troop of baboons started mocking me from the bush behind me. A group of women walked past and started shouting and pointing straight over my head at the baboons. Had they seen me? Should I take action? I decided to remain dead still and eventually the women turned around and strolled off, still laughing at the agitated baboons. They had no idea I was lying right there under their noses. I have never been so happy to be flatly ignored!

Kloppies had to endure a similar ordeal, as the same group of women stopped to study the drag marks of his sleeping bag on the road. Miraculously, they did not notice him lying three metres away, under a thorn bush, covered with dry leaves.

At the time every action we took and every idea we implemented were done on a trial-and-error basis, as we did not have any "small team" manual to learn from or any other experience to tap into. Little did we even understand, during those deployments, that we were actually conducting small team operations, at a time when the concept was considered quite revolutionary in the Reconnaissance Commandos.

The technique Kloppies and I used to sustain ourselves and still remain undetected was to cache the backpacks about 200 m away from the road, at an easily identifiable position that also served as the crash RV. We would then move forward to our positions before first light, with only webbing and a small pack (a "SWAPO bag", as we used to call it) containing a day's food and water. Come daylight, we would both be dug in and as comfortable as possible in a position where the slightest movement could expose us.

Meals consisted of cold food, with packaging that would not make any noise when opened, and that would not smell once opened. We took water through a plastic tube from a water bottle in the SWAPO bag, which was well concealed with the rest of the webbing on our bodies. Relieving oneself would be out of the question, although I managed to let it out bit by bit into the hole that served as my hideaway, not entirely without messing up my trousers and boots.

At last light we would both withdraw to the RV, establish comms with the Tac HQ, have a quick meal, relieve ourselves and move into a hide for the night, just to be ready before first light to repeat the previous day's routine.

The operation was a success, as Kloppies detonated the mine at exactly the right moment under the nose of a vehicle approaching from the south. The targeted vehicle turned out to be the Land Rover of a senior SWAPO official. During this trip I learned the importance of patience. And I discovered how easy it was to conceal your body with a bit of creative deception.

While operations such as these were conducted at a tactical level and were probably not central to the wider war effort, they provided invaluable learning opportunities. We slowly but surely amassed a wealth of experience and established a unique modus operandi for deployments to come.

In my mind, the two-man concept soon became synonymous with reconnaissance missions. Initially it took a massive mind-switch to leave the rest of the team, the bulk of the ammunition and the support weapons behind. Now it became second nature. Any team bigger than three became a potential giveaway. With only two in the team, stealthy movement and anti-tracking became easier, as each individual was now more alert and would automatically pay attention to every little detail.

By this time my colleagues in the recce wing had accepted the small team concept as the ideal for close-in recce missions. Fortunately, Commandant Opperman and Major Oelschig at Sector 70 (Katima Mulilo), because of their close involvement with the recce wing, allowed the team leaders a free hand in the composition of their teams for missions into Zambia.

However, as we started to deploy into southern Angola, in mid-1980, we discovered that the commanders of Sector 10 (Oshakati) and Sector 20 (Rundu) were not too eager to deploy teams smaller than eight. This was probably based on conventional thinking that any group smaller than an infantry section of ten soldiers would be too vulnerable.

5

The Realities of War:
Fighting Patrols into Angola

IN DECEMBER 1980 SWAPO was active in the area of Eenhana, a settlement and forward military base in central Ovamboland, close to the border. According to intercepts, SWAPO's Eastern Front was positioned northeast of a cluster of Angolan villages called Mulemba. Their very capable commander, known only by his combat name, Mbulunganga, had deployed his forward detachments roughly 30 km from the border with South West Africa, a distance SWAPO considered far enough to be safe from South African retaliation. One of Mbulunganga's most competent detachments was deployed at Chana Ohaipeto. This area served as a staging point for infiltrations into the farmlands of South West Africa during 1980 and 1981.

The SWAPO detachment was on high alert because 32 Battalion had been operating in this area throughout 1980. Moreover, the insurgents appeared to be exceptionally aggressive. Numerous contacts with the SADF were initiated by SWAPO – at times and places of their choosing.

During 1980, elements from 31 Battalion started deploying more frequently in the Sector 10 area of responsibility, including Ovamboland and areas immediately north of the border in Angola. The reason for this was twofold, firstly because cross-border operations into Zambia had been terminated after Zambia's government gave SWAPO the boot, and secondly because the Bushmen had steadily been building up a sound track record and were now in high demand in other operational theatres.

Although reconnaissance was the recce wing's bread and butter, fighting patrols offered a welcome break from the continuous pressure of small team operations. During one such deployment in the area of Chana Ohaipeto during December 1980, we decided that we would apply the same stealth and spoor discipline as during any recce mission.

We were a fighting patrol of three six-man teams with a small HQ element – myself, the radio man and the RPG gunner. Since there was a lot of enemy activity, we would establish a temporary base for one night only and move out before first light. We left no sign of our presence and applied anti-tracking techniques to deceive anyone who might find our spoor. During the day we would set up an ambush site along the edge of one of the chanas, the large open flood plains common in the area, and deploy an observation post to keep watch across the open plain and the kraals along its edges.

One day, while sitting in one of these ambush sites, three SWAPO cadres unexpectedly walked into our position. Two of the team leaders and I were crouched over a map in the middle of the all-round defensive position when somebody shouted, "SWAPO!" The three guerrillas had their rifles slung over their shoulders and couldn't get them into action fast enough. As soon as they realised they were not among their own comrades, they just pelted out of there in all directions.

One of the team members grabbed the RPG-7 and, in the heat of the moment, applied it without considering his mates. The three of us who had been stooped over the map rushed to fall into attack formation but suddenly realised we were running straight into the backblast zone of the RPG. I heard a voice shout "RPG!" and had the presence of mind to go into diving mode.

The backblast of the weapon threw me backwards with the other two. Except for burnt eyebrows and damaged egos, no one was injured, and we collected ourselves once again to move into extended line, although by now there was nothing to attack. We packed up fast and moved out on the enemy spoor, knowing that the larger group had to be in the area.

The three SWAPO cadres had been in light order, with only their weapons and chest webbing, a clear indication that they had been on a security patrol around the edge of the chana. Twice we found positions where the detachment had made camp, complete with shallow trenches and good escape routes. Numerous fresh tracks dotted the area, but by nightfall we hadn't found any more enemy and decided to move away from the chana to bed down for the night.

But there would be no rest for us that night.

By midnight SWAPO declared its presence by bombarding the position along the chana edge, where we had been searching for them earlier. Then, gradually, after there was no response from us, they moved their fire further into the bush in the direction of our hide.

Anyone who has been under mortar bombardment at night will know the sickening fear that comes with the uncertainty of not knowing where the next bomb will drop. There is nothing more unnerving than hearing the thump of an 82-mm mortar leaving the tube some distance into the night, and then waiting for the bomb to explode. In that instant the same question is on your own and the bomber's mind: will the bomb find its target?

Yet I decided not to retaliate, since our 60-mm patrol mortar did not have the range of their 82s. Besides, we had only a limited number of bombs and I did not want to give our position away. We knew from experience that the tree branches overhead would trigger some airbursts, and we could only pray that the bombardment would not come closer. We were not dug in, since we would be on the move before first light (although once we heard the first mortar leave the tube we dug frantically into the soft sand).

In the end, the 82-mm bombs did not find their target, but it was still an unnerving experience. I had been in many contacts with the enemy, and had been at the receiving end of much more accurate mortar and artillery fire, and later even fighter aircraft attack, but the uncertainty of that night remains vivid in my mind.

Before first light we were on the move and soon found the enemy's deserted positions – 60 well-prepared dugouts in an

L-shaped ambush formation, complete with mortar pit at the junction of the lines. As we inspected the surprise SWAPO had prepared for us, we could only thank our lucky stars that we hadn't charged in there blindly. The detachment had been ready for us, and, had we followed the tracks of the three SWAPO cadres further the night before, we would have walked straight into their ambush. That day we followed the tracks for ten kilometres north, but had to abandon the effort when we reached our boundary, as the spoor led into 32 Battalion's area of responsibility.

When I reported this, the Tac HQ ordered us to move to a safe area and secure a landing zone for a resupply. I found it strange, since I had not requested a resupply, and we did not really want our position to be compromised. But we went ahead and secured an area. At 17:00 that afternoon a Puma from Eenhana dropped off, for each of us, a warm chicken wrapped in tin foil, an ice-cold Coke and a carton of long-life milk.

It was 26 December 1980, and that resupply was a wonderful Christmas gift. We had our feast in a last halt, well spread out, with buddies covering each other. At last light we shifted our position into a hide. Under a brilliant starlit sky, I thought of my family, who would be together and the night before would have shared gifts and rejoiced in the message of Christmas.

That night, despite the pent-up fear and the uncertainty about what the next day would bring, I developed a personal philosophy that would become a yardstick for as long as I did clandestine deployments into countries harbouring hostile forces. In my mind's eye I would step out of my body, look down at myself lying under the stars in that foreign land and ask myself one question, "Where would you rather be at this moment?" If the honest answer was, "Nowhere. This is where I want to be", I would find peace in spite of my fear and uncertainty, as I knew that everything was exactly as it was supposed to be. I had made the decision to be there, and I was prepared to take full responsibility for it.

This was often easier said than done, but this philosophy guided and remained true for me for as long as I did special operations. In later years with Special Forces I went through periods of constant and extreme pressure. During those times I would relive all the old fears – and even had flashbacks of close encounters during my time with 31 Battalion recce wing. But the essence of the philosophy has carried me through many challenging situations, not only during special operations but also in a later phase in my life when I participated in extreme adventure sports events, and ultimately during a 200-km solo hike through one of the most barren sand deserts on earth, the Rub' al-Khali, or Empty Quarter, in Saudi Arabia.

That night I fell asleep with a full tummy and happy memories of my loved ones, knowing that I would face the challenges of the new day refreshed in body and spirit.

In 1981 SWAPO's Western Front launched a number of infiltrations from its headquarters in the vicinity of Cahama across the border into the Kaokoland, the barren semidesert bordering the Namib. The recce wing of 31 Battalion was tasked with a series of operations into Angola along both sides of the Cunene River. The purpose was to find SWAPO forward deployments that would serve as staging points for the groups infiltrating deep into South West Africa.

These operations, staged from Ruacana, differed in many ways from my experience up to that point. For starters, the area was covered in mopane trees and the ground was hard, unlike the thick sand that covered the whole of Ovamboland to the east and the central parts of southern Angola. Undergrowth was relatively sparse, which meant that we rarely found a good hide, and would therefore never outstay our welcome. Another difference was the rugged mountainous terrain to the west of the Ruacana Falls. This was a world apart from the tree savanna of Ovamboland.

Not unlike the Tac HQ we used to establish at Katima Mulilo, we had a cosy little ops and radio room in a bunker that served as operational headquarters at Ruacana. Initially our deployments were tentative, as we had to get to know the area and, more importantly, convince the Sector 20 bosses at Oshakati that we were up to the job. Therefore our early deployments were all on the "safe" side of the Cunene River, mostly shallow incursions to determine if SWAPO had been bold enough to cross over to establish forward bases or penetrate deeper into South West Africa.

At that point the strategic position of the SADF was somewhat restricted, since Pretoria's official position was that no South African troops were deployed in Angola. The capture of a South African soldier on the wrong side of the border would therefore have been a grand prize for the Angolans. At the same time, Pretoria was struggling to convince a sceptical world that ours was a just cause, and trying to obtain proof that the MPLA was supporting SWAPO. As always, politics prescribed the war effort.

To reduce the risk of South African troops being captured, South West Africa Territorial Command issued an order that South African regular forces were not allowed to deploy in any subunit smaller than a section, or ten men. This rule was also to be applied by all the units permanently based in the operational area, including 31 and 32 battalions.

I thought the order had to be a joke. A section of ten guys would be extremely exposed, especially if they were not trained in the finer arts of minor tactics. They would leave a track as clear as a highway, make unnecessary noise, and would still not have the firepower to fend off a large enemy force.

After discussing the issue with my superiors, both at Sector 10 and at 31 Battalion, we came up with a compromise: all reconnaissance missions would henceforth be done in ten-man sections, combining two five-man recce groups into a section-strong team – but each under its own team leader. Usually a ten-man section would be deployed under the command of one Tac HQ. However, we decided that the two five-man teams would operate separately and each in its own area of responsibility, but within so-called support distance of each other. This solution appeased everyone, and we managed to stretch the "support distance" somewhat.

During the time we were operating from Ruacana I was out of action for several weeks after I contracted malaria. One day, while doing PT with the ops personnel from the base, I suddenly started to feel very ill. Afterwards I had a vicious headache and started vomiting uncontrollably.

The malaria took me down. While lying in the cramped, hot sickbay at Hurricane, the airport and gunners' base outside Ruacana, I lost consciousness as the fever took my mind to terrible places. I was overcome by strange hallucinations of hordes of SWAPO fighters falling from trees onto my secret hideout. The next moment I would be back in green pastures along the Orange River with my family. I remember how, at some point between these bouts of fever, my comrades came in to greet me, and I realised with a shock that they were saying their goodbyes. But slowly I emerged from this ordeal, and steadily regained my sanity over a three- or four-day period.

I was too weak to deploy, and, since there had been a number of reports of cerebral malaria in the operational area, I was admitted to Oshakati hospital for observation. Upon my discharge, I took two weeks' leave, flew home and spent some precious time with my folks in Upington.

On numerous operations into both Angola and Zambia I had the privilege of having Xivatcha Shekambe by my side. To this day I consider him one of the best soldiers in the bush I ever came across. He had an amazing sense of awareness that often bordered on a foreboding, a sixth sense that made him able to understand and predict tactical situations.

Xivatcha's tracking skills were almost superhuman. The story was told in the unit of how his previous platoon commander in A Company, a young lieutenant, was challenged by some of the white South African trackers while on a training course at Kamanjab. Our young lieutenant boasted that there was no track his Bushman trackers could not follow. The white trackers then appointed their best tracker to lay a spoor for a Bushman from 31 Battalion to follow. Xivatcha was appointed to do the tracking.

Unknown to him, the white trackers had decided to win the bet at all costs. The spoor was laid across some open ground, and then onto a large lawn in front of the mess building to lead Xivatcha astray. The white tracker stationed himself in the bar, from where he could watch the Bushman struggle to find his way. Xivatcha hesitated only slightly at the point where the track led onto the grass, and then headed straight for the bar, following the line across the lawn that the white tracker had used ten minutes earlier.

Xivatcha often saved an operation from disaster through his calm and decisive reactions. This was the case when we conducted a reconnaissance of a suspected SWAPO base in the area of a forward FAPLA detachment at a settlement called Chiunga, in southern Angola.

As part of a large offensive against SWAPO detachments, Sector 10 had established a forward helicopter base known as a helicopter administrative area (commonly referred to as an HAG, after its Afrikaans name, *Helikopter Administratiewe Gebied*) inside Angola. The purpose of the HAG was to provide a quick-reaction capability to 32 Battalion companies deployed to hunt down the enemy, while twelve-man paratrooper sticks were placed on immediate standby at the helicopters.

Our recce team from 31 Battalion, under the command of a newly trained lieutenant from the recce wing, was flown in from Ondangwa to the HAG and tasked to locate the SWAPO base. I was to act as the team's second-in-command. From the HAG we had to cover 20 km on foot to the target during the night, find the base by first light and call in the reaction force for the attack the following morning.

Little did we realise that the reconnaissance was meant to provide a reason for the commander to initiate offensive actions against the FAPLA company at Chiunga, as they were suspected of harbouring SWAPO cadres. At that time FAPLA troops were not considered enemy, but the South Africans were frustrated by the fact that SWAPO shared facilities with FAPLA elements. Often it was impossible to distinguish between the two forces, as they used the same weapons and equipment.

By first light we hadn't located the base, and we realised we were in trouble. Now we had to find the enemy base in broad daylight, a predicament compounded by the fact that our vision was restricted as we moved east towards the rising sun. By mid-morning we found evidence that we were close to the base, but we had not seen any enemy yet. Suddenly, across an open stretch of omuramba, we spotted a group of soldiers running away from our position. Two of us, the team leader and I, moved forward to establish an OP in a tree on the edge of the omuramba, leaving the rest of our patrol in the relative cover of the bush.

To have a better view across the omuramba, the team leader insisted on scaling one of the young mopane trees, an effort accompanied by much huffing, puffing and swearing. Above the commotion I suddenly noticed another sound, coming from the direction where we had left the rest of our team. It initially sounded like the far-off barking of dogs, but we quickly recognised it as the high-pitched yelling of people moving in on the hide. Then some shots were fired, and the two of us started sprinting back to the hide.

By the time we reached the team, the skirmish had developed into a full-blown contact. We automatically started to withdraw and fell into a well-rehearsed routine of "buddy-buddy" (or fire-and-movement, where one person in the buddy pair would move under cover of his buddy's fire), eventually splitting into two groups to peel off to both flanks of the advancing enemy. Soon my team was out of the line of fire and we made good our escape by circling behind the enemy's advance.

The team leader, Xivatcha and a third member of the team were not so lucky. By this time they had been caught against the open omuramba on their right flank, and as a result had to withdraw while squarely in the line of fire. The team leader, not knowing whether we were dead or still fighting, realised that he had to establish radio comms to call in the reaction force. However, they now found themselves in a desperate fight, pinned against the open omuramba and with no way of disengaging from the contact.

At some point during this extended battle, Xivatcha shouted at the lieutenant to stay down, insisting that they set up the radio and establish comms, even if it meant making a stand against the advancing and much superior enemy force. He then took it upon himself to defend the position while the other two got the radio into action.

As Xivatcha kept a constant volume of fire going, the other two established comms, with the result that the parabat reaction force could soon be trooped in by helicopter to engage the enemy from behind. Heavy fighting ensued and lasted for most of the day, but our two teams were soon reunited and evacuated to the HAG.

On another deployment, Xivatcha again saved the lives of his team members by correctly assessing the situation and responding appropriately. Under the code name Operation Carnation, the recce wings of 31 and 32 battalions had to do the route reconnaissance for some of the combat groups that would advance into southern Angola during Operation Protea in August 1981. Operation Protea was aimed at neutralising FAPLA bases at Xangongo, Ongiva and Peu-Peu through semi-conventional attacks by mechanised forces and to destroy SWAPO in the area between the Cunene and Cubango rivers.

My team did the reconnaissance for Combat Group 30 from Beacon 16 north of Ombalantu to the tar road leading from Ongiva to Xangongo in southern Angola. As part of the larger offensive, Combat Group 30 had to approach Xangongo from the east, then swing north in order to neutralise FAPLA forces at Peu-Peu, while three other combat groups would attack Xangongo. This time I was compelled to take a six-man team, so that we would be able to "make a stand" in an encounter with the enemy. Fortunately, the idea of a ten-man team for reconnaissance missions had by then been exposed as ridiculous.

At the time I did not argue the matter, as a route recce did not require the same levels of secrecy and stealth as a point-target recce. In fact, I decided to approach the job more aggressively and prepared the team as a fighting patrol. Everyone therefore kitted up with support weapons and loads of ammunition. The real reason for this was that we would most likely end up in contact situations alongside elements of the combat group, and I had nightmares about running out of ammunition and having to quit in front of our national servicemen.

Once again, Xivatcha was part of the team. During the recce we painstakingly worked out, logged and memorised a route we would be able to follow at night, leading the combat group in towards Xangongo in the pitch dark. To ensure that we would follow the correct route, I took rolls of toilet paper and wrapped it around trees and bushes all the way up to the tar road. We had quite a laugh trying to imagine what message a SWAPO patrol might have gleaned from the wrapped-up trees – anything from "the shit is coming your way" to "begin solank gat skoonmaak [start cleaning your arse, or get away while you can]".

On the third day of the mission, instead of running out of ammunition, we ran out of battery power for the radio. With the last bit of battery life, I called in a resupply. This was done by Alouette, which didn't need a large landing zone, so I left four guys in the hide among the trees and headed off with one Bushman to an open area a few hundred metres away. The resupply went smoothly and soon the noise from the two Alos died away as they disappeared to the south.

I was still speaking to the pilots on the VHF radio when two Bushmen suddenly dashed into the open from the direction of the hide, eyes wild and thumbs pointing down from their closed fists in the familiar sign for "enemy". Xivatcha and his buddy were nowhere to be seen.

"SWAPO, baie, baie [many, many] . . .!"

"How many?" I demanded and they cried out, "Maar baie, baie, Luitenant. Miskien twintig of veertig [A lot, Lieutenant. Maybe twenty, or forty]."

I immediately called back the two retiring choppers, just managing to get a signal through by holding the radio above my head. The pilots, keen for some action, didn't hesitate.

At that point I was expecting the worst, thinking that the other two members of our team had been overpowered by the enemy. We rushed back to the area of the hide in line-abreast formation, going low as we approached. They were still there, Xivatcha and his buddy, guarding our packs and watching the enemy moving past them to form up for an attack. Suddenly the choppers were there, circling overhead.

The six of us broke cover and advanced towards the positions where the bulk of the enemy was last seen. As we approached, we donned our bright orange Day-Glo panels so the pilots would recognise us – standard practice for troops in combat zones at the time. Then the contact erupted, with shots fired from every direction. A chaotic firefight ensued, and the thick bush made it impossible to determine the enemy's direction of attack, as we were now right among the SWAPO fighters. Amid the shooting, the shouting and the two gunships circling and pumping 20-mm rounds into the bush, I desperately tried to hold the team as close together as was tactically safe.

The pilots, trying to distinguish friend from foe in the chaos below, requested that I show Day-Glo and keep my team together. The more I told them that we were already doing this and were keeping together in a sweepline formation, the more they countered that we were more than six and not exactly in line. It transpired that some of the SWAPO cadres, knowing that they had no chance of survival once they were isolated and spotted by the gunships, cleverly fell in with our formation, moving from cover to cover in the thick undergrowth on the flanks of the sweepline.

Applying fire-and-movement, or "buddy-buddy", we advanced through the contact area, shouting battle commands and delivering a constant volume of speculative fire into the undergrowth. After a few hundred metres the bush opened up and we realised that there was no more opposing fire. Then bursts of AK-47 shots erupted from the contact area from where we had just emerged. The pilots called us back into the killing zone and circled the area as we advanced to contact once again. Soon we engaged at short range with SWAPO cadres who had been hiding and were probably as confused as we were, not knowing which direction we were attacking from. With the lead gunship circling overhead, we eventually swept through the contact area no fewer than four times while the other chopper covered probable escape routes further out.

I never got into the habit of counting heads, or "kills", as subconsciously, and later deliberately, I could not bring myself to believe that three or four dead could influence the outcome of a war. But the Air Force claimed six kills, for what it was worth, and they loaded the bodies and stacks of AK-47s on board the Puma helicopters dispatched to the area after the contact – for the intelligence guys to analyse. The team received a resupply of ammunition and water, and continued with the route reconnaissance mission.

At our last halt that evening, I sat down with Xivatcha's buddy and asked him why they had stayed at the hide earlier the day in the face of such an overwhelming enemy force.

"Xivatcha," he said, "it was Xivatcha that insisted that we stay. When the Bushmen ran away, we didn't know if you were aware of the terrs [SWAPO cadres], and that they were forming up for an attack. So he wanted us to guard the equipment and open fire when they came – so that you would be warned in time."

After the reconnaissance, we withdrew to the border and met up with Combat Group 30 to prepare for Operation Protea. The recce team was divided between the two lead Ratels.[7] At last light on 23 August 1981 Combat Group 30 crossed the border into Angola. Because there was no space left inside the Ratel, Xivatcha and I had to sit on top, clinging to weapons and handrails. It was bitterly cold; we were given blankets, but the cold penetrated to the bone. However, we led the battle group all the way up to the tar road leading to Xangongo, passing toilet-paper ghosts in the darkness on our route.

When the combat group eventually reached the tar road and turned west towards Xangongo, it was daylight. I felt frozen, but there was no time for self-pity, as these guys were heading for a fight and were quite serious about it. By now I was the only pumpkin sitting exposed on top of the lead Ratel, since Xivatcha was ordered to sit inside, but there was still no room for me. I lay down behind the turret as the machine gunners started delivering speculative fire into the bush left and right. Every time they let off a burst, I shrunk away even further.

Fortunately, the resistance was relatively weak, as the defenders had already withdrawn by the time we passed their positions, probably realising that they would be cut off once the main attack force had taken Xangongo.

Combat Group 30 did not participate in the fighting at Xangongo, as its job was to neutralise Peu-Peu and then act as cut-off during the attack on Xangongo. My recce team was eventually airlifted to join up with the rest of 31 Battalion, which formed the main component of Combat Group 50, under the command of Frans Botes, the OC 31 Battalion. Combat Group 50 would be involved in mobile area operations as part of Operation Daisy deep into SWAPO-held territory in the areas of Evale and Nehone.

Operations Daisy and Protea

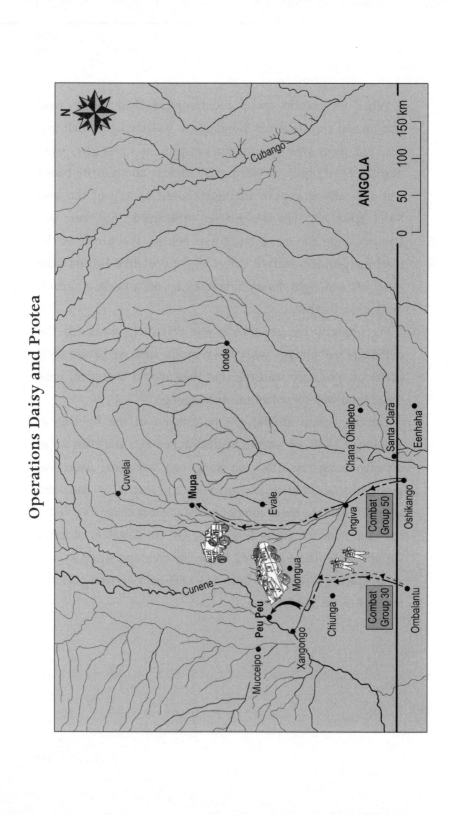

6

Operation Daisy
November 1981

OPERATION DAISY was essentially an area operation aimed at neutralising SWAPO forces in the terrain between the Cunene and Cubango (Kavango) rivers in Cunene province. I remember Daisy as a series of contacts along the route as we pushed deeper into Angola. During his final briefing, Commandant Botes told subordinate commanders: "We follow this route past Evale and Mupa towards Cuvelai, and we give them a bloody nose as we go along . . ."

We joked about this, because we could not imagine that the SWAPO detachments would sit and wait for us to "give them a bloody nose". To our surprise, it turned out exactly the way Botes had predicted. It transpired that the detachments north of Mupa were waiting for a resupply on the very day and on the same route that we approached from the south. We realised afterwards that they must have confused the noise of our vehicles with that of their own. Throughout that day we bumped into elements of SWAPO and engaged in running skirmishes.

We even captured a Volvo staff car and the replenishment truck, a Russian GAZ 66 loaded with bags of maize and dried fish.

The route the battalion took followed a lush green dry river-bed from Mupa towards Cuvelai. The recce wing led the way in two Buffels,[8] followed by one of the companies, the HQ and support vehicles and then the rest of the companies. Suddenly we heard shooting, followed by "Contact left!" over the radio.

We rushed towards the contact. By the time we arrived at the scene, at the side of the omuramba, the first recce team had already disembarked and was doing a hasty follow-up into the thick undergrowth. A single shot rang out, and I immediately thought one of our guys had been ambushed. As we closed in, we discovered a young SWAPO cadre who had shot himself in the head.

The dead cadre lay in the short grass, his clothes and kit in a sorry state. In his breast pocket was a Bible. For the first time – although I did not acknowledge it then – I was unsettled by the scene. He had clearly killed himself out of fear of what the South Africans would do to him had he been caught alive.

In those years it was still easy for me to distinguish between right and wrong. We were fighting on the side of the righteous; we were the God-fearing Gideon's band defending our country from the threat of communism and the anti-Christ. SWAPO represented evil. They were the dark force that would bring communism and an immoral world order to South West Africa and, eventually, to South Africa. At least, this was the mould in which I had been brought up, and it was easy to believe that I was on the "right" side.

But finding a pocket Bible on a young SWAPO cadre, who had killed himself out of terror for what I, a God-fearing South African, would do to him, flipped a switch in my mind. Never again would I see the Border War, and my later operations with Special Forces, in simple black-and-white terms. From this point onwards I would also start to question the reason for many of our actions during the war.

For the next few days we steadily worked our way towards Cuvelai, sweeping wide for SWAPO deployments. Information about a large SWAPO camp that served as detachment headquarters and training base in an area about 20 km northeast of our location was confirmed and the combat group established a temporary base (TB) to prepare for an attack. The TB happened to be in the exact location of a long-abandoned SWAPO base.

During the afternoon before the day of the intended attack, one of the guys found a roughly drafted map in one of the bunkers. This depicted the layout of a minefield, with 98 antitank mines and a large number of antipersonnel mines apparently in close proximity. What made this discovery even more alarming was the fact that we found 98 dust covers for Russian TM-57 antitank mines; the dust cover has to be removed to insert the fuse into the fuse well. This meant the mines were armed.

But, for some reason, our commanding officer was not too disturbed by this information, and ordered the combat group to be ready to move out by 04:00 the following morning. We would reach the enemy base by first light and deploy for the attack as we engaged in combat – two companies in attack formation and the third in reserve. The recce wing would form the cut-off group to the side, while the HQ would remain behind the attack force, with the indirect fire support group, the 81-mm mortars, in close proximity. Four Alouette gunships would be dispatched as close air support from an HAG south of us once the attack commenced. This was not uncommon for the type of operations we were conducting, as there was no time for a pre-recce and we did not know the exact location and layout of the base.

So it happened that the two recce wing vehicles moved out at 04:00 the next morning, crossing the narrow omuramba that led out onto our route. C Company followed, with Lieutenant "Swazi" Naudé's Buffel leading the way. Naudé, a dedicated young officer and second-in-command of C Company, had meticulously prepared his equipment for the day's fighting.

Suddenly a loud explosion tore through the morning air, followed by a commotion among the C Company vehicles behind us. Then Swazi's voice broke radio silence, which was supposed to be in force until the attack.

"Fokken landmine. I have just cleaned my rifle; now it's all messed up again."

Swazi's Buffel had hit a landmine as it moved out on our tracks. The two recce wing vehicles must have missed it by millimetres as we passed a few minutes before. Although stunned and full of dust, Swazi and his fellow passengers had not been injured. They collected their kit and moved away from the vehicle to shelter nearby, while everyone else debussed and moved into all-round defence while the damage was assessed.

Since the vehicle had been moving into its position in the convoy at a walking pace, it had not been overturned by the powerful mine. The front left wheelbase had been ripped off, but other than that there was little damage. With a little time and innovation the "tiffies" (mechanics) could get it running again. By now everyone was thinking about the minefield on the map we had found the previous day. Captain Gunther voiced his concern over the radio, asking the OC whether he wasn't worried about the possibility of more mines. But our combat group commander had his mind on the forthcoming attack and was adamant that we move on.

"Radio silence from now on!" he ordered over the VHF network. "No word until we hit contact. I don't want the enemy to sit and wait for us."

The damaged vehicle was left with a protection element until after the attack, so Swazi and his team of rattled and dusty men got onto the next C Company vehicle in the convoy.

It was daylight by the time we moved out again, the recce wing vehicles leading and Swazi trailing. I watched as Swazi and his team moved out across the omuramba, almost hesitantly, past the stricken Buffel. I was still looking when the next landmine went off. A massive dust cloud engulfed the Buffel, which was blasted onto its side this time. It all happened as if in slow motion. Fortunately everyone was ready and strapped in, and, once again, there were no injuries.

When the OC's voice came over the radio, he made his announcement in a calm and collected voice: "Stop! All stations, stop. We are in the middle of a minefield . . ."

But by now Swazi was fuming. He refused to get out of the overturned vehicle until the engineers had cleared the whole area, and by the sound of it he could have killed an entire SWAPO detachment barehanded. Later, it transpired that while Swazi waited for the damage to the first vehicle to be assessed and a decision made regarding the attack, he sat under a tree and meticulously cleaned his rifle. By this time he didn't need a radio to convey his disgust to everyone in the combat group – or any enemy who might have been listening in.

For the rest of that day everyone stayed either on his vehicle or in cover, waiting for the engineers to clear the area. By that afternoon they had lifted exactly 96 TM-57 landmines and 12 antipersonnel mines, the exact complement depicted on the map (minus the two that Swazi had detonated). The attack on the base had to be postponed for a full day while the tiffies fixed the two Buffels and the engineers ensured that we had a clear road back to the SWAPO logistics route in the main omuramba.

The attack on the detachment headquarters turned out to be a dud, as the area had been evacuated a day or two before. The combat group circled round to approach the base from the north, but as we advanced on the location, we realised that the enemy had already withdrawn. All the spoor were older than a day, and vehicle tracks indicated that their retreat might have been a hasty one.

Over the next few days the combat group was ordered to conduct area operations, and then to start sweeping south through the areas where we had engaged the enemy earlier on. It was considered too dangerous for our combat group to move any closer to the FAPLA and Cuban deployments in the area of Jamba and Techamutete, since we were essentially a guerrilla force armed only for combat against SWAPO in the bush. We had neither the arms nor the armour to engage tanks or armoured cars in conventional combat. At this point we were also well within range of the FAPLA MiGs operating from Menongue.

Strangely, on our way back to the border, we had a number of skirmishes with stray groups of SWAPO. This might have been because their command and logistics system had been disrupted by the earlier operation, or because the cadres did not know what was happening and had returned to the supply route for replenishment.

One day I was driving behind the HQ package, taking a breather from the stress of driving point and having to be vigilant all the time. The peace was short-lived. "Enemy right!" came the voice over the radio, followed by the sound of AK shots from the side of an omuramba.

I could see the HQ vehicles in front of us being bogged down by enemy fire. A voice cried over the radio, "They're shooting at me, they're shooting at me!" while the pressure switch was held down, preventing the rest of the force from communicating. But this didn't deter us. Without hesitating, we swung into the direction of the incoming fire and charged head on, followed by B Company's vehicles. In the absence of proper radio comms, the commander of A Company, which was in the rear, had the presence of mind to swing sharply to the right in an attempt to outflank the enemy and cut them off to the north.

The recce wing vehicles arrived simultaneously at the enemy positions, which by then had already been vacated. The ambush had been set up with well-prepared firing positions, good arcs of fire and good escape routes into the thick undergrowth beyond. Unfortunately for the ambushers, a group of about twenty, our combat group passed too far across the omuramba, thus rendering their fire ineffective.

We didn't waste any time; I took twelve recces onto the tracks into the thick vegetation, leaving the rest to protect our vehicles. We knew from previous experience that the enemy would run for one or two kilometres, slow down to listen, and then try to anti-track or deceive their pursuers by splitting into smaller groups. After three kilometres, they would settle into a steady pace on a route until they reached relative safety. This trick was all too familiar to us, as we had all done it ourselves many times before.

We therefore ran at breakneck speed on the clear tracks left by the running SWAPO soldiers. Soon enough, we found the spot where they had slowed down. From that point on the tracks were not as clear, and soon we could see them dispersing. We continued our chase, knowing that they would expect to hear vehicles first. I spoke to the HQ on the run, requesting choppers as air support and to act as telstar (an aircraft that would be dispatched to establish comms in case of an emergency) once we ran out of comms with the main column.

Contact!

Two SWAPO cadres were leaning leisurely against a tree and drinking from their water bottles when we ran straight into them. We opened fire before they could even put down their bottles. The first one didn't have a chance and died in his tracks, the other hit the deck and tried to crawl out of the field of fire, but to no avail. By this time we were like a pack of hounds, hungry for prey. We didn't stop, but just went on hunting once we had checked that the two cadres had passed on to greener pastures.

We knew that the shots would have alerted their comrades, who would be more vigilant, but we maintained a steady pace on the three or four tracks we were following. Suddenly the lead pilot of two Alouettes came on the air, calling for our position and ID. They had been on their way to our combat group when the call for assistance came through and were therefore instantly ready for action.

We gave them yellow smoke on the ground and I quickly briefed them over the radio. On the run I gave the choppers a compass bearing of the direction the enemy was heading. While one chopper circled overhead and maintained a close air support posture for our group, the other flew on the bearing and circled two to three kilometres further ahead in an effort to locate the fleeing enemy and also to keep their heads down. It wasn't long before we found where the cadres had been ducking and hugging trees as the chopper swept over them, trying to hide from the prying eyes of the crew.

When the 20-mm machine gun of the lead chopper started stuttering its deadly song, we knew we were onto them. We spread out wide, sweeping vigilantly through the thick undergrowth. The helicopter in the close air support role engaged, kicking up plumes of sand barely 30 m ahead.

I heard someone shout: "He's shooting . . . he's shooting! Down!"

In that instant I saw a SWAPO soldier taking aim at one of my team buddies from behind a fallen log. Our man was virtually on top of him, but didn't have time to train his weapon on the cadre at his feet. Instead, he just rushed at him like someone possessed, jumped the log and kicked the AK-47 from the wounded terr's hands, all in one mad, wild move. The rest of the team then opened up, killing the cadre instantly.

By now we were all fairly wasted, having run about twelve kilometres at almost full speed. We quickly regrouped in all-round defence and I ordered the Bushmen to find the rest of the tracks. The lead pilot reported that they were low on fuel and had to return to the combat group, but promised that they would be back with water. Soon it became apparent that the remaining two or three insurgents had dispersed and were now running individually. There would be no sense in following one track at a time, especially since the cadres had been given the fright of their lives and were now probably doing some serious low flying through the bush.

We started our withdrawal, exhausted and thirsty, but happy with the day's work, knowing that we had achieved the almost impossible: we had outrun fleeing SWAPO soldiers on their own turf. The choppers soon returned with our water, and the pilot was kind enough to talk us back to the vehicle column via an easy route.

During Operation Protea two mechanised combat groups had led the attack on Angolan forces at Ongiva. The town had been left in a shambles. All FAPLA elements had evacuated their positions, the town's administration had been completely disrupted and the population were battling to survive. Command of the salvage operation in town, as well as the defensive positions around the perimeter, was given to 31 Battalion. The whole unit converged on Ongiva and established a TB some 20 km to the southwest, from where mopping-up actions would be conducted. The unit had the unenviable task of systematically working through the abandoned FAPLA defences to collect remaining weapons and documentation, as well as to destroy bunkers, infrastructure and any foreign ammunition not used during the battle.

Although I was not keen on the job and did not want the recce teams to be exposed to the relaxed atmosphere and relative ill-discipline of the regular troops, it did offer us a well-deserved break while still attuned to the war. In the end it was a great experience, as we got to know our brethren from the companies more intimately, and generally had a pleasant time at the HQ in the bush. To keep their hand in, the recce teams did security patrols around the TB, and often found the familiar chevron tracks, a spoor pattern commonly used by SWAPO cadres, in the vicinity of the camp – just to keep the hair on our necks standing up.

During the mopping-up operations, we regularly found civilians who had been injured in the attack on the town four weeks previously, and our medics diligently attended to them. One incident that will always stay with me was when we found a woman lying in a dark little hut with a massive wound to her upper right leg. Gangrene had set in and her leg had swollen to twice the size of her frail body. The stench in the hut from the advanced infection was almost unbearable, and the poor woman would not let anyone touch her, as the pain must have been excruciating.

She also had a little girl, no more than five years old, who wouldn't leave her side. We explained to the husband – who had led us to her – that we were going to evacuate her with the girl. He protested strongly, but there was no alternative, as the little girl did not want to leave her mother's side. Without proper medical attention the woman would have died a slow and painful death. He eventually accepted, after we promised him that both his wife and his daughter would be returned.

It was easier said than done, though. Firstly, we struggled to get her out of the narrow door of the hut once we had moved her onto a stretcher, and had to break down part of the wall. Secondly, it was nearly impossible to get her on top of the Buffel, as she screamed in pain at the slightest movement. The trip across the uneven terrain was pure agony for the wounded woman, and she wailed constantly as we bumped along.

Knowing that the helicopters would not enter the 20-km no-fly zone around Ongiva, we pressed on to find a suitable landing zone (LZ) before last light. In the meantime I pleaded with the OC to have the choppers dispatched, because I knew the evacuation of civilians was not a priority for the South African Air Force.

When the OC asked if we were out of the no-fly zone yet, I faked a grid reference and assured him that we were in a safe area. Finally we heard the Pumas and marked our position with yellow smoke.

"Kilo Sierra, this is Giant," the lead pilot's voice came on the air. "Is that your yellow smoke?"

"Giant, Kilo Sierra, that's affirmative. I'm due northeast," I said.

"You are still in the danger zone, man," he responded. "You want me to come in?"

"That's positive. The LZ is secured and safe. No problem," I answered, and went on to describe the size of the LZ, wind direction and open quadrants.

Such was the nature and quality of our pilots that he didn't query my decision or the safety of the area. He moved in swiftly and set the aircraft down, giving me a thumbs up through the canopy. They were flying off again in less than a minute. The last thing I saw before the doors closed was the wide-eyed little girl clinging to her mother's dress, staring dumbfounded at the strange machine around her.

The story had a happy ending, as I learned some months later when I visited the Sector 10 operations room in Oshakati. The woman lost her leg, but was given a prosthesis to which she responded very well. The child was temporarily adopted by one of the nurses and was sent to school in Oshakati. Upon recovery, the mother was given a job at the sickbay – to assist and teach patients who had lost limbs and had to adapt to artificial ones. She was also allowed to go visit her family at Ongiva.

7

End of an Era

IT IS STRANGE how we are often connected to people even before we meet them. The regimental sergeant major (RSM) of 31 Battalion was a former member of the Reconnaissance Commandos and he often used to tell us about life in the Recces and about some of the characters he got to know there.

His firm favourite was a certain Diedies, whom he had allegedly recruited and who turned out to be a legend in the Special Forces. According to the RSM, André "Diedies" Diedericks and his buddy, a guy called Neves, operated only at a strategic level, conducting highly secretive and extremely sensitive operations far behind enemy lines.

I would listen intently as the RSM shared his experiences during his time with the Recces. Whenever he told us about Diedies and the small team reconnaissance group, I would pepper him with questions. The RSM often urged me to find a way to get in touch with Diedies, to do Recce Commando selection so I could join the Small Teams, but at the time I was too young and inexperienced to consider it seriously, and besides, I loved every moment with the Bushmen.

Little did I know then that this larger-than-life figure, who by the end of his operating career would be awarded two medals for bravery – the Honoris Crux Silver and the Honoris Crux Bronze – would become a comrade and close friend. To me, he was to become the personification of skill, dedication and sheer guts.

Those days at 31 Battalion were of the best any young soldier could hope for. We deployed on one operation after the other, steadily building up experience. Two weeks back at Omega would see us preparing for the next deployment. At Fort Vreeslik we invented new techniques, new pieces of equipment and fresh tricks to deceive our enemy.

The only way a bushwise guerrilla force like SWAPO could be matched in the African bush was for us to live as close to nature as they did – and to outwit them at their own game. I developed a firm belief – which I still hold today – that a guerrilla force in the dense bush of southern Angola and Zambia could not be beaten by firepower, at least not by firepower alone. After all, what would you direct your firepower at if your enemy was constantly on the move, or would "run away today to fight another day", as we frequently encountered?

So we became masters in the application of tactics, in everything from silent movement to stalking, tracking and anti-tracking, patrol techniques and contact drills. We also became masters in reconnaissance, simply because that was what we did – day in and day out. When we were not on a deployment, we would stage exercises in the Caprivi and simulate different types of targets, or use the neighbouring bases to observe and infiltrate.

When I look back today, I can honestly say that there never was such a closely knit, dedicated and professional team as 31 Battalion recce wing. Obviously, I cannot compare the 31 Battalion recce teams with other professional outfits out there, such as the 32 Battalion "recces", or even similar specialised groupings abroad, but, given that I spent the rest of my operating career in the Recces, I can compare them with the best reconnaissance teams in the South African Special Forces. I am immensely proud to have had the privilege of being part of such a unique band of brothers. It was an extremely valuable learning experience that laid the foundation for my career in the Recces.

At the end of 1981, my short-service contract expired and my military career got sidetracked for a while. By this time my father and two older brothers were all qualified ministers of the church, and were serving their respective communities. When my contract with the Defence Force expired, I had to make a decision about my future career. There was mounting pressure from my family to follow in the footsteps of my dad and two brothers, so I registered for a degree in Theology at Stellenbosch University and started my first year in 1982.

During my studies at Stellenbosch, I managed to slip away every holiday – to go back to Omega, the bush and my old comrades. Military call-ups provided valuable income, but more importantly offered a welcome break from the monotony of my studies. The first year, I managed to operate with Xivatcha every time I went back to 31 Battalion. In 1983, at the beginning of my second year at Stellenbosch, Xivatcha was suddenly not there when I arrived at the unit for the call-up.

I was told that he had gone on a drinking spree while sitting in front of his hut at Omega with his three little children. At some point he got so drunk that he picked up a bottle of hydrochloric acid that was standing next to his beer – and emptied it. He died five or six days later. In the hospital at Omega he crawled from the bed to the lawn, and when he couldn't crawl any more he insisted that they carry him outside. He refused to die in a bed.

PART 3

Special Forces

*"Self-pity doesn't jibe with power. The mood
of a warrior calls for control over himself and at
the same time it calls for abandoning himself."*

— Carlos Castaneda, *Journey to Ixtlan*

1

Special Forces Selection and Training

ALTHOUGH studying at Stellenbosch University was a pleasurable experience and, in a sense, a welcome break from three years of cross-border reconnaissance missions, I found that my passion was elsewhere. I felt the call to join the Recces, and realised after a year that I had been away from the books on military call-ups once too often.

One morning, while my fellow students were wrestling with Greek and Hebrew in class, I drove to Gordon's Bay and spent the rest of the day on the cliffs above the sea. While huge waves rushed in and broke on the rugged rocks far below, I peered out over False Bay and came to a decision.

No longer would I resist the nagging sensation that I belonged elsewhere. I would quit my studies, apply for Recce selection and commit myself to a career in Special Forces. There would be no turning back.

The first thing I did when I got back to Stellenbosch was to phone my dad. While I knew that he would be deeply disappointed, he did not say anything. He only asked if I had made up my mind and if I was dead sure. We spoke at length, and in the end I had the peace of mind that my father would stand behind me and support my decision.

The Special Forces pre-selection programme was a week-long series of tests done at the South African Medical Services Training College in Pretoria, where about 300 hopefuls gathered from all the arms of service across the country. Pre-selection was virtually a selection in itself. To thin out the field, the physical tests were concluded first. These consisted of a battery of fitness tests (six different PT tests done in quick succession), a fifteen-kilometre hike with kit and, finally, a range of biokinetic tests in the gym. This was followed by a full medical examination and a series of psychological and aptitude tests.

We stayed in the barracks of the medics' training college, where I had a bizarre experience with a guy whom I had met on the first day during the initial admin phase. Peter was a lieutenant from the Air Force's security squadrons – tall, handsome and with distinct athletic features. He had huge calves and a torso like a gorilla's – the kind of physique I knew I could not compete with. He was also an exceptionally jovial and easygoing person, and everyone took an immediate liking to him. For some reason he latched on to me, and we ended up sharing a cramped room in the barracks.

After the medical and biokinetic tests, Peter boasted about his performance. According to him, one of the pretty young nurses commented on his abnormally large chest capacity, apparently just the right thing if you wanted to become a Special Forces diver. His fine figure had clearly made an impression on the medics, since they were already referring to him as the "Air Force Recce". Little did I know that my roommate would apply his skills in other related diving spheres. That night he sneaked a girl into the barracks, and had her screaming in ecstasy on the bed barely half a metre away from me, with no shame or consideration for the other person in the room. With the erotic aromas in the air and the hushed panting and the vibration of passion, I had my own little fantasy adventure.

As soon as we heard that we had passed the test series, we were to report to 1 Recce in Durban. Of the initial 300 candidates who reported for the tests, 30 were found suitable to continue with the Special Forces selection. Peter did not make it and I never saw him again, but strangely enough the memory of that one night has stayed with me.

And so I began a whole new chapter in my life. At the end of May 1983 I drove down to Durban in my little Toyota Corolla, and passed through the gates of 1 Reconnaissance Regiment – known simply as 1 Recce – on the Bluff. Here I was at the epicentre of Special Forces training in South Africa, the very heart of the elite. I didn't know what to expect. I moved into the officers' mess and was, to my surprise, treated by all the mean-looking Special Forces officers as a fellow human being!

Within a week we moved to Dukuduku, a training area close to Lake St Lucia in Zululand, for Special Forces Orientation, a five-week preparatory course before the actual selection. The aim of this course was to level the playing field, since candidates came from all sorts of backgrounds, from all the different arms of service and even from civilian life. The programme was aimed primarily at building up strength and fitness, but it also addressed the elementary military skills of musketry, map reading and navigation, basic fieldcraft, communications and weapon handling.

During one of the communications classes where we practised Morse code, a fellow student called Werner, who had a rather pronounced stutter, became the target of our instructor, Taffy. He started barking out the letters of the alphabet to the class, then pointed at someone to respond to the "Alpha?" or "Bravo?", or whichever letter he chose to spit at his victim. The poor bugger at the receiving end then had to respond with the Morse equivalent, namely, "dit-dah" or "dah-dit-dit-dit".

Everyone waited in anticipation for Werner's turn. And, sure enough, when Taffy attacked him with a vicious "ALPHA?", Werner rose weakly from his desk and started stuttering, "dit-dit-dit . . .", to which Taffy responded by screaming, "Sit down, you fool, it's only one 'dit'!" Everyone roared with laughter and Taffy had to stop the lecture for us to come to our senses.

Each week we walked progressively further and with a heavier pack, and the PT became more strenuous by the day. At the end of the programme eighteen guys were left from the original pre-selection group. We were in top shape and in good spirits. No selection could stop us now!

The Special Forces selection course, also presented in the Dukuduku State Forest, was intense, but it was way too short for me to ever think of giving up. In addition to the eighteen candidates who had passed Special Forces Orientation, eleven medical doctors were earmarked to do the selection with us.

In 1983 the demand for qualified doctors during special operations forced the authorities to allow doctors to join Special Forces – and do the actual selection – while doing their national service. Once they passed the selection, they would do selective Special Forces training so they could be deployed on certain special missions. As an incentive, they could work in a hospital of their choice after completing their national service to specialise in a specific field of interest. Many of the young doctors doing national service saw this as a way to advance their careers, and did not mind sweating a bit of blood to make it happen.

Over three days we were exposed to a series of the most strenuous physical exercises – intended also to be psychologically taxing. One particularly challenging test involved a team of five having to carry a fuel drum filled with water over a distance of 12 km. The team had to improvise a way to carry the drum using two logs and some rope. Since two of the guys in my team were tall, they took one end while the shorties (myself and another midget) took the other. It was up to the team to decide how to rotate the fifth person. The shorter guys ended up taking most of the weight. This was character-building stuff, as we were also carrying our full kit and rifles. The end never seemed to come.

There were other exercises, like Octopus and Iron Cross, that were physically quite tough, but since they were all group exercises I found them relatively tolerable. For me the only really demanding test was the interrogation phase, towards the end of the course. The instructors concocted a devious plan to capture us, one by one, as we patrolled through a stretch of thick undergrowth. With our arms tied behind our backs and our faces hooded, we were transported to the base where the "interrogation" commenced – and lasted throughout the night.

I was expecting this, but nothing had prepared me for the shock of the extreme cold. My clothes were removed and I was tied to a post on a bare gravel surface. Then the agony started, as some sadist kept pouring ice water over me. At about midnight I discovered that I could retain some body heat by lying flat in the mud that was forming beneath me, and by keeping my legs closely pressed together. But my tormentor had obviously seen this trick before, as he ordered me onto my hands and knees. By kicking my legs open, he could shoot buckets of icy water up my backside – right up into the core of my body where I kept the last warmth, and where he knew it really mattered.

Relief came in the form of the interrogation sessions, where they placed us one by one in front of a blinding white light while an interrogator peppered us with nonsensical questions. Since the movement had warmed my numb limbs and the rays of the light were pleasantly warm on my naked body, I found this quite a treat and tried to extend my time with the interrogator by babbling on and on. This was subsequently held against me: my report after the course stated that I might be a security risk as I was "prone to giving secrets away"!

The South African Recce selection course in those days was known to be physically extremely demanding, as the weight of the equipment and the distances covered were beyond the abilities of the average soldier. But, indeed, so were most of the Special Forces operations executed at the time. The purpose of the programme was to select the very best – those who showed the physical and mental stamina to cope with the demands of operations deep inside hostile territory.

Over the years it was often asked whether the rigorous Special Forces selection process didn't eliminate candidates who might not have had the physical ability but who could have been assets in other respects. To me this was no argument, since I believed that physical endurance and mental ability went hand in hand. And in any event, I felt that the psychological pressures during those few days were the proverbial "cup of tea".

In my opinion three aspects made the selection relatively easy compared to my first selection at 31 Battalion a few years before. Firstly, everyone knew that it would be over in three days, as the same pattern had been followed in previous selection courses. Secondly, all the exercises were done in teams, which ensured that you consistently had a measure of peer support. Thirdly, we had an audience all the way through; the constant presence of psychologists, medics, instructors and operator-evaluators probably inspired many of us to keep up the performance.

After the Special Forces selection was completed, eleven of the original 300 candidates were left. I had a strange sense, similar to that when we finished the 31 Battalion recce wing selection, that the programme should have lasted another two or three days – to sort out the borderline cases that were not meant to become Recces. I was convinced that a few of my comrades made the selection purely on peer support. Had their buddies given up, they would not have seen the end of selection either.

Special Forces HQ and deployments

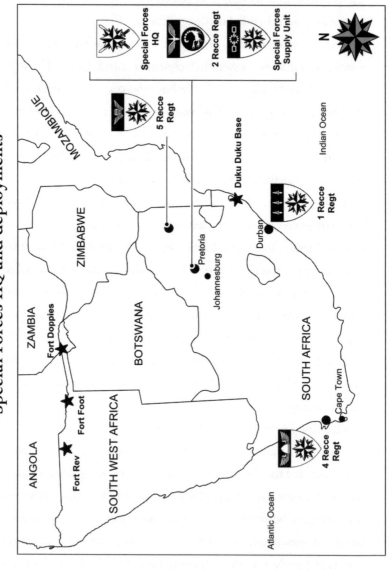

2

Special Forces Training Cycle

THE YEAR-LONG Special Forces training cycle was designed to produce a highly skilled soldier who would be prepared for the demands of specialised operations conducted outside the borders of the country. It was a year filled with fantastic new experiences. The wealth of knowledge I gained on the different courses, the extraordinary people I met, the new technology we were exposed to – all of it added up to a year of high adventure. I also met extraordinary leaders of men, made lifelong friends and visited the most beautiful parts of our country.

Over the course of that year, we did the toughest training imaginable. Following selection, the next phase was the Special Forces Individual course, once again in the Dukuduku State Forest. After that followed Basic Parachuting, Small Boat Orientation and Know Your Enemy, and then Air Operations and Basic Demolitions. The training cycle was concluded with the bush phase, first a Bushcraft, Tracking and Survival course and finally Minor Tactics.

Special Forces Individual

Now that we had passed selection, we were considered part of the Special Forces family. Attitudes towards us changed overnight. There was to be no more shouting and swearing. Objectives were given in a calm and mature manner, and it was up to us to achieve them. On the course we were introduced to Special Forces equipment – radios, backpacks, boots and an array of gadgets I was not familiar with. The content of the course focused on the application of weapons and equipment used by Special Forces. We were therefore also exposed to a variety of foreign-made weapons, and had the opportunity to apply them, initially on the shooting range and later during actual exercises.

Our fitness level was maintained by two PT sessions per day. These were meant to build us up for the demands of the rest of the course, and I found them quite enjoyable. While we didn't do any more route marches, the backpack was now a constant companion during exercises.

After Special Forces Individual we went back to 1 Recce to prepare for the next three courses: Basic Parachuting at 1 Parachute Battalion, Bloemfontein, Small Boat Orientation at 4 Recce, Langebaan, and finally Know Your Enemy at 5 Recce, Phalaborwa. The group was allocated two brand-new Toyota Land Cruisers, and we drove across the country to the different units where the courses were to be presented.

Basic Parachuting

Since the eleven of us had passed the Recce selection, we did not have to do the Parachute selection, then known as PT

course, but we still had to do the tough parabat entry tests –
again, a series of physical tests to measure candidates' potential. Four of us had done parachute training before, and
therefore did not fall in with the actual training course, or
hangar phase, as it was popularly referred to.

During the third and last week of the course, we joined the
group for some progressive jumping. Those few weeks in
Bloemfontein were quite carefree, and I used the time to maintain my fitness with long runs and hard physical exercise.

After the parachute course we drove through the Karoo to
Langebaan, on the West Coast. The ocean was a new envi-
ronment to me, and would certainly bring new challenges.
Secretly I dreaded the thought of the icy waters of the
Atlantic Ocean.

Small Boat Orientation

But 4 Recce turned out to be a breath of fresh air, literally,
as Langebaan is renowned for its ever-present wind, and fig-
uratively, since the unit was unique. The main base, with
the headquarters, accommodation, logistics and administrative capacity, was the public face of the unit. Across the lagoon, on the northern tip of the Langebaan Peninsula, was
the secretive operational base at Donkergat, an area naturally out of bounds to the public, from where operations were
launched and where all training was conducted.

Donkergat used to be a whaling station, and the operational base was built over the remnants of the old structures.
In fact, the main quay was formed by concreting the hull of

one of the trawlers. It also had a quay specially designed for the docking of South African Navy strike craft and Daphne-class submarines, both used extensively for deploying the Recces during operations.

Because of its specialised role, 4 Recce was not an Army unit in the normal sense. Aside from the array of operational boats kept at the boat yard at Salamander, across the lagoon, it had its own little fleet of ferries and a well-equipped boat workshop on the waterfront at Langebaan.

The unit was a world apart. Not only was it set in beautiful surroundings but it also had a different heartbeat. The sense of purpose and professionalism of both operational and non-operational personnel I encountered there remained with me for as long as I soldiered with Special Forces. Years later, I experienced it again when I served as the second-in-command of the unit.

For the duration of the Small Boat course we stayed at Salamander in an old hotel converted into a training facility right on the tip of the Langebaan Peninsula. The course was no walk in the park: the Benguela current makes the coastal waters extremely cold, and we spent the best part of our days and nights either in or on the water. In those three weeks we swam and kayaked more than any sound-minded person would in a lifetime. We became adept at handling inflatables, the operational rubber boats, and were exposed to various infiltration techniques from sea to land, as well as through watercourses like rivers and estuaries.

Know Your Enemy

After completing the Small Boat course we drove from Lange-baan to Phalaborwa, bordering the Kruger National Park, for a course then called Know Your Enemy, or Dark Phase. During this course we immersed ourselves in the doctrines, tactics and history of the armed wings of the freedom movements at the time considered enemies of the state. The idea was to recreate a guerrilla base so we would be exposed to a setting that resembled an enemy encampment. All activities would be based on the routine in a freedom fighter camp.

Black instructors from 5 Recce were our commanders and trainers, and would lead us in singing, marching, weapon handling and tactics. The unit contained many former guerrillas – from SWAPO, Umkhonto we Sizwe (MK) and even ex-cadres from ZANLA and ZANU-PF in Rhodesia. We therefore got a good dose of Marxist indoctrination, and had to learn slogans from old masters like Mao Zedong and Che Guevara.

Aside from learning about the doctrine and tactics of the revolutionary forces, the course provided in-depth background on the origins and history of the freedom movements of southern Africa. From schooldays we had been taught that there was a communist-inspired onslaught against God-fearing white South Africa. I had been indoctrinated to fear *die Rooi Gevaar* (the Red Peril) and believed in the proverbial "communist behind every bush". We were made to believe that the African National Congress (ANC) was quite literally the anti-Christ, and that we had to combat the organisation on all fronts – with mind, body and soul.

However, the Know your Enemy course gave me a completely new outlook on these so-called enemies of the state. In an ironic twist, right there in the heart of one of the best fighting units of the South African Defence Force, I started to understand that most of the freedom forces were fighting, at least from their perspective but also in the eyes of the world, for a noble cause. For the first time I learned about the origins and founding principles of the ANC and the South African Communist Party, as well as about the leaders of the early years of black resistance – Oliver Tambo and Nelson Mandela. It brought a different perspective to life as I had known it.

During that course we were taught a striking song about Solomon Mahlangu, who was executed by the apartheid regime in April 1979 and became an ANC martyr. The song, which lauded Mahlangu as a hero of the struggle, became embedded in my mind. One dark night several years later, during a highly secretive small team mission deep inside Angola, I would be surprised to hear it again.

On the course we were also introduced to the kinds of heavy weapons used by enemy forces at the time. The course was too short to master the details of all the antiaircraft machine guns, recoilless guns, rocket launchers and anti-air missile systems, but we at least learned to recognise and apply safety measures to Eastern Bloc weapons like the ZPU-23 anti-aircraft system, the DShK 12.7-mm machine gun, the SA-7 and SA-9 missile systems and recoilless rifles like the SPG-9 and B-10. We also had the opportunity to fire the machine guns and some of the antitank weapons.

Both Small Boat Orientation and Know your Enemy provided ideal opportunities for would-be operators to be exposed to two other operational units, having already become acquainted with 1 Recce on the Bluff. The idea was for the candidates to experience the environment they would eventually operate in, be it in water or in the bush, and to make up their minds as to where they wanted to be. For me there was no choice. Even though I liked the no-nonsense and professional approach at 4 Recce, my only mission was to get to Small Teams as soon as possible after the training cycle. Besides, 5 Recce appealed to me immediately. It was an "African" unit, with troops hailing from all over South Africa and as far afield as Rhodesia, Angola and Mozambique, and I fell in love with the much more informal and laid-back style of the unit.

Air Operations

For the Air Operations course we had to drive back to Durban, as the first week covering the theory was presented on the Bluff. By now the bright lights of the coastal city didn't appeal to me; I had visited the operational units and was eager to get back to the bush.

Air Ops was a cleverly structured course intended to expose us to all the intricacies of clandestine work with an array of fixed-wing aircraft and helicopters. The course leader, an experienced skydiver and head of the air operations branch at 1 Recce, put us through the paces of working with all kinds of aircraft.

The course covered a whole series of subjects related to cooperation with the SAAF. We learned to prepare landing zones (LZs) for various aircraft, to choose and prepare a drop zone (DZ) for para drops behind enemy lines, to call in aircraft for resupply or pick-up, and to control various aircraft during close air support in a combat situation. Although I had worked closely and extensively with the Air Force while at 31 Battalion, the exposure to the full range of SAAF aircraft was a new experience. I especially enjoyed collaborating with the fighter jets, as it introduced a completely new dimension – and little did I know how handy it would be during small team operations later in my career.

The course concluded with a practical phase, this time at the Hell's Gate training area close to St Lucia, where we put into practice all the procedures we had learned.

Basic Demolitions

Although I had done demolitions while at 31 Battalion, the Special Forces course had a specific focus. While the normal demolitions course presented by the School of Engineers was generally aimed at the destruction of large-scale infrastructure, the Special Forces course focused on sabotage – where a relatively small group of operators would infiltrate their target clandestinely and render it unserviceable, causing maximum damage with the minimum amount of explosives. To achieve this, we were taught techniques ranging from the use of shaped charges to the correct placement of explosives. Another part of the training included improvisation techniques, where the operator had to apply innovative ways of setting up charges with the minimum equipment at his disposal, or to use improvised techniques to set time switches and booby traps.

A further addition to the course was exposure to custom-made demolition charges designed and manufactured by EMLC, the highly specialised (and later controversial) engineering company that worked exclusively on devices and equipment used in special operations.[9] The EMLC array of charges included various initiation devices, ranging from time switches to light-sensitive and anti-tilt mechanisms. We were also exposed to different forms of explosives, such as the highly effective PE4 and PE9, and to a liquid explosive called "Slurry", which could be poured into confined spaces and turned solid when exposed to air. I would use many of these devices and explosives extensively during small team deployments later in my career.

Bushcraft, Tracking and Survival

The day finally arrived when we deployed to Fort Doppies, on the banks of the Kwando River in the Caprivi Strip, for the final phase of our training. The nine-month training cycle would be concluded with two courses – Survival and Minor Tactics. The nine remaining students, plus two guys who had joined us from previous selection courses, flew by C-130 from Waterkloof Air Force Base to Mpacha in the Eastern Caprivi.

Ray Godbeer, a seasoned operator from the erstwhile Rhodesian Selous Scouts, presented the Survival course. To our surprise, on the first day our clothes and equipment were taken away, leaving us with only PT shorts, T-shirt, a cap and a rifle to face the African bush and survive the chilly nights. We were dropped off about fifteen kilometres from the survival camp, and then our shoes were also taken away; we had to cover the distance back to the camp barefoot. I couldn't comprehend the logic of this, but I realised later during the course that it was aimed at stripping us of all the comforts of civilised life to force us into survival mode from the outset.

Soon enough everyone started improvising by making rudimentary shoes from leaves, grass and strips of bark. Apart from providing protection against the burning hot sand, it taught us that makeshift feet covers could also serve as anti-tracking devices, since no clear footprint would be left. Wearing only PT clothes forced us to respect the bush, to move carefully around thorny shrubs and quietly through the undergrowth. In the long term the effect of those three weeks in PT kit under the African sun, at least for me, was that I would take great care to move cautiously through the bush, and to wear protective clothing during operations.

During the first week we established a base camp at the "Horse's Shoe", a peculiar-shaped bend in the Kwando River, where we were given lectures on the wide variety of fauna and flora, their uses in a survival situation, and what to avoid and what to exploit. Tracking formed an integral part of the course. After the initial lessons on spoor recognition, determining the age of a track, counting the number of tracks and, eventually, how to follow a spoor, we would always move out in two groups, the first laying a track and the second following. Soon it became second nature – to be aware of signs indicating human presence.

In the heat of the day and during the evenings we received further detailed lectures on the plant and animal life of the region. We would learn how to locate water in tree trunks or in the bends of dry riverbeds, and how to collect water using a "desert still", or a simple method called a "tree still", where we would wrap a plastic bag over the wet leaves of a branch and leave it overnight for the water to condensate.

Food was systematically reduced from one tin per day to nothing, as we learned to set snares and traps for birds and small game. The Kwando River also yielded freshwater mussels, while the small nuts from the dried-out fruit of the marula tree provided some relief from the persistent hunger. Also in abundance at that time of year was the raisin bush, which provided edible berries as a supplement to our meagre diet.

At the end of the first week we were taken by vehicle and dropped off individually in a remote area along the Botswana border. It was time for Exercise Egg – Ray Godbeer's unique way of exposing his charges to Mother Nature. Each of us was given two eggs, one match, a small piece of flint and two rounds of ammunition (meant only for protection against lions, which were abundant in the area). The idea was that we had to get a fire going, cook the eggs and sleep out alone under the stars.

I have spent countless nights in the bush on my own, so for me the experience was a positive one and merely a test of my ability to be completely at ease alone in nature. But for someone from the city who had not been exposed to the thrills of night life in the African bush, this could turn out to be a somewhat scary experience, and in subsequent years I have heard hilarious stories about would-be operators' hair-raising encounters during Exercise Egg.

After I had been dropped off, I went on a recce down a nearby omuramba and soon found water holes with some muddy water left from the rainy season. I was hoping to use some green leaves to make a crude wrapping for my two eggs, and then drench it with water, bury it under a few inches of sand and cook it up by covering it with coals from my fire. But at the water hole I found two rusted tins that I put to good use. I carried water in the tins to my "camp", made a fire with my match and flint, and simply boiled my eggs.

As a child, while hunting with my father on farms in the Kalahari, I had been taught the art of making a "Kalahari bed" to survive the bitterly cold winter nights – a trick I applied again. I gathered enough wood before last light and stoked the fire, then dug a shallow trench long enough to lie in. Once I had a good supply of coals from the fire, I scraped them into the trench so that the entire bottom was covered. Taking care to cover all the coals, I then worked a layer of sand across the bottom.

Then I made a second fire on the other side of the "bed", hoping that any hungry lion with the intention of having half-cooked human flesh as a midnight snack would be discouraged by the flames. I also piled up a sizeable heap of sand and a supply of firewood, knowing that I would need to restock my "blanket" before the early-morning chill set in.

Finally I collected dried grass, which I used to cover myself once inside my cosy cradle.

By the time the instructors arrived in the morning, I was refreshed from a good night's rest and presented them with my boiled egg (having eaten the other the previous night). A number of the other students had been unable to get a fire going and endured a cold and scary night out in the bush, while most of them lost their eggs trying to cook them in the fire. One colleague had discharged both his rounds at what he thought was a lion, and then climbed a tree where he spent the rest of the night trying to maintain his balance and get some sleep.

Back at base camp our routine involved tracking, checking our snares in the evening and receiving lectures on a range of subjects. But unfortunately I fell violently ill with diarrhoea, possibly caused by drinking contaminated water out of the rusted tins. Already weakened by a lack of proper nourishment, my body packed up. I was evacuated to Fort Doppies where I was put on a drip and nursed back to health over a couple of days.

We were halfway through the Survival course and my biggest fear was that I would not be allowed to continue with Minor Tactics, which meant that I would have to wait another year to complete the training cycle and qualify as Special Forces operator. Fortunately, Ray Godbeer stood up for me, and convinced the bosses that I had done all the theory and only needed to pass my exams to complete the course. While recovering from the diarrhoea at Fort Doppies, I asked for my notes to be sent from the survival camp and used the time to study.

After about five days in bed, I rejoined the course for the assessment phase. I passed the theory and recognition exams easily, and then went on to do the practical tracking evaluation. I was completely whacked from the diarrhoea, but managed to follow the track with relative ease and convince the instructors that I was actually a born tracker. Ray let me pass the course, albeit with a little bit of TLC, for which I am eternally indebted to him, and I was allowed to continue with Minor Tactics.

I consider the Survival course as a learning experience on a par with the training I had received from Frannie du Toit at 31 Battalion. Even after my three years with the Bushmen, I had to admit that I had never learned so much about the bush in such a short time.

Minor Tactics

This was one long route march from beginning to end. For the students it turned out to be a second selection. When not slogging through the Caprivi bush with a 35-kg pack, we were doing fire-and-movement, so the course became a long drawn-out battle with an "enemy" that was persistently following us through the bush, with the eleven of us trekking and fighting consecutive battles day after day. Since I had done the course previously under the capable Frannie, and in fact had developed my own approach to tactics and a specific style of patrolling in the bush, the course was particularly challenging, since I dared not oppose the conventional wisdom at that late stage of our training.

During the long fire-and-movement "battles", which were all conducted with live ammunition and loads of mortar, RPG and machine gun support, all sorts of strange methods were applied to stoke the students' aggression. One specially favoured technique was to walk behind the student and hit him with a stick, presumably to make him move faster, shoot straighter and take better cover. This was not only counterproductive but also bred resentment against those instructors who indulged in the practice. Unfortunately it remained a favourite method to induce aggression, one that I encountered repeatedly in subsequent years at Special Forces training.

There were other peculiar features of the course, such as the extended ambushes, where we had to lie in wait for hours on end in the bitter cold of night, or during the heat of day in the sun, for the "enemy" to appear. Having done this in real life more times than I could remember, I battled with the concept, since I believed it was a waste of time. To my mind the ability to wait out a real-life enemy could not be taught superficially; it demanded a certain mindset that every soldier who had passed the selection should naturally possess.

Another feature of the course was the harsh punishment for any transgression, whether committed on purpose or not. Any accidental discharge of a weapon or cheating during exercises would earn the punishment of a "spes ops", where the candidate would be taken by vehicle to the Botswana cutline 20 km away, and dropped off with his weapon, backpack and a case of ammunition weighing 25 kg, which he then had to carry back to base. This was regularly done on a Saturday evening, so the transgressor had the whole night and the next day to think about his sins while transporting his uncomfortable load back to Fort Doppies.

I had the honour of doing a "spes ops" once, but since my transgression – an accidental discharge of the LMG on the firing range – was not considered life-threatening, I was dropped off only ten kilometres out and was back in time to catch a solid night's sleep.

During the Minor Tactics course I met Captain André "Diedies" Diedericks, the legendary Small Teams operator I had been told about years before during my time at 31 Battalion. With his long-time buddy, Neves Thomas Matias, Diedies had conducted several two-man deployments, over extended periods and extreme distances, into neighbouring countries. Diedies and his group had established a camp somewhere in the bush and were rehearsing for a deployment when I met him one Sunday during a break in our training at Fort Doppies. The guy had a very focused aura about him; in Diedies a sense of purpose combined with a delightful sense of humour. It immediately struck a chord with me. I was surprised to find that he had heard of me when I was still at 31 Battalion recce wing. He also seemed to be aware of my dream of joining Small Teams. From that first meeting I felt a close attachment to this man who had become a legend in his own lifetime.

Diedies informed me that Small Teams might soon be relocated from Pretoria to 5 Recce, based on his recommendation that the Small Teams elements of all the units should be united under one command. The three active Special Forces units – 1 Recce at Durban, 4 Recce at Langebaan and 5 Recce at Phalaborwa – each had its own field of specialisation: as the founding unit, 1 Recce harboured the Special Forces Training Commando and specialised in airborne and urban operations; 4 Recce specialised in seaborne operations; and 5 Recce focused on bush operations. Both 4 and 5 Recce also maintained an inherent airborne capability. Each of the regiments had a reconnaissance element that was meant to conduct strategic-level recce missions.

At the time Diedies and his Small Team grouping formed part of the secretive D-40, code-named Project Barnacle and based outside Pretoria (it was the forerunner to the Civil Cooperation Bureau, or CCB). But Barnacle's undercover status would soon cause Small Teams to be relocated to one of the regiments, as the operators were constantly exposed to the overt structures of Special Forces. Diedies often had to visit Special Forces HQ for intelligence briefings and liaison, while the operators had to do their specialised military training at the Reconnaissance Regiments. For me, the planned relocation of Small Teams to Phalaborwa was good news, as I knew by then that I would be heading for 5 Recce soon after the training cycle.

From that first meeting with Diedies at Fort Doppies, a long and true friendship flowed. It continued in subsequent years when we operated together on a number of extremely demanding and dangerous Small Teams operations, and beyond that through periods of very trying times of a different nature.

I knew that I had to get to Small Teams as soon as possible, as this had been my sole purpose for joining Special Forces. I didn't want to waste any more time. But I had to stick it out on the training cycle and get the Special Forces operator's qualification before I could move on. Fortunately the final stages of the course went by quite quickly. There was a fantastic team spirit among the students, and we worked hard to support and motivate each other.

The last exercise – escape and evasion – flowed naturally from our perpetual fighting and moving of the previous days. We reorganised at a rendezvous way down the Western Caprivi, about 50 km southwest of Fort Doppies, where we took in a hide for the night and prepared for the next day's "mission". A company from 703 Battalion at Katima Mulilo was brought in to take up the chase, while local Bushmen from the Kwando would do the tracking.

The idea was that, as a Special Forces team that had been compromised deep inside enemy territory, we would evade the follow-up force while moving back to the safety of our base. The "enemy" would apply all sorts of techniques to catch us, following us back towards Fort Doppies. They had an assortment of vehicles, a helicopter and the advantage of knowing where we were heading.

Our hide was "attacked" by the instructors at 05:00 the next morning, which was the sign for us to start our evasion. The eleven students were given a thirty-minute head start, so we wasted no time in getting away. As soon as we were on the run, I split from the group, veered off to the right and started anti-tracking in a southerly direction, knowing that the follow-up would be directed at the main grouping heading northeast towards Fort Doppies. The follow-up force would certainly use the road to the left of the follow-up axis to leapfrog ahead and dispatch teams to cut us off. I also had no intention of being located by the helicopter, as that would mean certain capture.

I soon slipped off my boots and anti-tracked in my socks in a wide circle back in the direction of the starting point, and then moved a kilometre south before putting my boots back on. To the north I could hear the vehicles starting up and the troops yelling to boost their own morale, for they knew that an encounter with a trapped operator could become a messy affair. I heard the Alouette start up, and before long it moved out in the direction of Fort Doppies. It circled wide and overflew my position twice, but there was no chance of their spotting me, and I knew from the flying pattern that they didn't have troops to call in to my location.

I used the rest of the day to jog on a bearing towards a spot on the Kwando River just south of Fort Doppies, not bothering to anti-track, as I knew that the main follow-up was now in front and some distance north of me.

Throughout the day I kept a steady pace and enjoyed the peaceful surroundings of the savanna terrain. Twice I encountered herds of elephant, but gave them a wide berth.

By late afternoon, when I finally hit the vehicle track running along the Kwando River, I turned north and headed towards camp. I knew for certain that the "enemy" would be deployed along the Chopper omuramba (named after the heli-copter landing zone that was situated there) south of Fort Doppies, as that would be the point where all of us would need to cross into the base area.

I watched the area for a while from the southern edge of the omuramba, and soon realised that there was no way of crossing unseen, as the observation posts (OPs) were sited every 100 m to block us off. I also realised that there was no time to circle the area, as our cut-off time to reach the base was 18:00, which gave me barely two hours to finish.

The only chance to make it in time was to walk straight into one of the OPs, "eliminate" the guards and make a run for the base.

What I did not realise was that these guys had been on edge the whole day, and were now fairly trigger-happy, since they had had to face two or three other lunatics trying to crash through their defences. By the time I reached their position, they were all nerves, wide-eyed and ready to shoot.

I took a sporting bet on my chances, and started running as soon as I reached them. But the long day's walking had taken its toll, and the thick undergrowth and loose sand made it difficult to break away from the well-rested and eager young men, and we soon agreed that I would stop acting like a mad-man and they would refrain from manhandling me. Besides, I was happy to be transported the last two kilometres to Fort Doppies in the back of a Land Rover, to arrive well before the exercise cut-off.

By that time I knew that I had passed the course. It was of no consequence that I hadn't got past the final hurdle of troop positions around our destination, as I knew it was a superficial barrier. Besides, I was confident that, given the time and the advantage of darkness, I would have easily reached the base undetected, as this is what I was really good at.

Of the original eleven guys who had started the course, nine of us passed and qualified as Special Forces operators. One student had withdrawn early of his own accord and another was taken off by the final assessment board on the basis that he was a safety risk.

The course was a satisfying experience, mainly because of the camaraderie and the exhilaration of being in the unspoiled bush of the Caprivi, but I was glad to be leaving, because I was ready to start living my dream. Since I had met Diedies at Fort Doppies and discussed my aspirations with him, there was no stopping me from joining Small Teams.

It was July 1984. We flew back to Durban and I soon departed for Upington for a few weeks' vacation with my folks. During those three weeks at home, quite to my mother's disappointment, I went on a solo hiking trip in the barren hills along the Orange River way downriver from Augrabies Falls. In the loneliness out there I came to find peace with my decision to give up my studies and take the bold step to join Special Forces. I had a new sense of purpose and felt immensely proud, because now I knew that I could master anything I set my mind to.

3

First Special Forces Operations

"And finally power is something in oneself, something that controls one's acts and yet obeys one's commands."
– Carlos Castaneda, *Journey to Ixtlan*

BUT MY DREAM to become part of Small Teams was not to be fulfilled – at least not yet. For my first deployment I had to join 53 Commando, one of the offensive combat subunits of 5 Recce. I had barely arrived at the unit early in August 1984 when we boarded a C-130 heading directly for Nkongo, an operational base in the far east of Ovamboland. At the time, SWAPO's Eastern Front had declared it a "liberated area", as the cadres roamed the bush around the villages freely, visiting the kraals and getting food from the local population at night. The locals supported the guerrillas, providing shelter, food and water, while warning them of any security forces in the area.

The vegetation was dense, with widespread thickets of *haak-en-steek* (thorn acacia). The sand was thick and soft. While this made tracking relatively easy, it also ensured that we left a clear trail, slogging with our heavy packs through the difficult terrain. Since SWAPO mingled with the population, they had the advantage of walking about in civilian clothes, often barefoot. They also had the cattle herders – young boys who wandered in the bush around the kraals with their cattle – as a regular source of information about SADF activity in the area, and they often used them to cover up signs of SWAPO presence by chasing the cattle over their spoor.

I stepped off the C-130 at Nkongo not knowing what to expect. I was assigned to the team of Sergeant Coen van Staden, a very experienced team leader. At the time it was quite acceptable for a young officer to be part of a team commanded by a senior NCO. I was fresh from selection and the Special Forces training cycle, and had a lot to learn – at least from the perspective of the Special Forces fraternity. I made a point of never mentioning my years at 31 Battalion or my experience in reconnaissance operations. The area we now entered, the "liberated" Nkongo region, had been my hunting ground three years before, and I knew the terrain like the back of my hand. But it felt good to be back in the bush, and this time it was different; as Special Forces we had all the equipment and support we needed.

My bush kit was exactly how I had drawn it from the stores the day before: large white plastic water bottles, shiny mess tins, unpainted backpack and webbing. My personal webbing was not tried and tested. It was new and noisy and too clumsy for me. The experienced operators in the commando checked me out like I was some kind of alien. I had to scrounge around frantically to get some first-aid plasters, paint and

171

rope to make my equipment presentable, camouflaging the shiny surfaces, tying the loose straps and webbing, and reducing the noise by tightening everything up.

The afternoon before the teams were deployed, the whole commando gathered in a corner of the base and was addressed by Sarel Visser, 5 Recce's bearded and much-respected chaplain. As a minister's son, I have listened to many sermons in my life, but Sarel's message that day, at a forgotten base in a SWAPO liberated area in Ovamboland, is the one I most vividly remember – almost word for word.

Sarel read from Psalm 125:2: "As the mountains surround Jerusalem, so the Lord surrounds His people now and forever." He explained how God protects His servants no matter where they are, as He remained with them just as the mountains surround Jerusalem. Everyone watched as our minister got down on all fours and started building mountains and valleys in the Ovamboland sand, drawing his congregation of battle-hardened soldiers – black and white, some believers and a few agnostics – into a vivid and beautiful picture of God's love and protection. This was a language all the men understood – the language of sand models, since that was how operational orders were given. And so the operators were glued to his words as he conveyed the powerful message in the simplest of terms, down on his knees in the white sand.

My relationship with Sarel would grow steadily over the years to come, as he would always conduct a "last supper" – a communion held with only the team and the Tac HQ commander – prior to a Small Team deployment. He became my spiritual mentor.

Our mission at Nkongo was to dominate the area by sheer aggression and try to regain full control. It soon dawned on me that we would patrol the bush in teams of twelve to sixteen, like regular infantry. There would be little of the anti-tracking, deception techniques, stealthy movement and other tactics we had developed so meticulously during my years at 31 Battalion.

Our stick sergeant, an Angolan Portuguese, was a master-snorer because he suffered from a minor medical condition. At night his snores used to cut through the cold still air and send shivers down my spine. As a standard arrangement each night the sentry had to take position next to him and wake him every time he started snoring. The poor bugger didn't sleep at all, as he started snoring the moment he fell asleep. We eventually requested that he be evacuated, as the situation started affecting the whole team.

Team leader Coen and I agreed that we would try some techniques to deceive the enemy, or at least not let them know our position. We started by avoiding the kraals and staying away from pathways. We moved frequently, and spent as little time as possible in static positions. Then we would close in on one of the suspect kraals, observing and search-ing for signs of enemy presence. I would often choose one of the soldiers to go on a close recce of the kraals and pathways, but soon realised that the men were extremely reluctant to do this. The idea of two guys alone in the bush was not their cup of tea.

Eventually we split the patrol in two; while the bigger group would guard the rucksacks in a temporary base (TB), the other ambushed the pathways leading to the kraals. I was lying in one of these ambushes one afternoon when the PKM[10] gunner started spraying bullets all over the treetops. A small group of SWAPO cadres had strolled down the trail – straight into one end of our six-man ambush. Unfortunately, the machine-gunner was in Sunday-afternoon mode, and only realised there was trouble when he and the SWAPO point man came face to face. Frightened out of his wits, he started shooting with the PKM still on its bipod, pointing upwards. The cadres did an about-turn and seemed to disappear into the thicket almost casually.

Two nights later we approached the same kraal complex for a close checkout and to replenish our water supplies at one of the wells. We placed listening posts at two of the kraals while the rest formed an all-round defence at the well. I was still busy filling my water bottles when all hell broke loose. Apparently a SWAPO patrol had had the same idea as us, and was approaching the well from the opposite direction when they bumped into one of the listening posts. Coen and I simultaneously started running towards the contact, but I stepped in a hole and sprained my ankle. One of the cadres was killed, while the rest disappeared into the night.

The following morning we found the tracks of a large group that had moved south past the kraal, and had obviously sent out the small patrol to replenish water. A follow-up was immediately organised, but I had to be evacuated back to Nkongo base, as my foot was swollen thick and I could not put any weight on it.

Back at the base I was treated with much suspicion and had to endure a fair bit of abuse. My swollen ankle meant I was immobile for two weeks, but it was summarily concluded that I had concocted a reason to return to base and avoid being deployed. After a while, I had had enough of life at the base, and I was preparing to rejoin the team in the bush, regardless of my injury, when I was informed that I was to fly out to Ondangwa to join 51 Commando at Fort Rev. This next step in my relatively short Special Forces career had also been planned without any input from my side.

4

51 Reconnaissance Commando

"A man should totally be where he is."
– Uncle Albertus in Dana Snyman, *On the Back Roads*

THE SPECIAL FORCES command structure had called on newly qualified, single operator-officers to serve at Ondangwa, as 51 Commando was running short of leader group. The unit specialised in pseudo-guerrilla operations and most of its operators were ex-SWAPO cadres who had been captured and "turned" to work for the South African Defence Force. Although I was dying to join Small Teams, I did not have a say in the matter. The concept of pseudo-guerrilla operations was foreign to me, but I was ready to learn and explore the opportunities 51 Commando offered.

The successes of the Selous Scouts in then Rhodesia were well known in the Recces, and a number of its operators were now serving with us. When I arrived at Ondangwa, Staff Sergeant Jim Lafferty, a highly experienced operator from the Scouts, served with 51 Commando. I was fortunate to learn from a soldier of his calibre. Soon Jim would share his experiences with me and lead me into the intricacies of pseudo-operations.

In 1984 PW Botha became state president of South Africa. The national effort to counter the so-called total onslaught against South Africa, a perceived all-encompassing threat posed by communist-inspired forces both inside and outside the country's borders, was steadily gaining ground. PW Botha was of course a strong exponent of the theory of the total onslaught, and established widespread countermeasures – of which the military effort formed but one – to combat the threat. Religion was used to instil a sense of patriotism among soldiers, who were told that South Africa was the last bastion of Christianity in southern Africa, since many of its neighbours were ruled by communist regimes after decolonisation. Soviet Russia, Cuba and East Germany also supported these governments and trained the guerrilla forces that were infiltrating both South West Africa and South Africa. By 1984 at least 6 000 insurgents were being trained and armed by the Soviet Union and Warsaw Pact member states in countries like Tanzania and Ethiopia. No fewer than 30 000 Cuban troops were positioned in Angola, though at this time still acting in a training and advisory role.

During February 1984 an agreement was reached at a high-level meeting of South African, Angolan and American observers in Lusaka. One of the provisions of the Lusaka Accord was the Mulungushi Minute, which determined, among other things, that the MPLA government would act to restrain SWAPO cadres from infiltrating South West Africa. The

Mulungushi Minute also provided for the establishment of a Joint Monitoring Commission (JMC) to oversee the withdrawal of South African forces from Cunene province and ensure that SWAPO did not reoccupy territory vacated by the SADF. However, the JMC was slow to materialise, and it soon became clear that the Angolans could not afford to go through with a process that would help to install a non-SWAPO government in South West Africa, especially given their own precarious position vis-à-vis Jonas Savimbi's UNITA.

So cadres from the People's Liberation Army of Namibia (or PLAN, the military wing of SWAPO) were still crossing the border into South West Africa, and it was 51 Commando's exclusive job to infiltrate the guerrilla structures and become part of the detachments penetrating Ovamboland.

Fort Rev, a completely enclosed and highly secretive camp, was conveniently situated next to the runway within the larger Ondangwa Air Force Base area. It served as the commando's headquarters and accommodation. Some of the ex-SWAPO insurgents were absolute masters in the bush: they knew the area intimately, spoke the language and blended in as easily as any SWAPO cadre. Once a cadre had been "turned", he would be given a whole new identity and deployed to areas of Ovamboland where he was not known.

Absolute secrecy was required about the base, for two reasons. Firstly, the conduct of pseudo-guerrilla operations meant that operatives were literally smuggled in and out of base, usually under cover of darkness and hidden in the back of a vehicle or helicopter, sometimes in South African military uniform or in civilian dress. Secondly, the base contained detention facilities with custom-made interrogation rooms where the captured SWAPO cadres were interrogated and eventually turned.

During my years in Special Forces, I worked with some outstanding intelligence officers, and Captain Dave Drew at 51 Commando was one of them. With his huge frame and overpowering personality, his knowledge of enemy structures and modus operandi, as well as his sixth sense for the enemy's intentions, Dave was the face of intelligence at Ondangwa. He was also responsible for turning the newly captured SWAPO insurgents and preparing them for their new role as pseudo-guerrillas.

I once saw Dave in action during an interrogation session and was dumbfounded by his shrewd combination of cunning, veiled threat and technique to draw information from his subject. By the time the captured cadres arrived at Fort Rev, there was no need for the old nail-pulling, thumb-twisting routine, since the idea was to win their confidence and to convince them that we were not as bad as they had been led to believe. Many of them arrived wounded and had to be treated, which the medics did with great care, as it was one sure way of instilling confidence in their captors.

Dave played carefully on the captives' fears of their communist-inspired bosses, as we knew that, once it became known that they had been captured by the "Boere", they would never be trusted or taken back into the SWAPO structures. Few of them opted not to work with us, especially when the incentive of a healthy salary and all sorts of extravagant benefits (for them!) were thrown in.

Once an insurgent agreed to deploy and to lead us back to his ex-comrades, preferably within two or three weeks of his capture, Dave would know that he had switched. He would then convince the guy that he was doing the right thing and that he would be in extreme danger if his former comrades were to find out that he had been caught. In the big man's favour was the fact that he knew the names of every single SWAPO commander, at every level, and in most cases where they hailed from and who their families were. He could therefore easily convince the captive insurgent that he had special means of communicating with Commander So-and-So.

Upon arrival at 51 Commando I was given a team of eight ex-SWAPO soldiers and deployed almost immediately. It was, to say the least, a massive culture shock for me. We were dropped off by a Casspir[11] in a sparsely populated area along the South West–Angolan border, and had to infiltrate to our area of operations in Ovamboland, acting as a new insurgent group that was moving into the area to establish itself.

The team acted as guerrillas and completely adopted the style and tactics of the SWAPO detachments. I was not prepared for this. There was no patrol formation, no communication signals, no semblance of tactical movement the way I had been taught. The team would stroll along in a single file, chatting away as they walked, weapons slung or just casually draped over the shoulder. When we passed a kraal, some would split off and pay the headman a visit.

Sometimes they would spend hours in the kraal while the rest of us waited under the trees outside. Then they would come out with food for the patrol – goat meat or *mahango*, a type of maize porridge, which we would all eat with our hands from the same bowl.

Already on this first deployment I had to readjust my thinking – in fact, the very essence of my being as a soldier. For me it was quite literally a matter of adapt or die, since this kind of operation was completely alien to me and in sharp contrast with the disciplined and methodical way I had developed over the past years. My equipment, for instance, was still organised in typical Special Forces style. To switch to the rag-tag manner and appearance of the cadres required a major shift.

The objective of the operation was to collect information and to establish the group as a new SWAPO element in the area. While we made some useful contacts for future reference, I had no way of verifying the bits of information I was fed, since I could not understand the language and did not have a proper grasp of the political and tactical situation in the area.

The deployment went without incident and I was grateful for the "soft landing" when we returned to base after a week. Back at Fort Rev I had to make some modifications to my kit, as well as to my thinking.

During deployments we didn't carry food – just one or two tins for an emergency. For food the team would rely entirely on the local population. While these guys were obviously used to this way of life, I never got accustomed to the erratic diet, and I became as thin as a rake. In an attempt to replenish my body's dwindling resources, I bought huge amounts of Wilson's toffees, which I would carry with me on deployments. In no time, they buggered up my teeth, as the toffee would stick to a tooth and cause it to pull out, root and all. I would end up in the middle of nowhere with a treasured tooth in the palm of my hand, and would have to carry it back to base for the dentist to fix.

My standard ops kit at this time was a small bag, resembling a rucksack, and the makeshift webbing worn by SWAPO cadres. On my head I generally sported an Afro wig, cut to size so as not to appear too conspicuous, and a large SWAPO hat that would cast a shadow over my Western features. A nicely groomed "Sam Nujoma" beard rounded off the picture. Instead of the good old "black is beautiful" camouflage cream, I used a brown cream similar to the stuff used by make-up artists. I applied it lavishly morning, noon and night, but the team would always keep me away from the local population or suspected SWAPO cadres. When we did encounter other people, they unobtrusively formed a shield and kept them occupied until I could disappear into the brush. Occasionally I came into direct contact with the local population, but we never detected any suspicion from their side.

However, I still slept with one eye open. I made a point of choosing a sleeping spot away from the rest of the group and always in a position where I would have some form of early warning, either in thick undergrowth or surrounded by a bed of dry leaves. Often I would change positions during the night. These were scary times, since I did not know the men and I had no idea who I could trust. We once deployed with a guy who had been on the other side scarcely one week before, and who, under Dave's subtle guidance, had agreed to lead us to a specific point where two SWAPO detachment commanders would meet. He was not given a weapon, but, since there was no way of knowing if he could be trusted, I avoided him. I made sure that he didn't know where I was bedding down, and I watched him closely as we approached the target area. The information turned out to be a lemon and I was quite relieved to return to base.

The lack of tactics and poor discipline – from my perspective, at least – inevitably led to a confrontation between me and some of the leading characters in the patrol. I became unable to tolerate the slack style and absence of discipline, as it appeared to be the norm even when we were back at base. The men would not listen to any advice or follow any form of tactics that I recommended. Basic drills, like moving from shadow to shadow when approaching a potential target area, were simply not observed, even after numerous rehearsal sessions. The excuse would always be, "but SWAPO wouldn't do this", or "SWAPO would do that".

In between deployments a few of the men challenged my authority, often induced by a bit of courage from the bottle. One Sunday, it led to a physical confrontation. We were to deploy that night and two of the team members were late. They eventually arrived two hours after the set time, totally intoxicated, which drove me over the edge. Long, senseless arguments with the two drunkards led to a fistfight, something I regret to this day, as it only served to turn the whole group against me. We deployed the following night, after I had charged the culprits with misconduct and reduced the size of the patrol.

I did have the opportunity to deploy on some memorable missions from Ruacana into southwestern Angola, where I used to operate with 31 Battalion. Jim Lafferty manned the Tac HQ at Ruacana, while I deployed with twelve ex-guerrillas into an area just south of Xangongo along the Cunene River. This time around, the deployment was of a different nature than three years before. We were dropped off by helicopter in an unpopulated area across the Cunene and started infiltrating along a traditional SWAPO infiltration route towards Ovamboland. The local population bought our story that we were there to reinforce the ranks of some cadres already deployed inside Ovamboland and steadily guided us along the route. On the west bank of the Cunene we discovered a large cache of mortar bombs and RPG rockets, and then were shown where the detachment had hidden their rubber boat.

The team learned from the locals that a contact man on the eastern shore was ready to meet us once we crossed over, and would put us in contact with the political commissar in the area. That night we crossed the river with the rubber boat. It took two boatloads and lots of swearing in Kwanyama to finally deliver everyone to the eastern shore. But the crossing didn't pass without incident. As the second boatload approached the shore, an RPG was discharged from inside the boat. My initial thought was that it was a contact, but the night remained quiet and I thought perhaps the guy shot at a crocodile. It transpired that the weapon had accidentally discharged, fortunately without injuring anyone or destroying the inflatable.

As we moved along during the following days, I started to think that the accidental discharge was perhaps not as accidental as they would like me to believe, since the contact man did not appear and the meeting with the political commissar did not materialise. But since I was constantly kept in the background and could not communicate with any of the local population, there was no way for me to determine the facts.

Eventually, after five or six days, we were set to meet the local commander. We established a hide in a thick patch of undergrowth and waited for the commander to pitch at a nearby kraal. As it got closer to the time, we moved to our meeting point close to the village. I was told to keep well back and make a break for it if things went sour. Two of the operators were assigned to stay with me.

I insisted on moving closer with the group, as my patience was wearing thin and my trust levels were falling. It went too smoothly: the team walked right in and chatted away with the "enemy". The "commander" was there already, laughing and patting everyone on the back.

It turned out to be one of our own pseudo-teams, which had arranged to meet an important SWAPO commander (that would be the very honourable me!) moving in from Angola. In a sense I was relieved; I did not want to end up in a contact with this ill-disciplined bunch on my side – especially since I did not quite know who was enemy and who not – and I believed that we had not been compromised and would be able to continue working in the area, as the locals had no reason to believe that we were not two SWAPO elements meeting each other.

When I tried to figure out, during the debriefing afterwards, how it was possible that two teams could enter each other's area, it was explained that the meeting place was on the border of the two so-called frozen areas, and that a lack of comms between the Tac HQs of the two teams had led to this potentially dangerous situation. I did not buy this, as it was obvious to me that the meeting had been prearranged – not by the local population, but by elements within our midst. I queried the explanation, but experienced operators explained to me that these kind of incidents happened in the shadowy world of pseudo-guerrilla operations.

The concept of frozen areas was a contentious issue during my time at 51 Commando. For a pseudo-team to deploy into an area, a warning had to be sent out a week in advance to the regular Army forces in the area, the Air Force and Koevoet, the controversial hunter unit of the police. The area would be declared "frozen", which meant that no other elements but Special Forces could enter. Koevoet, however, often chose to ignore this and, as a result, hunted down 5 Recce teams on a number of occasions.

One good thing about the time I spent at 51 Commando was the exposure it gave me to a range of Reconnaissance Commandos. Every one of the three regiments, or elements of them, would pass through Fort Rev on operational deployments, and I had the opportunity to see all of them in action. It only made me more determined to get to Small Teams as soon as possible.

When the OC 5 Recce, Colonel James Hills, paid a visit to Fort Rev, I requested an interview and explained my situation: I was not interested in pseudo-operations, I was not cut out for that type of mission and I did not take kindly to the poor discipline of the ex-cadres. The colonel's response was that I needed the experience and that Fort Rev needed me. I would stay at 51 Commando for a year, after which a decision would be made regarding a possible redeployment.

My stint at the commando was made bearable by the fact that I worked alongside a few highly skilled pseudo-operators, the likes of Captain Roes Terblanche, Sergeant André Meyer and Staff Sergeant Jim Lafferty. While I learned a lot from them and realised the merits of pseudo-deployments, I never liked the idea of the white team leader being kept at a distance, and I never got used to the poor tactics and relaxed ways of the ex-SWAPO soldiers. I also doubted my own ability in the field as a white person, given that I did not speak the language and didn't have any in-depth exposure to the Ovambo culture. I would never truly fit in with the pseudo-teams, and consequently I always felt exposed.

By late 1984 André Diedericks was in the process of moving from Pretoria to Phalaborwa to establish Small Teams as a subunit of 5 Recce – soon to be named 54 Commando. Up until then Small Teams had operated under the auspices of the covert D-40, or Project Barnacle, which collected intelligence and launched disruptive actions against enemies of the state. Diedies realised that a Small Teams outfit could not function effectively in a covert environment, where any links with government or the military were denied.

All the while, I remained in contact with Diedies and continued writing letters to the OC, telling him what I was destined for and urging him to let me go, but with no luck! By now Diedies had started his own campaign to get me to 5 Recce. Since Small Teams resorted directly under the GOC Special Forces, as far as operational tasking was concerned, Diedies had a direct line to General Kat Liebenberg. At this time it also transpired that the Small Teams elements from 1 Recce were destined to move to 5 Recce, and so I knew my time was coming.

Sadly, although it was an interesting experience, I cannot claim any breathtaking operational successes during my time at 51 Commando. I never had the opportunity to do my own thing, to deploy on my own terms. I was always at the mercy of the SWAPO ex-cadres and somewhere in the background so the enemy would not recognise my white face.

My time at 51 Commando tested my personal mantra, developed so meticulously during my years at 31 Battalion, to breaking point. No longer could I say that this, and nowhere else, was where I wanted to be. But I endured because I believed it was a necessary stepping stone to get to Small Teams. I also knew that I was gaining invaluable information about the way SWAPO operated from men who had recently roamed the bush as PLAN cadres.

Another source of inspiration that made the time at Ondangwa worthwhile was the presence of Dave Drew, who was like a walking encyclopaedia and would share with me his intimate knowledge of SWAPO structures and tactics. Little did I know that Dave would soon be transferred back to 5 Recce and would serve as intelligence officer for the majority of Small Teams deployments I would be involved in over the next five years.

PART 4

Small Teams

"Whenever a warrior decides to do something he must go all the way, but he must take responsibility for what he does. No matter what he does, he must first know why he is doing it, and then he must proceed with his actions without having doubts or remorse about them."

– Carlos Castaneda, *Journey to Ixtlan*

Chřisto Rei
Lubango

Koos Stadler

1

Into the Fray

*"Send men to spy out the land of Canaan, which I am giving
to the people of Israel. From each tribe of their fathers you shall
send a man, every one a chief among them."*

— Numbers 13:2, *The Bible* (English Standard Version)

THE DAY I FINALLY drove through the gates at 5 Recce, my
heart was thumping in my chest. Over the course of six months
I had nagged Colonel James Hills so much to let me join the
newly formed 54 Commando that eventually he had to concede.
The persistent prompting by André "Diedies" Diedericks from 5
Recce also must have helped. I could hardly conceal my excitement, but at the same time I was anxious, mostly because I did
not quite know what to expect.

Diedies welcomed me like a long-lost brother and the Small
Team operators made me feel at home from the outset. The first
thing that impressed me at the Small Team office block – and in
fact the whole of 5 Recce – was the friendly and apparently
relaxed atmosphere. There were no cowboys, no unfriendly
stares, no holier-than-thou attitudes. Instead, seasoned

operators came round to introduce themselves, which immediately made me feel part of the 5 Recce family. From the outset I also noticed the competitive tension between Small Teams and the two offensive commandos, but this was evidently the result of a healthy rivalry, and probably because Small Teams lured some of the best away from the commandos.

I was introduced to my team buddy, Sergeant "CC" Victorino, an exceptionally strong operator originally from Angola. Vic and his wife Christobel lived with their two kids in a house in Hebron, the village especially built for the married men of the unit. Vic took me in like a son, and his house became a regular stopover for a lonely bachelor.

The second thing that struck me was that Small Teams was clearly no Sunday-school picnic. There was a predominant air of urgency. The normal weekly routine was like an intense military course. We'd start the day with PT at 06:00. At 07:30 there was a quick roll call and order group. Every morning there would be lectures or group discussions. Portuguese lessons were a standard fixture of our morning routine. Since Portuguese was widely spoken in our theatres of operations the white operators had to gain a working knowledge of the language. With the aid of a "Learn-Portuguese-in-three-months" pocket guide, one of the Portuguese-speaking operators would guide us through the intricacies of the language, covering mostly pronunciation, vocabulary and some common phrases. During rehearsals before deployments we would concentrate on learning specific phrases to give us the edge in crisis situations – an advantage that would more than once in my Small Team career save the day, if not my life.

At the time, the majority of 5 Recce operators were black, about half of them were Portuguese-speaking soldiers originally from Angola and Mozambique. Most of the Angolan operators came from 32 Battalion, the highly acclaimed fighting unit established by Colonel Jan Breytenbach and made up of former FNLA fighters. The operators from Mozambique were recruited from Renamo, the Mozambican resistance movement, and were secretly brought to South Africa to be trained in special operations techniques. Given their experience in their home countries, these Portuguese-speaking operators were exceptionally suited for reconnaissance missions into those countries, and a select few were accepted into Small Teams. The rest of the operators were former Special Air Service (SAS) and Selous Scouts from Zimbabwe and a few were South African.

Signals lessons by Dave Scales, at the time a staff sergeant and the most senior NCO with Small Teams, would follow. Subjects such as antenna theory, electronic counter-measures (ECM), electronic counter-counter-measures (ECCM) and Morse practice were drilled into us. Dave had made the move to Phalaborwa with Diedies and acted as both the commando warrant officer and Tac HQ signaller. Having served with C Squadron, SAS and the Selous Scouts' "Recce Troop", Dave had extensive experience in small team operations. Aside from being exceptionally dedicated and highly professional, he had a sharp wit.

But Dave's real claim to fame was signals. His knowledge of the subject was second to none. He came from a line of experts in the field of electronics in combat: his grandfather had been a signaller in the British Army during the First World War and used Morse code based on HF radio communications; his dad had been a signaller and paratrooper in the British Army in the Second World War and parachuted (among other significant feats) into the Netherlands on 17 September 1944 during the biggest parachute drop in history.

The signals lessons would alternate with sessions on Soviet-bloc weapons, aircraft and vehicles. Since all our target countries were supplied by the Soviet Union, or in some cases China, we focused all our efforts on the recognition of their military hardware. Along with the recognition of arms and equipment, a lot of time was spent on the analysis of Soviet-bloc doctrine as applied in the so-called frontline states.

After lunch, during the proverbial "graveyard session", teams had time for kit preparation. Endless hours were spent preparing, altering, camouflaging and fine-tuning packs and webbing. Once the fierce lowveld temperature had subsided slightly, teams would depart for practical work; buddies could sort out their patrol formations and tactics, invent new anti-tracking methods and rehearse their team drills and standard operating procedures (SOPs). A lot of this practical training was spent on radio work and comms procedures.

At least two nights a week were set aside for night work. All the teams would report to the headquarters at 19:00, and then one of us would lecture on the theory of night operations, covering aspects like stalking, rendezvous (RV) drills or radio procedures in low-light conditions. Thereafter the teams would disperse into the training area for an exercise. More often than not we would sleep out in a hide after the night's exercise and report for PT at 06:00. I did it because I loved being out in the bush, Vic probably because he did not want to disturb his family after the exercise ended around 02:00.

As Vic and I worked on our team skills, a relationship of mutual trust was established and a close bond developed between us. Vic was a big man, perhaps 20 kg heavier than me, and as fit as a fiddle, so I really suffered when we did buddy-PT together. While he could pick me up like a feather and run as if my weight didn't bother him at all, I used to stagger under his weight.

Diedies and I were the only two living-in officers in Small Teams and we clicked immediately. He lived up to everything I had heard about him. The eternal optimist, Diedies was unstoppable when a new challenge presented itself. Every minute of each day he was busy working out new schemes, thinking of ways to outwit the enemy, inventing new tricks and planning new operations. He also felt a great sense of responsibility towards his comrades and subordinates, and would not expect anything of them he wouldn't do himself. His outstanding leadership qualities have always served as inspiration for me. But it wasn't until I had the opportunity to deploy with him that I realised why he was such an outstanding soldier.

Commandant Boet Swart, 5 Recce's second-in-command, also lived with us in the mess. Soon a close camaraderie developed, as the three of us shared the same interests. Every morning at 05:00 I was kicked out of bed by the old man. I then had to make coffee and serve him and Diedies in bed. "Oom Boet" as he was affectionately called, was a delightful individual, with a fine sense of humour and contagious enthusiasm. He was also a highly professional soldier, having served in various units in the then Rhodesia. Boet was also the best Tac HQ commander I ever came across.

Initially we were four two-man teams. Diedies and his long-time buddy from many previous deployments, Neves Thomas Matias, formed the first team. The others consisted of Lieutenant Jo-Jo Bruyns and José da Costa, Paul Dobe ("Americo") and José dos Santos, and me and CC Victorino. While Da Costa, Dos Santos, Americo and Victorino were by then South African citizens, they all hailed from Angola, having served with the FNLA during the civil war. They later joined 32 Battalion in the Caprivi until they volunteered for Special Forces selection.

These guys – all experienced soldiers – formed the backbone of the Small Team capability at the time. They were all Portuguese-speaking, strong-willed, motivated and highly capable, and had joined Small Teams of their own free will. During my five years with Small Teams the group remained relatively small and contained. We never had more than six teams at a time.

This period saw a number of people coming and going again. Mike Mushayi, along with two other ex-Rhodesian soldiers, also joined Small Teams then. Not all operators were cut out for Small Teams, as they not only had to cope with the demands of a rigorous routine while on the base but also had to manage the stresses that came with deployment in small groups. The base routine was taxing, and the months away from home, either on rehearsals or actual deployments, would place great strain on the family life of a married operator.

Our first exposure to the joys of Small Team ops was a training exercise in the Mariepskop area, at the northernmost tip of the Drakensberg range. Diedies, Dave Scales and Corné Vermaak, the intelligence officer dedicated to Small Teams, were to run the Tac HQ, while two teams deployed in the most rugged and thickly vegetated terrain imaginable – the steep mountains and deep valleys of the Blyde River Canyon.

The exercise was cleverly worked out around a scenario whereby ANC insurgents had infiltrated the area from Mozambique and established weapons caches in the secluded valleys, utilising donkey trains to transport their goods. The intelligence picture was indeed based on fact, although the teams never knew exactly how much was fact and how much fiction. We expected to encounter enemy at any time during the deployment.

At first I did not realise the significance of this first deployment, but it dawned on me much later that Diedies was already preparing us for deployments in the mountainous terrain around the town of Lubango in southwestern Angola – an area that would become the focus of Small Team deployments in years to come.

For some reason I didn't fare well on that exercise, and felt like a complete failure afterwards. Vic was a strong man, and I had to work hard to keep up. Down in the valleys the vegetation was subtropical, virtually impenetrable. The first night we spent eight hours in the pitch darkness to cover 700 m, trying desperately to crawl through the undergrowth with our huge, heavy packs. It was literally a matter of one step forward, three steps back – as the frames of the packs got tangled in the vines and roots.

I struggled to master the new challenges of comms procedure, one-time letter pads and Morse code. Our comms with Dave were mostly poor – partly due to the deep ravines we were deployed in, but also because we were inexperienced and not well prepared. At some point Vic and I had a difference of opinion about the position of our observation post (OP), which we would use to watch a cave supposed to be one of the targets. Then we argued about the best route to take. Having studied the map, I insisted that we go up a dry waterfall during our exfiltration. But when I took a nasty fall while attempting to scale the almost vertical cliff, I realised my mistake. Luckily I fell directly backwards onto my pack. Mildly concussed, I tried to stand up. Vic quietly walked up to me, lifted my pack and pulled me to my feet. Then we followed the route he had suggested from the beginning.

As could be expected, the debrief at the Tac HQ on Mariepskop was not a positive or rewarding experience. Diedies pointed out our navigational errors, poor choices of OP sites and a number of tactical mistakes. Dave was not at all happy with the standard of our comms, particularly the fact that we were repeatedly late with scheduled times, or "scheds", as well as the poor quality of our Morse.

Driving back with Diedies from Mariepskop to the unit at Phalaborwa I fell quiet. Eventually Diedies broke the silence:

"What's the matter?"

"I don't know," I said, "but I think I messed up."

He was wise enough not to take the matter any further and simply said, "Sleep on it tonight and we'll talk tomorrow."

By the next morning I felt significantly better. I realised that, while the other guys had been with Small Teams much longer than I had, they hadn't fared substantially better on the exercise. What I needed to do was to cover a few basics and master the technical challenges that were new to me.

So Vic and I got stuck into a serious learning routine. We spent hours sending and receiving Morse, as well as improving our radio work, incorporating field repairs, the use of various types of antennae and ECM/ECCM procedures. Knowledge of enemy weapons, aircraft and vehicles turned into a bit of a status symbol among the teams and we had daily slideshow competitions to test each other's knowledge.

We also meticulously prepared our equipment and were fortunate to have at our disposal the services of Sergeant Major "Whalla-whalla" van Rensburg, the unit's tailor. With his heavy-duty sewing machines, Whalla-whalla could redesign any piece of webbing and turn it into a masterpiece. The result was chest-webbing and kidney pouches designed to our own taste, with a special pouch for each item of survival kit, strobe light, cutting pliers, torch or whatever else the operator considered vital enough to keep on his chest. Whalla-whalla also made canvas and cloth bags for just about everything, from toilet paper to peanuts. The much-treasured "Whalla-whalla bag" soon became a hallmark of Small Teams.

In addition to the rigorous training, we used the time at base to brush up on our first-aid skills. We'd set aside a week for the unit doctor to guide us through the ABCs of resuscitation, the contents and application of the priority 1 and 2 medical packs, improvised techniques for applying slings and how to stop bleeding. A casualty scenario was built into each exercise, with the result that we ended up punching each other (and ourselves!) full of needle holes in an attempt to get a drip flowing. I became quite adept at administering a drip to myself, even with the sweat running and the adrenaline pumping.

Not all training exercises were as challenging as the one in the Mariepskop area. Once, Small Teams was commandeered to take part in a countrywide exercise run by the Air Force to sharpen their command and control systems and fine-tune the integration of different resources.

Operation Golden Eagle was a typical blue-on-red exercise, with red ("enemy") bases spread along the eastern border with Mozambique and blue forces based in the interior. A request arrived from Pietersburg Air Force Base for the Recces to do a close-in reconnaissance of red bases at Punda Maria, on the edge of the Kruger National Park. The mission entailed the placement of command-detonated flares to guide bombers to their targets. One flare would be positioned 20 km away to guide the aircraft on their initial run-in, the second 100 m away and the third on the perimeter of the actual target. The jets would detonate the first flare while in the holding area, and the second and third on the approach to the target.

The flare had a separate radio receiver, which was to be connected to the detonator and then armed for action. Little did I know that I was actually testing a new system that would later be used in our reconnaissance missions.

A day before the deployment, Sakkie Sibanda, one of the intelligence NCOs, and I were picked up in a Puma helicopter and taken to Pietersburg. A team of technicians were waiting for us at the base. We went through a quick training session on the flares and tested the systems with the fighter pilots. Just before we departed, Sakkie and I each had a freshly baked pie and a Coke from the Air Force canteen.

The helicopters first took us to a point 20 km east of the target where the first flare would be set up to serve as the initiation point once the air strike came in. I was dropped on a rocky outcrop and had no difficulty in preparing the flare and connecting the receiver while the choppers circled. With the initiation point prepared, Sakkie and I were taken to our respective landing zones (LZs) for the final infiltration to the "enemy" bases, where the target markers would be planted. I was dropped first, just before last light, and started navigating my way through some scattered villages and fields towards the target.

Everything went smoothly. I found the target easily and planted the first flare 100 m out, and the second one at the perimeter fence. I decided to stay put to see how it functioned. Not realising how powerful the explosion would be, I fell asleep right next to the flare, and was rudely awakened by the blast. The "enemy" must have gotten an equal fright, as the huge flame leaped about two storeys into the air. Afterwards they claimed they had located and almost caught me, which was nonsense, as I quickly disappeared into the thick shrubs surrounding the base. The fighter planes came thundering directly over the target in a simulated attack, "bombing" the red base into the proverbial smithereens.

The next morning I exfiltrated and was picked up by the choppers at the prearranged LZ. Mission accomplished.

It was only then that I heard Sakkie didn't have such a smooth ride to his LZ the day before. The flight engineer told me how, after dropping me, they suddenly got the smell of freshly baked pies. Looking forward past the co-pilot, he tried to locate the bakery.

"You know, Lieutenant," he said, "I'd never realised you could actually smell a bakery in a chopper. I looked down to see if we could land somewhere to buy a fresh loaf of bread. But the next thing I see are these pieces of what I thought was bird flesh and stuff on the perspex. It was the first time I had seen a bird strike from inside the chopper. So I reached past the co-pilot to see what it was. Then I felt the back of my helmet and it was all wet and sticky – and smelling of fresh pie."

It turned out that Sakkie had been sitting in the open door of the helicopter until he couldn't keep his lunch in any longer. But then, as he puked into the rushing wind, everything whirled back inside and into the cockpit. The crew's helmets were plastered with fresh pie, as was the cabin interior. Since the Air Force crew were not too impressed with the Recces' performance, we had to buy the drinks during the "debriefing" in the bar that night.

2

Operation Cerberus
September 1985

BY 1985 – my first year as a Small Team operator – the Border War had escalated and SWAPO was aggressively pushing its political agenda while its detachments infiltrated deep into South West Africa. Some of the worst fighting of the war took place in central Ovamboland, while across the border the civil war between the MPLA and UNITA had reached a peak.

The Joint Monitoring Commission (JMC), established in February 1984 under the terms of the Lusaka Accord, consisted of personnel from both the SADF and FAPLA. Its mandate was to monitor the systematic disengagement of the opposing forces in the conflict. After Operation Askari in December 1983, South Africa had indeed withdrawn its forces from Angola. However, SWAPO immediately deployed its fighters into the areas the SADF had evacuated, violating the terms of the disengagement agreement. Since the JMC could not fulfil its mandate, it soon became dysfunctional. Then Wynand du Toit from 4 Recce was captured and two of his teammates, Louis van Breda and

Operation Cerberus

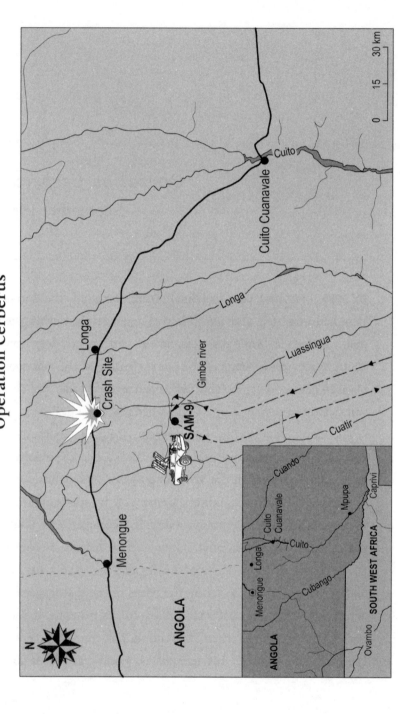

Rowland Liebenberg, were killed during a Special Forces raid on a Gulf Oil installation in the Cabinda enclave of Angola. Politically this was a disaster for South Africa, as the Minister of Foreign Affairs, Pik Botha, had just proclaimed that all SADF troops had been withdrawn from Angola. The MPLA of course exploited the situation and accused the South African government of being liars who could not be trusted in any peace negotiations. Following the failure of the JMC, the SADF moved its forces back across the border into Angola, launching attacks on bases SWAPO had established.

It was against this backdrop of political turmoil and strategic manoeuvring that I was sent on my first mission with 5 Recce's Small Teams. One evening in July, after we had gathered at the block for a night training session, Diedies called three teams into the intelligence briefing room. Dave Drew, by then the unit's intelligence officer, was also there, along with Eric McNelly, a counterintelligence officer from Special Forces HQ in Pretoria. We knew immediately something was up.

First we got the usual counterintelligence brief from McNelly: that the enemy was out there listening and that we should keep our traps shut. We had heard this message often without fully comprehending the reality of the threat. The need for secrecy was only brought home a year later when Major André Pienaar from Special Forces HQ was caught spying for "an African country". He was arrested at Jan Smuts airport (today OR Tambo International) when he tried to travel to Zimbabwe with seven top-secret files from Military Intelligence. Pienaar had been working in none other than the counterintelligence section, which had to keep us in check, and as such was privy to all the information regarding Special Forces deployments. (Pienaar remained in custody and was only released in the early 1990s.)

Dave Drew first gave us an overview of air traffic between Lubango and Cuito Cuanavale in southern Angola. Since the railway line running east from Lubango to Menongue had been rendered useless by UNITA, the MPLA was now relying heavily on air transport to get their logistics to the front. Daily flights of Soviet Antonov cargo planes transported huge amounts of logistics and troops to Menongue in support of the MPLA war effort. SWAPO's Eastern Front also benefited substantially from this, as their logistics were ferried by truck from Menongue to their base southwest of the town – an area I would get to know intimately during later deployments.

By June 1985 the MPLA had initiated two large-scale offensives against UNITA, one in the Cazombo salient in the east and the second against Mavinga in the southeast, forcing Jonas Savimbi's forces to fight on two fronts. Soviet and Cuban advisors guided the MPLA operations, and large numbers of SWAPO's semi-conventional troops and ANC cadres, who were being trained in Angola, took part in the operations. The SADF viewed these offensives as part of the total onslaught and a direct threat to stability in South Africa.

After Dave's overview, Diedies gave a brief outline of the mission, though not covering any details of timings and positions. We would deploy with UNITA to shoot down MPLA transport aircraft, utilising captured Russian SA-9 missile systems attached to the BRDM-2 armoured vehicle. Should we shoot down an aircraft, UNITA would claim the success. Although this was not a classic Small Team mission, I was grateful for the opportunity to learn. I had heard much about deployments with UNITA and was eager for first-hand experience.

Diedies and I drove to Pretoria for briefings and to marry up with the Air Force's anti-aircraft specialists handling the missile systems. Back at Phalaborwa the operational teams started preparing their equipment under the guidance of Dave Scales. Dave maintained a modular Tac HQ that could be reduced or augmented depending on the requirement – whether on foot, in a vehicle or in established headquarters. He took care to pack equipment that could be transported by air and deployed at Rundu. The operators prepared their equipment, rations, water and a reserve for possible resupply. Then, under the pretext that they were going on a training exercise, the operational team went to Sawong,[12] a secluded training area on the banks of the Olifants River outside Phalaborwa, for a two-week rehearsal.

While I was in Pretoria I met up with a friend who told me he wanted to introduce me to a girl he thought I would get along with. "She's a teacher, she's fun and she's also a fitness fanatic . . . runs road races and stuff," he explained.

"Thanks," I said, "but you know I'm a bit tied up and will be going away for a few months."

At the back of my mind I was also thinking of our unspoken policy that, once a guy got involved in a serious relationship, or wanted to marry, he would quit Small Teams of his own accord. I didn't want to get bogged down in a relationship when I had just started what I had so long aspired to do.

"Well, think about it . . . You can always just be friends," my friend persisted.

So I agreed to meet Zelda the following day. And because she was beautiful, clever, fun-loving and a fitness fanatic, I was hooked right from the start. While my friend had obviously informed her that I was a Recce, I did not volunteer any further information. Zelda was smart enough to realise that she shouldn't prompt me for more details, and accepted from the outset that I would often be away.

After a week of planning and briefings at Special Forces HQ, Diedies and I returned to Phalaborwa to join the rest of the teams for final preparations and rehearsals at Sawong. Once we were ready, we were picked up by C-130 from Hoedspruit Air Force Base and flown to Pretoria, where the SA-9 missile systems were loaded onto two C-130s under the cover of darkness. The Tac HQ and all our personal equipment went in with the vehicles.

The flight to the operational area was scheduled for the afternoon so that we would arrive at Rundu, the headquarters of Sector 20, after dark. The SAM-9s were offloaded and we moved our equipment to Fort Foot, where we would stay for a few days before the deployment. Fort Foot, 1 Recce's operational base at Rundu, was situated inside the perimeter of the larger headquarters base. Adjacent to the fort was the Chief of Staff Intelligence (CSI) base, from where all liaison operations with UNITA in eastern Angola were coordinated.

The next morning Diedies and I went to meet our UNITA guide, a young captain only introduced to us as Mickey, at the

CSI base. Mickey was an amiable guy with whom we would cooperate closely for years to come. He spoke English well and had an intimate knowledge of the situation in Angola. He knew the locations of the FAPLA deployments in our area of operations and, even better, knew personally all the UNITA commanders of the bases that we would travel through.

The SAM-9 crews used the opportunity to do a final rehearsal on the systems, locking on to just about every aircraft that came in to land at Rundu. This initially caused some consternation and a few near-crashes, as the pilots of the fighter jets had not been informed, and got some nasty missile scares. In the meantime Dave Scales had set up Tac HQ in Fort Foot and was testing and monitoring the frequencies we'd be using. As always, he had the most practical and well-coordinated system going, and had us rehearsing comms procedures endlessly.

Oom Boet Swart, the Ops commander, kept us in good spirits all the way. I loved the old man dearly, even more so because we shared a love of classical music. In those days, the SADF had a fifty-fifty language policy for formal communications, which required English and Afrikaans to be used in alternate months. As it was the English-speaking month, Boet, whose real name was Mathewis, insisted on being referred to as "Matthew Black". He reckoned this pseudonym would enhance the clandestine nature of our mission, since no one would suspect he was a "regte Boer".

The time for the deployment came and we crossed the Cubango (Kavango) River with a UNITA pontoon at night, taking the heavy BRDM-2 vehicles across one at a time. Most of the

211

Small Team operators had made themselves comfortable on the camouflage netting next to the vehicle's turret. We actually tied ourselves to the superstructure so as not to be wiped off by branches. And so began the long and tedious journey along a sandy vehicle track, from one UNITA base to the next, to our final destination along the Gimbe River.

During the afternoon of day three, there was a grinding of gears and the vehicle I was riding on suddenly packed up. Diedies, in consultation with Lappies Labuschagne, our vehicle technician, made the call to move on with one BRDM and a UNITA escort. I would stay behind with the disabled vehicle and a contingent of UNITA soldiers. As soon as a recovery vehicle could be organised, I would move on and meet up with the main force at a UNITA headquarters base 100 km further along our route. If the vehicle could not be recovered, Diedies would continue the operation with the one SAM-9 and a UNITA protection element.

During those few days on my own with UNITA, I realised how much could be done with almost nothing. I was astonished by the sheer genius, clever improvisation and perseverance of the UNITA soldiers. Since Captain Mickey had departed with the main group, I was left without an interpreter and in the company of the UNITA detachment commander whose English was about as limited as my Portuguese – which was nonexistent. Nevertheless, he told me not to worry, as they were just waiting for a vehicle and some shovels. I couldn't figure out what purpose it could possibly serve, as the BRDM-2 weighed at least 8 tons. There was no way of towing it through the dense bush on the sandy vehicle track. I honestly couldn't see a way out and was dismayed that I would probably miss out on a great experience.

Early the next morning I heard a Kwêvoël arriving. A swarm of youngsters, each armed with a pick or a shovel and cackling excitedly, jumped off the back of the truck. The commander approached me with a big smile on his face. They clearly had a plan, but for the life of me I couldn't figure it out. Then a heavily loaded Mercedes truck arrived and my enthusiastic colleague indicated to me that we should move all the equipment from the BRDM onto the Mercedes.

I was still baffled. I thought they were about to abandon the missile system and take all the equipment away. I started to protest and tried to explain to the commander that I needed to stay with the SAM-9.

But my worry was short-lived. The Kwêvoël was driven to the front of the BRDM and parked about two vehicle lengths' away. To my astonishment the shovel-bearing youngsters cleared a stretch of sand between the two vehicles and started digging. Throughout the rest of that day, they methodically sunk a pit in front of the BRDM, working rhythmically to a song they sang. Every now and again a fresh hand would jump in and grab a spade from one of the group. It was beautiful to watch – the harmony of the labour, the rhythm, the ease with which they accomplished a task that for most Westerners would have been impossible.

A trench sloped down from the Kwêvoël towards the BRDM, levelling out a few metres in front of it. By that afternoon the pit was deep enough for the Kwêvoël to reverse into, and for the BRDM to run forward onto the back of the Kwêvoël. Now they were faced with the challenge of how to get the unserviceable armoured car onto the back of the Kwêvoël. However, they also had this worked out. Two technical geeks started unwinding the winch from the BRDM's front, looping the cable straight across the armoured hull of the Kwêvoël to where the Mercedes truck was waiting some distance away. With the cable fully extended and hooked onto the Mercedes, this became a simple operation. The Mercedes inched forward, pulling the BRDM slowly but steadily onto the Kwêvoël.

Once the BRDM was snugly on top, the next job was to get the Kwêvoël out of the pit. But even that turned out to be a minor challenge, as they simply let the Mercedes, with the winch cable still attached to the BRDM, move forward slowly, assisting the Kwêvoël with its massive load to get onto level ground.

We were ready to go, but as we started rolling I immediately saw that there was no way the huge combined structure of the two vehicles would pass under the tree canopy. But, again, I had underestimated the resolve and genius of these people of the bush. They simply placed two capable axe handlers on the Kwêvoël's hardened roof. These guys patiently and methodically chopped away at any branch, whatever the size, that blocked the way. It took us two full days (and probably five times as many axe blades) to cover the distance to the base where the rest of the team was waiting. Disregarding the time and huge amount of effort it required, the UNITA soldiers literally cut a path out of the tree canopy for the BRDM to slide through.

But still our woes were not at an end. On the morning of the second day the Mercedes truck, my taxi, suddenly came to a halt with a flat rear tyre. We were stuck in the deep soft sand of the vehicle track. Then it transpired that there was no jack. With the vehicle fully loaded with bags of maize and all our equipment, and without proper tools to change the tyre, I assumed we were stuck for good.

Yet again I was proven wrong. Twenty young men jumped on the vehicle and offloaded every item, including all the bags of food. In the meantime, two of the axe-men started chopping down a Y-shaped tree with a trunk about a metre in diameter. Once the tree was down they cut off the two main branches, leaving a distinct and solid-looking Y-shaped part of the tree to serve as a base. While they took time cleaning away the smaller branches from one of the remaining poles, a few of the men dug a hole about two metres from the truck. In this they inserted the long end of the Y, burying it halfway so that the forked part was next to the vehicle.

Next came the tree trunk that had been stripped of branches. This was laid into the V-shaped base with the short end under the truck body. Bingo, we had a crude crowbar that proved to be amazingly effective. A group of UNITA soldiers got onto their comrades' shoulders and, slowly and tentatively, started to hang on to the long end of the "crowbar". Suddenly the Mercedes lifted, and with a loud shout everyone still standing around grabbed a piece of the tree trunk and held on as a few good men swiftly changed the wheel – in a matter of five minutes.

The whole tree-felling, jack-rigging and wheel-changing operation took no less than three hours. When we finally arrived at the UNITA main base, a team of Special Forces technicians had already been flown in by helicopter with a new gearbox for the BRDM. It took the tiffies a day and a night to lift the old gearbox out and fit the new one. Once they were done, the vehicle was as good as new.

Two days later we reached our target area, high ground overlooking the flood plain of the Gimbe River. That night Diedies deployed the two missile systems right in the open, about 40 m from the tree line. We cut branches from trees way into the bush line and camouflaged the two vehicles until they appeared to be clusters of loose-standing thickets. The Small Team guys and the missile operators dug in just inside the tree line, while Captain Mickey established his headquarters higher up on a dune sloping down to the river, close to our mini-HQ where the intelligence officer, the tiffies and the doctor were deployed. The UNITA company served as protection element and were deployed in a rough half-circle to our rear.

We hadn't even properly set up our little camp when two "swing-wing" MiG-23s suddenly appeared from nowhere, flying almost at treetop level and generally just making a nuisance of themselves. I was frightened, lying dead still in my trench, expecting the pilots to see me at any moment. They kept on fooling around, one moment coming over slowly with the wings extended, then screaming down with wings pulled in and breaking the sound barrier. Later I heard that the UNITA soldiers wanted to open fire with their small arms, which would have given away our vulnerable position and ruined the operation. We were not armed for defence against fighter attack, and our mission was to shoot down a transport, not a fighter plane.

The very next day we heard the Antonovs flying over, sometimes directly over our positions. There were many flights, often as many as five or six a day. Over the next six weeks we recorded more than 140 flights. Unbelievably, over that whole period the missile operators were unable to get a single lock-on. The rainy season was approaching fast and the days were cloudy, making it impossible for the heat-seeking infrared systems to lock on to the engines of the aircraft.

I learned much from Neves Matias and CC Victorino during this operation. Right from the beginning they settled into a routine they diligently stuck to throughout the deployment. They took it upon themselves to organise the daily tasks of placing security details, collecting information from UNITA, camouflaging positions and sending patrols to fetch water from the Gimbe River. Every second day Victorino ensured that the missile systems were covered with fresh foliage and that the dry branches were removed and hidden under the tree canopy. He painstakingly effaced all the tracks that led to and from the missiles. I soon realised that these guys had been moulded by years of experience, and that the base routine was borne of a simple understanding of its importance.

After six weeks, we were ordered to withdraw. We had many scares that FAPLA had located our position and were on their way to intercept us with a large force or that they had identified our camp and were about to launch an air attack. However, aside

217

from occasional random bombing by the MiGs in the area, we were never targeted. Diedies requested an extension, stating that we had not been discovered and needed two more weeks.

And so it happened that one morning, during the extension period, Christie Smit, the medical doctor, was leading the morning dedication. He read from Ephesians 3:20: "Now to Him that, through His grace working in us is able to do so much more than we can think of, or even pray for, to Him be the glory."

Then someone shouted, "Antonov!", the usual warning for the missile operators to get into action. Most of the guys were gathered at Diedies' trench. We looked up. The sky was clear, with not a cloud in sight. An AN-12 was heading straight towards us.

"This is it, *manne*!" Diedies shouted and ran to place himself between the two missile vehicles.

I fixed my binoculars on the approaching aircraft. The wings had to fit into 18 mm on the instrument's reticule to be within striking range of the SAM-9s. As I started shouting, someone else also called out: "It's within range!"

"Get it!" Diedies ordered the gunner.

The missile left the launcher in a cloud of smoke and dust, blasting most of the camouflage off the vehicle. Our eyes were fixed on the smoke trail of the missile, which seemed to bear way off track and then appeared to explode far behind the aircraft.

"It's a hit!" the gunner shouted as he climbed out of his vehicle. "It's a hit!"

"Okay," Diedies ordered, "Get this vehicle camo'd up again and move to your positions. We'll wait and see if there's any reaction."

All the while I tracked the aircraft through my binoculars. Suddenly it started to veer off course and a thin trail of smoke appeared.

"It's hit!" the rest of us shouted simultaneously. "It's going down!"

After ten or fifteen minutes the plane disappeared behind the tree line, having circled in a wide loop to the north. It was obviously in trouble. Then, as we watched in silence, a massive cloud of smoke appeared above the trees. The aircraft had crashed.

We kept a low profile for the rest of that very long day, waiting and watching as the MiG-23s did their meticulous searches. As soon as it was dark we packed and got the vehicles ready. We could not afford to stay in the same position any longer. That night we drove 20 km south and found a suitable spot, on the edge of a flood plain, where we redeployed the missiles. By first light the SAM-9s were ready and camouflaged and everyone was dug in.

Over the following days, while waiting for another target to present itself, I contemplated our success. I felt sorry for whoever had died in the crash. Killing an enemy in a fair fight was one thing. But this was different. The crew and passengers of the aircraft had no chance. In fact, we did not even know who'd been on board. I discussed these thoughts with Diedies and found some consolation in his reaction.

"I don't even think of the people killed," he said. "I just look at the bigger picture. There was a reason why we got this job. The task was executed successfully and the goal was obtained. That's it. Get on with your life."

Diedies was always the pragmatic one. By this time I had gotten to know him as a very sympathetic person, and I realised that he probably felt the same measure of guilt as I did. This reassured me and helped me to work through my own feelings.

A week later we exfiltrated along the same route we drove in on. Aside from the occasional MiG flying at high altitude, no more aircraft bothered us. After a full two-month deployment we finally reached the border. It was the longest I had been without a wash, and I desperately needed one. But my sense of accomplishment was great, not so much for the successful operation but because at last I felt I had settled in with the Small Teams group.

Diedies and I also formed a lifelong bond, and for years to come we would work closely together. Every single day of those two months he had me drafting and sending intelligence reports covering movement of ground forces as reported by UNITA, as well as the details of aircraft passing overhead. Little did we know at the time that these reports would greatly assist the intelligence community in compiling an accurate picture of the build-up of enemy forces at Menongue and Cuito Cuanavale.

It transpired that the Antonov had been carrying a Russian crew and eleven senior Russian advisors. Radio intercepts indicated that the Russian officers had been directing operations against UNITA on the Eastern Front and were heading back from Menongue to Lubango for a break. This was a serious setback for the Angolan-Soviet-Cuban war effort. To us it was clear proof of Soviet involvement in a war that, in our view, had nothing to do with them.

3

Operation Killarney
December 1985 to January 1986

---

*"The first principle of the art of stalking is that warriors
choose their battleground. A warrior never goes into battle
without knowing what the surroundings are."*

– Carlos Castaneda, *The Wheel of Time*

BY THE MID-1980S the civil war in Angola was at its height.
The MPLA focused its efforts on Jonas Savimbi's UNITA in
the eastern part of the country, while South Africa supported
UNITA with rations, equipment, ammunition and vehicles.
Behind the scenes, the Americans directed substantial finan-
cial aid to UNITA because they were still concerned about the
communist threat, especially in light of Russian and Cuban
support for the MPLA.

The supply lines in support of the MPLA offensive against
Savimbi relied on the delivery of huge amounts of stores and
equipment to the ports of Namibe and Lobito. In the case of
Namibe this material would then be transported by train into

221

Operation Killarney

Team 1   : Victorino & Stadler
Team 2   : Matias & Da Costa
Combined Team: Matias, Da Costa & Victorino

the interior to Lubango. From Lubango, Russian cargo planes ferried supplies to the forward airfield at Menongue.

The Namibe–Lubango railway line carried a substantial part of the logistics for both the Angolan forces and their SWAPO brethren, which of course made it a priority target for the SADF. The Recces had indeed launched a number of operations to render the logistics ineffective, one of which was an attempt to demolish the rail tunnel at Humbia, another to destroy the road over the Serra de Leba pass in October 1979. There were also several unsuccessful attempts to destroy the road bridge at Xangongo.

Diedies had previously convinced the bosses that two-man teams could disrupt rail traffic for substantial periods at low cost and with minimal risk. Over the course of two years two Small Teams – Diedies and Neves, and Tim Callow and Paul "Americo" Dobe – had repeatedly deployed in southwestern Angola, laying mines along the exposed railway line and bringing traffic to a virtual standstill.

During the same period EMLC conducted wide-ranging research on various types of explosive charges and methods of detonation that could effectively derail a train, destroy the engine and cause enough damage to the track so it could not be repaired easily. However, there were certain challenges that had to be considered. The Angolan forces patrolled the line on a daily basis, checking for disturbances on the track. Intelligence confirmed that an empty carriage was also placed in front of the engines to detonate any charge before the engines could set it off. All trains carried armed escorts, while culverts and curves in the line were especially well monitored as they were considered vulnerable or potential targets.

By the end of November 1985, barely a week after our return from the previous deployment, we were back in the ops room at Phalaborwa to be briefed for the next mission. Present were Dave Scales, Neves Matias, José da Costa, CC Victorino ("Vic"), me and some intelligence support guys. Operation Killarney was aimed at causing maximum damage to the railway line. EMLC's latest invention also had to be tested.

Our ops briefings always started with the counterintelligence brief, followed by an intelligence overview, after which the ops commander would convey the mission. Eric McNelly, taking personal responsibility for Small Team deployments, was again there for the counterintelligence brief. He explained the details of the security risks we would be facing once we were at Ondangwa, since SWAPO ran a comprehensive spy network in Ovamboland and any new activities in and around Fort Rev would be reported.

Then Dave Drew gave us an overview of how SWAPO received its logistics. Supplies went mainly by train from the port of Namibe via a distribution base at Lubango, then to the operational front headquarters, and eventually by truck to the detachments on the ground. He zoomed in on the area between Lubango and Namibe, describing the topography and vegetation of the semidesert terrain, and finally highlighting the railway line, the types of trains that were used and the frequency of the log runs.

Since Diedies would be on a course during our preparations for Killarney I was appointed mission commander, while Oom Boet would be the Tac HQ commander.

Top: The famous five-course meal served to Small Team operators after a deployment. From left to right: Graig Trethewy (second from left), Dave Scales, Neves Matias, Col. Terence Murphy, Boet Swart. My back is to the camera.

Bottom: A Small Team operator's personal equipment. All items were secured to the chest webbing with a string.

Right: The Small Team operators who took part in Operation Caudad in May 1986. At the back are Jo-Jo Bruyns, Dave Scales and André Diedericks. In front are me and CC Victorino.

Left: In the helicopter before take-off for Operation Caudad to Zimbabwe. On my left is sergeant-major Eddie Edwards.

Operation Caudad was aimed at conducting pre-emptive stikes at ANC facilities in the so-called frontline states. Our mission to Harare, during which two ANC offices were attacked, caused an international uproar. This headline is from the *Pretoria News*.

Top: CC Victorino and me during Operation Killarney in December 1985. Our goal was to disrupt the railway line that was also FAPLA and SWAPO's supply line between the harbour town of Namibe and Lubango in the interior.

Bottom: Neves Matias, José da Costa and CC Victorino formed a combined team after I injured myself during Operation Killarney. This photo was taken back at the landing zone – note the empty backpacks.

Top: A train on the Namibe-Lubango railway line – this shot was taken from one of the team's observation posts near the town of Caraculo.

Bottom: I took this photo of the railway line at Caraculo, stretching east towards the Serra de Leba mountains, when I visited the area in 2002.

Top: Our "guesthouse" at a UNITA forward base during Operation Abduct 1 in early 1987. Our aim was to bring an end to FAPLA's air superiority in southern Angola by blowing up MiGs at the air base at Menongue.

Bottom: Prior to deployment on Operation Abduct 1: André Diedericks, a UNITA liaison officer (standing), Neves Matias (sitting in the doorway), Daves Scales (in civvies), me, and our UNITA contact known to us only as "Captain Mickey".

Top: The Kwêvoël en route to the forward UNITA temporary base during Operation Abduct 1.

Bottom: With André Diedericks (second from left), UNITA's Captain Mickey and Neves Matias during Operation Abduct 1. Note the sheepskin padding on the operators' knees.

Top: Small Team operator José da Costa points to the position of the cache during Operation Abduct 2.

Bottom: The team back at the landing zone: André Diedericks, me and Da Costa.

Left: This wooden cross was still at the mission station, near the town of Huila, in 2002. During Operation Abduct 2 in 1987 we passed this cross during our infiltration of the target area.

Bottom: This shot of an MPLA Ural truck was taken from an observation post during Operation Abduct 2.

Top: This photo of the church at Huila was taken from one of our observation posts. We had to pass the settlement to get to the air base at Lubango.

Bottom: The same church in 2002.

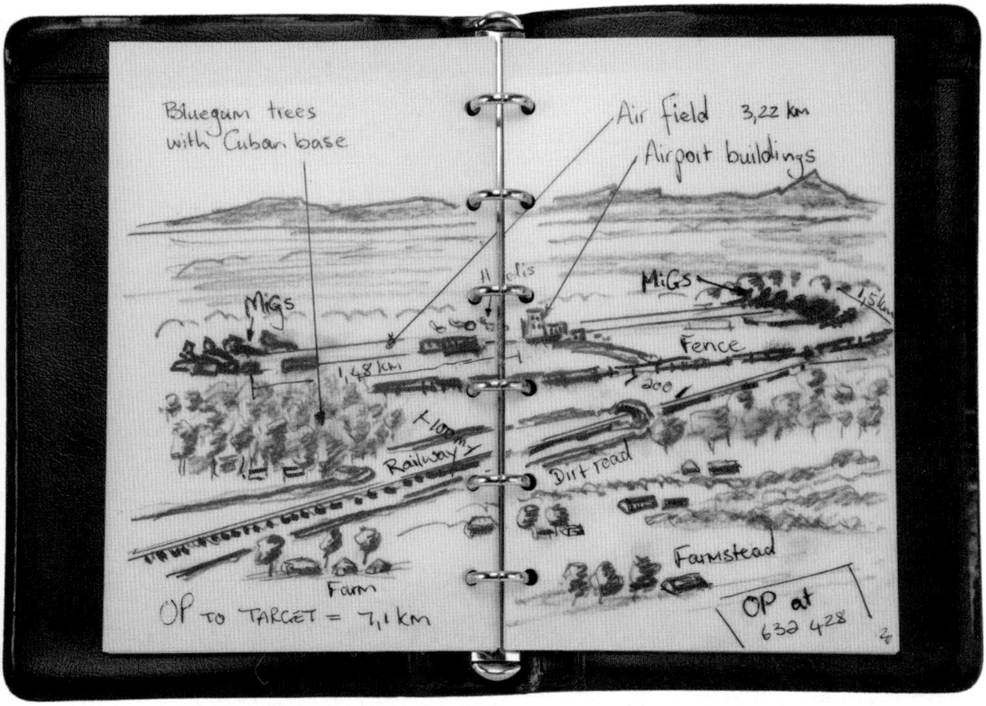

Bluegum trees
with Cuban base
Air field 3,22 km
Airport buildings
MiGs
MiGs
1,5 km
1,48 km
Fence
200
Railway
Dirt road
Farmstead
Farm
OP TO TARGET = 7,1 km
OP at
632 428

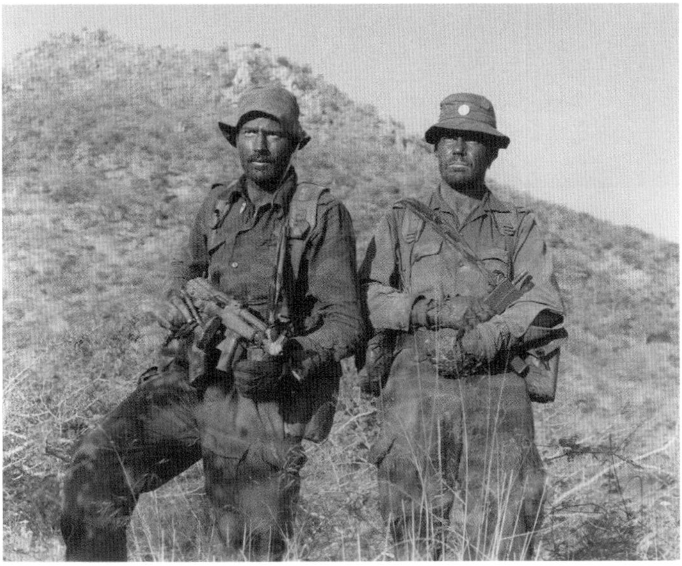

Top: My sketch of the target area during Operation Abduct 2, made in a pigskin notebook, which ensures that the drawings stay intact when exposed to water or adverse conditions.

Bottom: André Diedericks and me at the landing zone just before we were picked up after Operation Abduct 2.

Above: Receiving the Honoris Crux (bronze) from then Minister of Defence Magnus Malan.

Opposite: The citation for the Honoris Crux I received for "several highly dangerous and top-secret operations" conducted "deep behind enemy lines".

Nommer	:	75230797PE
Rang	:	Kaptein
Naam	:	Jacobus Johannes Stadler
Eenheid	:	1 Verkenningsregiment
Korps	:	Suid-Afrikaanse Infanteriekorps

Kaptein Stadler het sedert 1985 as lid van 'n tweeman-verkenningspan aan verskeie uiters gevaarlike en hoogs sensitiewe operasies diep binne vyandelike gebied deelgeneem. Die nadering van die teikens het soms oor etlike weke oor lang afstande deur onherbergsame terrein plaasgevind wat deur die vyand oorheers word.

Tydens 'n operasie in September 1986 is kaptein Stadler as missiebevelvoerder die taak opgelê om 'n vyandelike gebiedshoofkwartier op te spoor en te verken. Tydens die uitvoering van die verkenning het hy, vergesel van 'n makker, vir etlike dae naby die basis vertoef en soms baie naby aan vyandelike stellings beweeg. Die akkurate inligting het tot gevolg gehad dat die vyandelike mag tydens die daaropvolgende aanval swaar verliese toegedien is.

Tydens 'n ander operasie was kaptein Stadler lid van 'n kleinspan wat die taak opgedra is om vyandelike vliegtuie te vernietig. Die operasie is onder groot psigiese en fisiese druk uitgevoer. Infiltrasie van die bewaakte teikens het plaasgevind in die nabye teenwoordigheid, soms binne enkele meters van vyandelike skildwagte en in situasies waar daar geen uitkoms in geval van opsporing bestaan het nie. Kaptein Stadler is tydens die operasie enkele meters vanaf 'n vyandelike vegvliegtuig deur wagte gestop en gedaag. Sy akkurate en kalm optrede in die situasie het die vyand verwar en meegebring dat die span veilig en sonder kompromittering kon onttrek.

Ten spyte daarvan dat verskeie terugslae tydens van hierdie operasies ondervind is, het kaptein Stadler op kenmerkende professionele wyse voortgegaan om sy take uit te voer.

Hierdie dappere optrede, terwyl hy in wesenlike lewensgevaar verkeer het, maak van hom 'n waardige ontvanger van die Honoris Crux-dekorasie.

L242(54)

Right: When I noticed this photo in an album, I simply knew I had to meet the girl. Karien subsequently became my wife.

Below: With my wife, Karien, and our twins, Kobus and Karlia, on a dune in the Rub' Al-Khali desert in Saudi Arabia where I was stationed as Defence Attaché between 2007 and 2011.

Greeting the Greek Defence Attaché at a reception during my time as Defence Attaché in Saudi Arabia. In the bottom image are my wife, Karien, and our friend General Abdullah Al-Sadoun.

In 2010, while still stationed in Saudi Arabia, I decided to do a 200-km solo hike through the Rub' Al-Khali, the "Empty Quarter" of the Arabian Peninsula – the largest sand desert in the world and one of the most barren places on earth.

"The cover story for the deployment is that you will be going on a Small Team training exercise to Sawong," Eric McNelly said, "which will actually be the case. You will spend two weeks at Sawong for rehearsals, and then move to Pretoria for the second stage of the rehearsals as well as final planning and briefings."

Rehearsals at Sawong followed the usual pattern of exercises to condition our minds and bodies for night work. We would use the hours of darkness to practise team drills and rehearse every contingency. Much time was spent on patrol tactics, anti-tracking and emergency procedures. In the early morning, after a full night's work, we'd do a strenuous PT session, carrying our buddy or running with backpacks. After catching a few hours' sleep in the morning, we'd brush up on first aid, often administering drips to ourselves. During daylight hours we honed our communications skills, concentrating on sending and receiving Morse code. During the hottest part of the day we worked on recognition of enemy weapon systems.

After two weeks of intensive preparation, we departed for Pretoria. I went in my own car since I wanted to spend time with Zelda before the deployment. Although I had battled with my feelings for her for a long time, our relationship soon grew into much more than a friendship. Whenever I was in Pretoria on business, I stayed with Zelda and her family in the affluent Waterkloof Ridge neighbourhood. We were very fond of each other and had wonderful times together, but soon the secrecy of my job and the uncertainty of our long-term deployments started to affect our relationship.

Hiding the true nature of our forthcoming deployment introduced some complications, since by then Zelda had some grasp of Special Forces and the type of operations we were involved in. Since she had met Diedies and some of my comrades, she was part of the "inner circle" of Small Teams and had a fairly good understanding of our job. As far as our families were concerned, I would be doing one of the regular long-term stints on the border, as was common during that time.

After the weekend with Zelda I moved back to the Karos Hotel in Pretoria, where we stayed at reduced rates when the officers' messes were full. Our rehearsals now became more focused, as we needed to master the technicalities of railway demolitions. Specialists from EMLC taught us the intricacies of working with a mine, code-named Pick, tailor-made for diesel-electric trains. To ensure that the charge would not detonate when an empty carriage was coupled to the front of a train, Pick was designed to activate only once a diesel-electric locomotive passed over it. The device could be programmed to remain in sleep mode for up to three months, and then to arm itself and wait for the approach of a diesel-electric unit. The device had a little antenna that would pick up the electromagnetic field generated by the electric motor (the diesel engine in a diesel-electric unit is primarily there to generate power for the electric motor that drives the train), thus activating the mechanism. It was also fitted with an anti-lifting device that would react to any disturbance of the mine.

The explosives used for trains, code-named Slurry, consisted of an RDX base washed out of PE4, then mixed with nitro-methane to form liquid explosives. Aluminium powder was added for incendiary effect. The advantage of Slurry, which we carried in thickly sealed plastic bags, was that it could be poured into a hole made in the ballast of the train tracks. It would trickle down into the open spaces and fill all the cavities among the ballast. When exposed to air Slurry would eventually settle and slowly turn into a solid. The complete charge, Pick and Slurry, would be positioned to derail the train and cause maximum damage to the diesel-electric unit.

Various other devices, some extremely advanced for their time, were invented by EMLC and tailor-made for operations. Working on a similar basis as Pick, a device called Shovel was designed for vehicles, while the charge accompanying it was Hydra, a robust explosive that could be formed into all kinds of shapes − even resembling elephant dung strewn on the road surface! Another device I would get to know intimately was the mechanism used for demolishing aircraft, called Tiller, and its specially designed charge, Havoc, consisting of the explosive Torpex based on a solid aluminium plate for incendiary effect.

We visited train shunting yards and various stretches of track to get a grasp of the new challenge. It was important for us to understand the impact explosives had when placed in different positions on the track. I learned that, due to its sheer weight, a train could not be derailed simply by an explosion under the belly of a unit or a coach. The rail itself had to be disrupted, while factors such as the curve of the line, the speed of the train and the height of the tracks above ground level had to be taken into account.

By that time we had invented a new technique to prepare the railway site and plant the device: Diedies and Neves had designed a small tent that could be assembled and positioned over the tracks within a few seconds. With the side flaps stuck together with Velcro, the tent was completely light-tight. The operator inside the tent would use a powerful headlamp, allowing him to work fast and effectively and to make sure that, once the hole between the tracks had been filled in and the site covered up, the camouflaging would pass close scrutiny.

One problem was that the top layer of the track ballast, through exposure to the elements, had a different colour and texture from the underlying stones. The operator therefore had to clear the top layer and keep these stones aside to cover the hole again once the job was done. Previously, operators had used night-vision goggles when replacing the ballast, but the unnatural green image created by the goggles often meant that some discolouration would be visible on the surface. Working with white light reduced the risk of poor camouflage, and it certainly boosted the operator's confidence when connecting and arming the detonating device.

One Saturday night, while I was staying at Zelda's parents for the weekend, we had a rehearsal on a disused railway line passing through a deserted stretch of land outside Pretoria. Da Costa, Neves, Vic and I spent the Saturday at Special Forces HQ preparing for the night's work, and departed for the target area as soon as it was dark. Since it was not meant to be a tactical exercise, two of the EMLC technicians joined us to provide technical support and advise us on the placement of the devices.

We got started straight away, but soon realised that digging into the ballast would not be an easy job. Until late that night we worked on various ways to remove the stones and dig into the

strata below, testing different types of tools for the job and practising different ways of inserting the devices. At about 02:00 we
packed up, satisfied with the night's work, and started towards
the parked vehicles.

We had to cross a dilapidated old fence line and, since my arms
were full of equipment, two of the guys held the rusted strands
down to help me get across. Then, unexpectedly, a single strand
snapped loose and ripped across my face, one of the wire knots
tearing open my upper lip, strangely enough on the inside, as I
must have had my mouth open at that moment. In an instant
blood was spurting all over the place. The operators rushed me to
1 Military Hospital, where the wound was stitched up. A heavy
dose of painkillers and antibiotics rounded off the treatment.

I wasn't a pretty sight when I quietly slipped into Zelda's
folks' home in the early hours of the morning, but everyone was
asleep and I got to bed without anyone noticing. But eventually I
had to get up and show my badly swollen face. I had barely slept
due to the pain and discomfort. I looked decidedly rotten as I
walked into the kitchen, where Zelda, her folks and her brother
were having their Sunday-morning breakfast.

Zelda's mom immediately assumed that I had been involved in a
bar brawl – "so typical of the Recces". There was no way of
explaining this one away, having disappeared from their home on
a Saturday and returned at some ungodly hour with a face apparently smashed to a pulp. To this day they believe I told them a tall
tale. It took much explaining just to convince Zelda, but eventually she accepted Vic's version, as she adored and trusted him. She
gave me a hard time for causing damage to my pretty little face.

We now moved to a phase of detailed planning for the deployment, spending many hours on the execution of the deployment, and on routes towards the target areas and the actual points on the line we wanted to attack. As usual, we meticulously worked out and rehearsed emergency procedures for every possible contingency. At the Joint Aerial Reconnaissance and Intelligence Centre (JARIC) at Waterkloof Air Force Base, bent over maps and aerial photos of southwestern Angola, we worked out the details of every leg, emergency RVs and escape routes.

JARIC had state-of-the-art facilities, and for the first time I had the amazing experience of "riding" the stereoscopes. Enlarged stereo pairs of photos covering the target area were laid out under a massive stereoscope. The operator would get into a seat and steer the scope across the photo sets, which would allow him to fly virtually over a landscape that would "jump" out at him in 3D. The experience was so realistic that I became nauseous after a few minutes' "flying" in the machine.

Then the day arrived on which I, as the mission commander, had to do the in-house ops briefing for the deployment. While I was mentally and physically exceptionally well prepared for the mission, presenting our plan seemed like an insurmountable hurdle. I couldn't imagine selling my story convincingly to General Joep Joubert, then GOC Special Forces, and all his staff officers. In those days the mission commander would normally do the "in-house" ops briefing to the GOC, followed by a briefing to the Chief of the Defence Force the next day, given that the mission had been approved at Special Forces level.

In attendance at the in-house briefing would be all the staff officers involved with the operation as well as representatives from other departments and arms of service. The Air Force would be represented by the air liaison officer (ALO) dedicated to the deployment, while the medics would be represented by the OC 7 Medical Battalion. The plan would only be approved if all these elements were able to provide support.

As it turned out, my first briefing as mission commander to the GOC Special Forces proved to be more challenging than crawling into enemy-infested targets in hostile countries.

Commandant (the rank was later changed to lieutenant colonel) Ormonde Power, the Ops officer dedicated from Special Forces HQ to the operation, started with the introductions and presented the mission, and then Dave Drew covered the intelligence picture. By the time he introduced me I was almost paralysed by nerves. From the start my transparencies got mixed up, which caused me to start fumbling around with my notes, and I lost my thread. Eventually General Joubert stopped me.

"Stadler," he said, "what's this circus? You want to do this operation or not?"

I was nearly in a state of panic. All our hard work, the long hours of preparation and nights of rehearsals were at stake.

"Yes, General, we want to do it, and we are very well prepared," I managed to blurt out.

"Forget your bloody notes; tell me the story," he exclaimed.

Then, probably to help me save some face, he started asking me questions about the deployment.

"I want to hear your mission again."

I ran through it without even glancing at the pinned-up mission statement.

"Now, tell me what it is you really want to do."

General Joubert was addressing me like the mildly impatient father of a son who had arrived home from school with poor marks.

"Okay, now take me through your execution, step by step . . ."

This I could do well, since the map of our deployment was ingrained in my mind, and I had every single detail of the mission at the tips of my fingers. I took the general through every phase, explaining the details of the infiltration, execution and exfiltration on the map in front of them. Knowing that the Air Force would take issue with it, I explained the emergency procedures in the finest detail – our escape and evasion (E&E) route, emergency RVs, when and where we would like the telstar (comms relay aircraft) to fly if communications were lost, identification procedures and emergency extraction requirements.

At the end of the briefing General Joubert half-turned in his chair and, in typical fashion, stared at the staff, and then asked: "Any issues, anyone? Can you support the trooper?" I didn't even blink at the sudden demotion. I knew I had stuffed up badly. But, aside from a few technical clarifications, there were no further issues and the plan was approved.

That, however, was not the end of my woes. Sitting quietly next to General Joubert throughout the presentation was the fierce and, I must add, much-feared Brigadier Chris "Swarthand" (Black Hand) Serfontein, then the second-in-command of Special Forces. As I packed up my aids, Swarthand walked up to me, gripped me firmly by the wrist and ushered me out of the ops room to his office.

"Where do you come from? Have you never learned to do presentations? Haven't you done Formative?" he asked, referring to the leadership and management course all young Permanent Force officers had to complete. Now I expected the worst.

I started mumbling, but the brigadier forced me to sit down at the conference table in his office, and then walked around and sat opposite me.

"Do you realise that, now that the operation has been approved, you are presenting to the Chief tomorrow?"

Swarthand was spitting fire, his eyes boring into mine.

"Ja, Brigadier."

"Are you going to stuff up as badly tomorrow as you did today?"

"No, Brigadier."

"Now listen carefully . . ." he said pointedly. "Go and fetch your aids and bring it here. Let me show you a few tricks."

To my surprise, Swarthand Serfontein then took the rest of that day to show me how to do an ops briefing, explaining the nuances of effective communication, style and language. He forced me to repeat every single part of the briefing over and over again, there in the privacy of his office, and patiently corrected me whenever he thought I could do better.

Late that night, at the Karos Hotel, I got a phone call from Dave Drew. "Koos, I hate to tell you this, but the general does not want you to present tomorrow," he said. "I am to do the Int *and* the Ops briefing – on your behalf."

I was furious, but what could I say? Dave was obviously just conveying the message from the general. I left it at that and went to bed, thinking hard about how I would handle the situation.

The next morning I phoned Serfontein. "Brigadier," I said, "this is *my* operation. If anyone is to present it to the Chief, it's *me* . . ."

And that was it. Swarthand Serfontein didn't hesitate. "You go ahead; I'll mention it to the boss. Just do your best," he said and put the phone down. Just like that, no questions asked.

Dave Drew picked me up at the hotel and we drove together to Defence HQ. He thought it wise not to argue the point when I told him that I would be presenting the ops plan. We arrived early and set up maps and other aids in the conference room of the Chief of the Defence Force.

The General Staff took their places, and I desperately looked around for a rank that I could more or less associate with, but the lowest was a brigadier. The Chief's aide-de-camp, a captain, was not even allowed near the briefing room. General Jannie Geldenhuys, then Chief of the Defence Force, entered and sat down at the top end of the table.

My moment of truth had arrived. As usual, Dave did a magnificent job of sketching the strategic picture and highlighting the enemy activity in our area of operations. Then it was my turn.

But this time I was prepared. I let the mission unfold on the map like some mysterious adventure, exactly as Brigadier Serfontein had suggested, then talked them through the resources required and ended off with a summary of the emergency procedures. Once I had finished, there was a brief discussion about the political repercussions if the operation failed, if a helicopter went down or if one of us got caught.

At the end General Geldenhuys sat back in his chair and addressed me across the room: "Lieutenant, tell me, what is your gut feel, is this going to work?"

By now I had worked up an overdose of courage, since, from the reactions round the table, I could sense that the operation was on. "Yes, General, we are very well prepared and I have no doubt that we'll pull it off," I said without hesitation.

The General seemed satisfied. The deployment was approved and the meeting adjourned, leaving Dave and me with a great sense of accomplishment. Back at Special Forces HQ Brigadier Serfontein called us in and congratulated us. He had been informed by the Chief's office that we had presented an excellent briefing and that the boss was impressed by our performance – apparently one of the best he had ever heard!

I felt like an upstanding citizen again, and I am forever indebted to Swarthand Serfontein for lifting me up from the gutters of humiliation that day and for restoring my pride!

A C-130 brought Oom Boet Swart, Dave Scales and all the Tac HQ equipment from Phalaborwa and picked us up at Swartkop Air Force Base for the flight to Ondangwa, where we had a week for final preparations. The Tac HQ was set up in one part of the old jail in Fort Rev, and Dave wasted no time in setting up comms equipment and testing frequencies. The operators made final preparations to their kit. The Pick and Slurry were prepared and distributed among the teams. Each operator would pack a minimum of 30 litres of water, while an additional 30 litres for each would be packed to cache at the drop-off LZ.

As usual, a lot of time was spent on emergency procedures. We talked endlessly through the contingencies and role-played various scenarios with the Tac HQ. The final kit inspection was done in minute detail: all equipment was unpacked and rechecked for functionality and non-traceability. Batteries were checked and recharged where required; radios and electronic equipment were once again checked and tested to ensure they were both serviceable and "sterile" (the term used for non-traceable).

On the afternoon of the deployment the teams were trooped with two Puma helicopters to Okongwati in Kaokoland. Oom Sarel Visser, 5 Recce chaplain, and Oom Boet accompanied us while Dave manned the radios back at Fort Rev. At Okongwati, in a secluded spot under the trees away from the helicopters, we changed into our ops gear – mostly olive green with some pieces of FAPLA uniform – while the crews refuelled the helicopters. As we waited for last light, Oom Sarel put on his United Church of the Conqueror cassock, read from the Bible and gave us a short message of encouragement before giving communion to the teams. This was a custom unique to Small Teams that not only lifted our spirits but also strengthened the bond between us.

We took off before last light and crossed the Cunene River into Angola while visibility was still good. Vic and I were in the first Puma, with Neves and Da Costa following in the second. While there was still enough light, we kept the doors open and helped the pilots observe the skies for enemy aircraft, but all seemed quiet. When it grew too dark to see, we closed the doors and the pilots switched to night-vision goggles.

The drop-off LZ was about 40 km from the railway line in the rugged desert terrain south of Caraculo, a little settlement on the plain between Namibe and the Serra de Leba pass. We had picked one LZ for both teams, since it would serve as both the main emergency RV and a cache for the reserves. From there the teams would split up to approach their different target areas, the idea being to cover a wider stretch of the line. Each team would plant three charges five kilometres apart. All charges would activate within 30 minutes of priming, but had been set with different time delays so that they would come "alive" at different times over the next six weeks, ready to be detonated by the first diesel-electric unit that passed over them.

The LZ, in a grassy valley between sloping ridges, had been carefully picked. The moon was approaching first quarter and the pilots found the spot easily enough. The landing went off without any glitches. While the second Puma circled the area, Vic and I quickly offloaded the backpacks, water bags and crates of reserves for the cache. Then we kept a lookout while the procedure was repeated with the second helicopter.

Once the helicopters had departed, we moved into a defensive position around the LZ and waited, listening carefully for any sounds that might indicate the presence of enemy or local population. To me, this was always the worst part of any deployment. As the noise of the helicopters faded away to the south and the silence of the night became almost tangible after the rush, I was overwhelmed by a feeling of loneliness. But I kept these thoughts to myself, as there was a lot to do before daylight.

After an hour's listening, we converged on the pile of reserve equipment and started caching the crates and water bags. It was slow, painstaking work, as we had to dig a separate hole for each item, bury it and camouflage it. Then the exact position was carefully logged by means of a sketch in relation to objects and features in the area. All the time one of us would be positioned on higher ground away from the activity to listen for any sound of approaching enemy.

By first light we had finished. The two teams had moved into separate positions on high ground overlooking the LZ area. Well camouflaged and with good vision on approach routes, we waited out the day, calling in on the VHF every hour to check if the other team was okay. All appeared quiet, and by late afternoon we decided to move out that night. Before last light Neves approached the cache to ensure that it was undisturbed and still properly camouflaged.

Vic and I would take the area west of Caraculo, while Neves and Da Costa would go 20 km further east. I had not expected the going to be as taxing as I experienced it that first night. My backpack weighed in excess of 85 kg, which was more than my own body weight, and it took great effort to get it on my back and to stand up. For a main weapon, I carried the Hungarian AMD-65, a modified version of the Russian AKM assault rifle, while Vic had a silenced weapon, the MP5 SD.[13] It had become standard practice for teams to have a normal (unsilenced) firearm and a silenced weapon as main armament. Each operator would carry a pistol of his own choice as a secondary weapon. I had also taken it upon myself to do the navigation, which I routinely did during subsequent operations, as it was a skill I liked to practise and which I believed I had perfected to a fine art. But on this first deployment it was a challenge to navigate the rugged mountainous terrain while carefully applying patrol tactics and anti-tracking techniques.

By midnight, having covered only two kilometres, we were already bone tired and decided to move into a hide and rest. At first light I went up the mountainside and kept a lookout for the day while Vic stayed with the kit. From my vantage point I could see our route stretching north through the barren countryside. It was very uneven terrain, and I realised that we needed to pick up the pace and at the same time preserve our precious water.

We moved out by late afternoon, utilising the last light of the day to make up for lost time. We had agreed to cover ten kilometres that night, although I knew it was a tall order. But in the valleys among the mountain ridges the going was comparatively easier and we finally settled into a steady pace.

But I was not destined to see my first operation through. In the early hours of the morning, having covered most of our intended stretch for that night, I stepped on a loose rock and badly sprained my ankle – the same one I had injured in the night contact with 53 Commando at Nkongo the year before. I tumbled down the slope with my kit. The moment I managed to disengage myself from the heavy backpack, I realised I was out of the game. Within minutes my ankle was swollen, and no matter how we strapped it up, it wouldn't fit into my boot. There was no way it would sustain the weight of the kit.

My predicament left us with few options. A helicopter evacuation so close to Caraculo would mean certain compromise, but Vic could not carry all the equipment and finish the job alone. The only solution was for Vic to join the other team while I waited in the area. So it was decided that the other team would move in to our position. We would then rearrange the equipment so that the newly formed three-man team – Neves, Da Costa and Vic – could carry five charges. I would remain in the area until their return.

Fortunately Neves and Da Costa, having made about the same progress as we had, were no further than four kilometres to our east. Through the Tac HQ we arranged for an RV at a prominent feature close to us, and late that afternoon Vic went to meet them and led them to our hide.

I kept enough food and water to last me another seven days and gave the rest to Vic, while I took the HF radio. The team also took one Pick and enough Slurry for one charge from me. Between the three of them they would still be able to place five charges.

At last light they disappeared into the night. After the noise and movement of the repacking, I decided to move out and find a new hide where I would feel more secure. I cut my boot open and forced my strapped foot inside, then wrapped it all up again with dems tape (an exceptionally strong adhesive tape used in the preparation of demolitions). Moving around was slow and painful, but I managed to cover about a kilometre and settled in a good hide halfway up the slope of a mountain.

What followed was an extraordinary experience, even though I was no longer taking part in my own carefully planned operation. I was used to being alone and doing my own thing; in fact, I took pride in being able to live with my own good company for long periods. In the past I had often gone on solo hiking and camping trips, which I enjoyed immensely and always used as opportunities to cleanse body and soul. But this was a new experience, as I now had to deal not only with the loneliness but also with the threat of discovery by the local population or FAPLA. Although the rugged mountainous terrain offered good cover and excellent escape routes, there was almost no vegetation, and I had to take great care not to expose myself during daytime. As I knew that I would be hampered by my injured ankle if located by the enemy, I carefully applied proper tactics. By that time anti-tracking formed part of my everyday routine, but I still made sure I left no sign of my presence.

We had agreed to stick to the same radio scheds so I could receive the team's messages and monitor their progress. Dave Scales was as prompt and efficient as ever. He got both teams in the hopping mode[14] simultaneously and let Da Costa transmit the team's message first. Then he closed them down and had me transmit my message. I was surprised to learn how much distance the team had covered. Two more nights and they would be at the target.

Over the next seven days Dave Scales became my closest companion. We had two scheds a day, but the afternoon call was aimed mainly at boosting morale and guiding me through the long hours of hiding. Dave would check if I was on the air and then start an extensive broadcasting regime. He shared snippets of news from home, read newspaper cuttings he thought I might find interesting, and told jokes. This was essentially a one-sided conversation, as I could not afford to transmit, both to save battery power and to avoid detection by enemy electronic measures. However, Dave, who broadcasted from the base station at Ondangwa, could chat away – an opportunity he wouldn't have passed up.

Every day Billy Joel's "Piano Man" would be carried to me on the airwaves, since the song is all about loneliness. To this day, whenever I meet up with Dave or call him on the phone, our opening line is always "And he's talkin' to Davy, who's still in the Navy/And probably will be for life", from that touching song.

The team made good progress, and, two nights later, after observing the railway line for a full day, they started placing their charges. They planted the first one west of Caraculo, and then started working east towards the Serra de Leba mountains. By the time the second mine had been planted, they were fifteen kilometres east of the position of the first charge, the area where Vic and I would have operated. Since they were still heading east, it wouldn't make sense for them to return to my position once the job was done. They were running low on water and had a long distance to reach the RV. I therefore decided to start moving back towards the LZ area so the team could head straight there.

I moved only at night and took exceptional care with my injured foot. Before first light I would find a hide as high up the mountainside as possible and spend the day observing the trail I had covered during the night. By this time I was also low on water, but kept a strict routine and refrained from drinking during the day.

I reached the cache area on the seventh night after splitting from the team, a few days before they would arrive. I was now out of water, but forced myself to observe the area for another day before moving in. Just before last light I approached the cache, having left my kit in a hide up the mountain. The area was undisturbed and all the caches untouched. Very relieved, I removed a water bag and took it back to my hide, from where I kept a lookout while I waited for the team.

When they arrived a few nights later, I had already taken some stock from the cache, as they were completely out of water and running low on food. They reported that they had used all the Slurry to beef up three charges planted over a distance of 20 km.

We were picked up by the two Pumas late the following afternoon. After refuelling at Opuwa, we headed straight back to Fort Rev, where oom Boet Swart and Dave Scales had prepared a five-course meal as a welcoming feast for us.

Over the next few months we received three reports from Intelligence at Special Forces HQ of diesel-electric units that had detonated charges on the line between Namibe and Lubango. Rail traffic came to a halt as the train drivers started to refuse to travel on that stretch. In spite of FAPLA's efforts to locate and destroy the mines, the charges kept exploding one after the other, always targeting the diesel-electric unit itself.

Operation Caudad

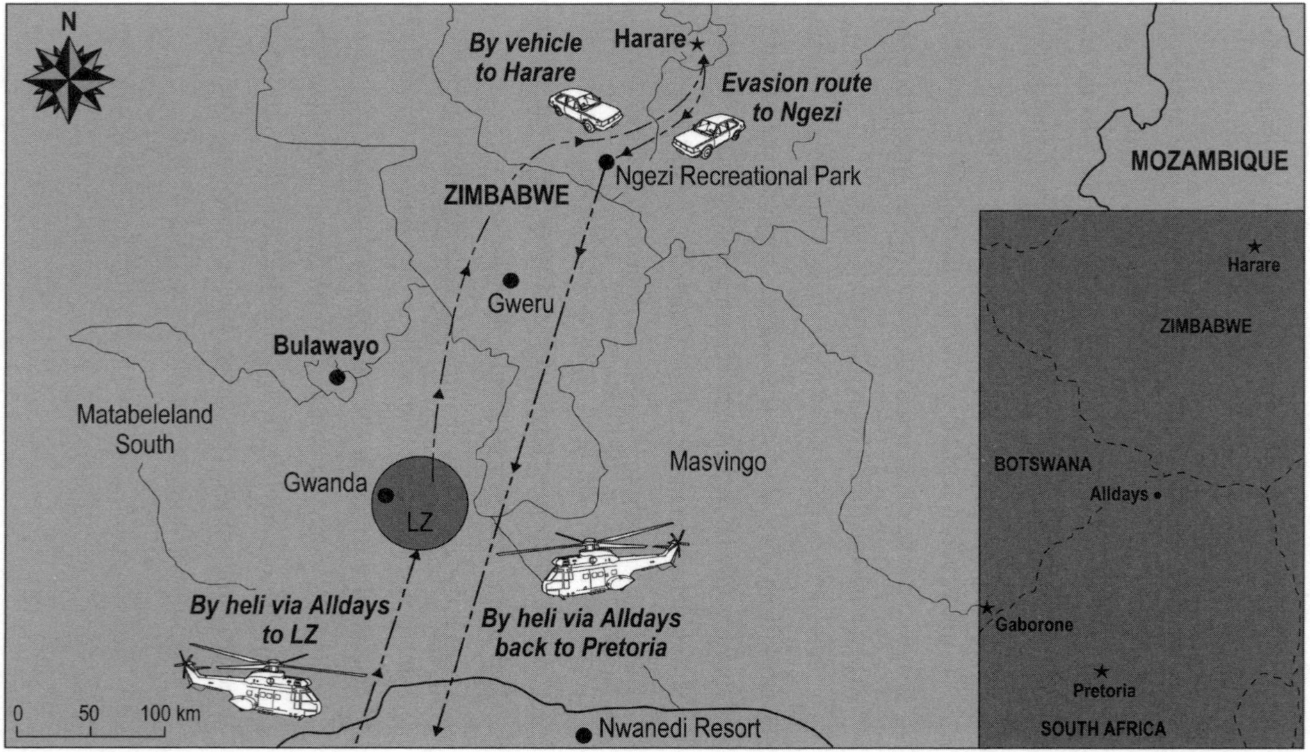

4

Operation Caudad
May 1986

IN THE 1980s many rumours had begun to do the rounds about the Recces. Because of the secretive nature of Special Forces training and their operations, little was known about the units. Whatever was written about the Recces in the media was often distorted or misquoted. One Afrikaans magazine in particular had a penchant for stories about the Recces. An article I kept for many years portrayed the South African Special Forces soldier as a silent killing machine, programmed to sneak into enemy bases to slit the guards' throats prior to an attack. We were depicted as superhuman warriors, fighting the enemies of our country in underhand ways.

I experienced first-hand the effect of someone taking these crazy stories too seriously. While on a visit to my folks in Upington, I picked up a lonely hitchhiker close to Vryburg, in what is today the Northern Cape. As soon as the guy got in I sensed from his body odour and scruffy clothes that he was one of the so-called knights of the road, vagrants who travel from town to town, making a living from benefactors and travellers who provide food and drink along the way.

Yet he told me how he studied Agriculture at Stellenbosch University and was travelling back for the start of the new term. After some time he noticed my uniform hanging in the back of the car.

"I also work for the army," he said, and from the conspiratorial tone of his voice I immediately sensed what was coming.

"Oh, which unit?" I asked innocently.

"You know, I'm not really at liberty to say, but I work for the Recces," he almost whispered.

"Sorry, I got you wrong there. I thought you were studying at Stellenbosch."

He had clearly played this game before and was unperturbed. "You see, that's just a cover. Special Forces have an agreement with the university authorities. Whenever there is a job, I would just disappear one night – and be back two weeks later. No questions asked."

By now I was starting to enjoy the intriguing tale that was slowly unfolding. "So what are these 'jobs' you are called to do?" I asked.

"Don't you know the Recces? We do the special jobs for the army. Dirty jobs, like silent killing."

I gave him some more rope: "So how do I sign up for these Recces?"

But apparently he had already summed me up and found me lacking: I was too skinny, too soft-spoken, definitely not Recce material . . .

"No, they have to approach *you*. And then you go through a very serious selection."

He proceeded to give an elaborate explanation of how each candidate is each given a puppy at the beginning of their selection, how they have to nurse the puppy for a year through the training period, and then kill it with their bare hands before they can qualify. He told me how realistic the training was, how trainees would often be killed because every exercise was like "the real thing". During operations you had to survive on scorpions and snakes, since you could not afford to carry unnecessary items like food.

After about two hours of listening to his heroics, I decided to give him something to really think about. In the middle of nowhere, in the semidesert between Vryburg and Kuruman, I slowed down and pulled into a gravel road off the main road.

I had retrieved my Beretta pistol from under my seat, but kept it from view. "Listen, brother," I said, "I am an officer with the South African Special Forces, your Recces, and before you ever share your shit with anyone else I'll just sort you out for good. Get out of my car."

Then he saw the pistol. And his face went white with fear as he started stuttering, "Sir, please sir, you can't shoot me. I'm just a poor man."

In a fraction of a second he had jumped out and retired into the sparse undergrowth. Like a frightened rabbit, he ducked and dived behind the bushes as I got out and pretended to chase him into the veld. He cleared out, no longer the fearless killer of a few minutes before. I dumped his kitbag along the main road and continued on my journey, hoping he had learned his lesson.

I then spent a quiet and restful week with my parents. My father was curious about the Special Forces, so I shared bits of information about selection and training with him, as well as snippets from operations I thought harmless enough. I returned to 5 Recce refreshed and ready to tackle training and preparations with new vigour.

I also got back into the routine of long-distance training and ran every marathon I could, either at Phalaborwa or Pretoria. Zelda and I used every opportunity to spend time together. She often visited Phalaborwa on weekends, and we always found something adventurous to do, either hiking in the mountains at Tzaneen or camping in the game reserves of the Lowveld.

The high command had decided that Small Teams from the other Special Forces units would join forces with Small Teams at 5 Recce. Since all operations were independent, strategic missions, it made sense to bring the teams together to streamline logistics and command and control.

And so three Small Team operators from 1 Recce (Piet Swanepoel, Menno Uys and Jakes Jacobs) moved from Durban to Phalaborwa to join 54 Commando. 4 Recce at Langebaan decided not to commit to the restructuring, since their reconnaissance missions were normally linked to seaborne operations and thus required specialised skills.

With our numbers bolstered, we threw ourselves into our work with a renewed sense of purpose.

By 1986 the ANC was fighting its revolutionary war against the South African government on all fronts: politically through its "hearts-and-minds" campaign and physically, through its armed wing Umkhonto we Sizwe (MK). MK had launched a number of incursions into the Northern Transvaal (today Limpopo), while sporadic attacks had been conducted on high-value targets in the interior of the country, like the Church Street bomb in Pretoria on 20 May 1983 and the attack on Magoo's Bar in Durban on 14 June 1986.

In response to these incursions, the National Party government had formulated a counter-revolutionary war programme that was enforced through a system of close cooperation between government organs and the Defence Force. In addition, the military was tasked to conduct pre-emptive strikes against MK facilities in the so-called frontline states. These were selective precision raids aimed at disrupting ANC structures and discouraging neighbouring countries from harbouring members of the liberation movements.

In May 1986 the Defence Force was tasked to conduct strikes against ANC facilities in Harare, Gaborone and Lusaka. The three raids would be conducted simultaneously, so actions had to be coordinated and timings carefully synchronised. While the Lusaka operation was to be an air strike by the SAAF, the Botswana and Zimbabwe raids would be conducted by Special Forces. Because of Harare's geographic position and the nature of the two targets in the city, the infiltration would be of a clandestine nature. The Gaborone raid would be a helicopter-borne strike launched from South African soil. D-day was determined by the Harare operation, as it was the most challenging of the three deployments and demanded intricate planning.

Diedies was selected as the mission commander for Operation Caudad, the raid on two ANC facilities in Harare. The teams consisted of operators from both Small Teams and 53 Commando. The first target, allocated to Jo-Jo, Vic and a third operator, was a set of ANC offices on the second floor of an office block in Angwa Street in downtown Harare. My team would be led by Bill Pelser, a highly experienced operator from 53 Commando. Our target was a residence, 29 Eves Crescent, in one of Harare's suburbs, which was used as a transit house for ANC cadres moving to and from South Africa.

While these targets were tactically almost insignificant, their destruction would signal to the ANC and their hosts that the South African government could get to the freedom fighters wherever they were harboured. A secondary task for all the deployments was to bring out as much intelligence material as possible, either in the form of propaganda pamphlets or actual operational planning documents.

Our rehearsals were conducted at the General Piet Joubert Training Area at Murray Hill, north of Pretoria. One of the old farmhouses had been converted to resemble 29 Eves Crescent, and we acted out every possible scenario in approaching, attacking and clearing the facility. Jo-Jo and his two teammates rehearsed at Special Forces HQ where they could place their ladder and practice the entry drills into the second floor.

Finally the teams were ready, and we were flown to Alldays by helicopter on the afternoon of 18 May 1986. The forces that would conduct the operations in Botswana and Zambia reported that they were ready, and we departed from Alldays in two

Pumas just before last light. The pilots flew nap-of-the-earth (below radar coverage) wearing night-vision goggles, a scary experience if you are a passenger looking out in the darkness at the ground rushing by. Agents from D-40, the highly secretive and covert military unit, awaited us at a prepared LZ in the area of Gwanda in Zimbabwe. From here we drove in a dilapidated old kombi to a deserted farm in the Matopo Hills, where we spent the next day preparing our kit and sorting out final details with the agents.

The D-40 operatives hired four vehicles from Avis in Harare to take the teams to their targets. Diedies had decided that the team leaders needed to drive by their targets to assess the situation first-hand, so a final recce was organised with the guys from D-40, while Diedies checked out the area where the mission HQ would be established, a hill close to Heroes' Acre in the centre of town. That afternoon the teams departed from the lying-up place and drove to Harare to meet Diedies and the team leaders at Lake Chivero, our predetermined assembly point outside the city.

Bill filled us in on the situation at the target: while he didn't see any enemy, the house had a high wall in front and the gates were locked with a padlock. The front yard was brightly lit and two large dogs were seen inside. Jo-Jo reported to his team that, while the office block appeared to be quiet, the street in front was abuzz with people from a number of hotels and bars in the area.

By 21:00 Diedies and the team doctor departed to take up their mission command post at Heroes' Acre. Just after midnight the teams started moving in on their respective targets in the hired vehicles. The infiltration went smoothly. We stopped just outside the gate at 29 Eves Crescent and jumped the wall using a short aluminium ladder. I immediately went around the right side of the house, while Bill and the assault element engaged the main building. One operator was assigned to cut the lock on the gate as soon as we were inside, to ensure a quick getaway, and the two dogs saw this as an ideal opportunity to opt out of the fight and take flight down the street.

On the side of the house I ran into an unforeseen obstacle, a makeshift fence that barred our entry. It took two of us to charge it down, and we literally fell in on the target. I jumped up and engaged the outbuildings, lobbing a stun grenade into the room and adjacent bathroom, but then my MP5 jammed after the first shot. I cocked and engaged again, but once again it had a stoppage. I quickly went down on my knees and changed magazines, cocked and fired into the dust-filled rooms.

By this time everyone had switched to white light on the weapons (by means of a powerful torch mounted below the barrel), as was the drill upon first engagement. I swept the outer room and bathroom with my torch and realised that they were empty, aside from stacks of ANC pamphlets spread out on a table. These I quickly collected in a bag each of us carried for this purpose, and then took up position outside with my teammate.

In the meantime Bill and the rest of the main assault team had followed us round and entered the house through the rear door, having found that the front was too strongly secured for a quick entry. The team encountered minor resistance inside, as there appeared to be only one person guarding the place. The house was cleared in a matter of seconds, and the piles of documents and propaganda material were hastily thrown into the plastic bags. Bill coordinated the setting of 4-kg charges in the house and the outbuildings, and on his command we initiated the timers. In less than two minutes the assault was over and the charges armed. Everyone cleared the house and got into the vehicles outside. We were barely two blocks away when the charges detonated. Twice we passed police vehicles flashing by in the opposite direction, but we reached the RV safely and waited for Diedies and Jo-Jo to arrive.

At the Angwa Street target the team found the street as busy as earlier that night. When they pulled their minibus (one of our hired vehicles) into a parking lot in front of the building, a security guard armed with a knobkierie ordered them away, apparently because the parking was reserved for police vehicles. When Vic told him to move aside, the guard became quite agitated and started shouting and threatening. Vic then produced his AK, which finally convinced the guy that he should rather stand down.

Jo-Jo's teammates placed the ladder and held it down while he quickly mounted to the second floor. The burglar-proofing posed a minor obstacle, but Jo-Jo managed to get the charges inside and armed the devices through the window. The job was done in less than a minute and the team got away safely. The ladder was left against the building and was on display for the world's media the next day.

All elements made it safely to the RV and we departed in a convoy towards the pick-up point in the Ngezi Recreational Park, south of Harare. A few kilometres from the city, a car overtook us from behind. The driver, a white man, inspected us as he drove past, then sped ahead and made a U-turn in the road, passing us again on his way back to Harare. We found this curious, but encountered no further obstacles on our route. Twice we stopped to strew the road with caltrops – multi-spiked metal "thorns" that would puncture any vehicle's tyres and delay a pursuit.

There was a thick fog in the area of our pick-up point, to the extent that we feared the helicopters might not be able to locate our strobes or make a safe landing. We offloaded our gear from the vehicles and prepared an LZ while the drivers wiped the vehicles clean of fingerprints. Finally, at first light we heard the lead pilot calling on the radio, and soon the noise of the aircraft became audible. The fog had lifted slightly and the helicopters were able to land and get us out of there. The cars were left at Ngezi but a call was made to the Avis office in Harare to thank them cordially and inform them where they could find their vehicles.

While the three raids conducted simultaneously in Harare, Gaborone and Lusaka had little tactical impact, the political fall-out was huge. South Africa was once again criticised by Western powers and African nations alike for its apartheid policies and its "flagrant acts of war" against its neighbours. The effect the raids had on the ANC was impossible to measure, although I believe that the message was conveyed that the South African Defence Force would strike at its enemies wherever they were hiding.

5

Operation Colosseum
October-November 1986

ON 25 OCTOBER 1986 the whole of 5 Recce converged on Oshivelo, a training area adjacent to the northern tip of the Etosha National Park. It was just across the so-called red line, dividing the farmlands to the south from the operational area to the north. The unit had come together to rehearse for Operation Colosseum – a deep penetration into Angola for a base attack on the headquarters of SWAPO's Eastern Front. A two-man recce team – José da Costa and I – would be inserted a week before the attack to locate the base and call in the attack force. This was to be our first Small Team deployment together, and both of us were a bit apprehensive, as each of us was unsure what to expect of the other.

José's huge frame had earned him the nickname "Mr T", after the character of BA Baracus in the popular 1980s television action series *The A-Team*. Depending on the big man's mood,

Operation Colosseum

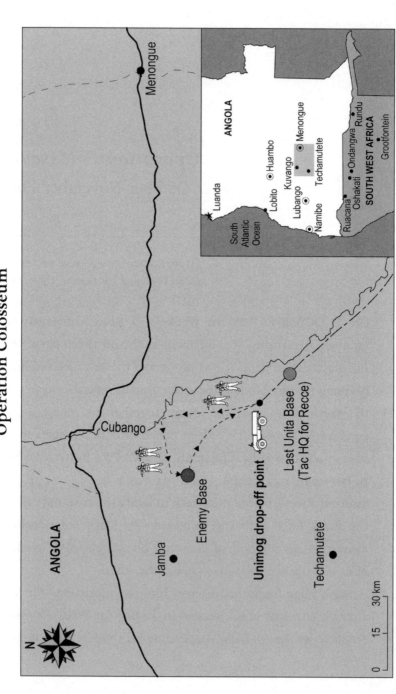

we would call him "Da Costa" or "Mr T", or simply by his first name. For Operation Colosseum Mr T became my team buddy, as Vic had to catch up on promotional courses, which every operator still had to complete for promotion, and was subsequently moved to another team.

Da Costa was born in Lobito, then a lively coastal town in the Benguela province of Angola, to a white Portuguese father and a mother from one of the local tribes. Before the Angolan civil war the town had been known for its carnival – not unlike that of Rio de Janeiro – which, together with the town's location and picturesque setting, attracted many tourists. But his blissful childhood was cut short by the civil war; Da Costa was only eighteen when the war split up his family and forced him and his sister to leave the country.

Over the years Da Costa has shared snippets of his life story and how he came to join Special Forces. I was amazed by what he had experienced by the time he was in his early twenties. It was difficult for me to imagine losing your home and your parents and having to flee for your life at such a young age. What happened to him and his family happened to thousands of other Angolan refugees. Their stories have not received as much attention from the South African media as those of former SADF soldiers, yet their experiences are just as much a part of the Border War story.

In early 1976 Da Costa arrived at Buffalo Base in the Western Caprivi with a group of ex-FNLA soldiers, who would later become the formidable fighting force known as 32 Battalion. Their familes were brought from Rundu and established in the *kimbo* (village) at Buffalo along the banks of the

Kavango River. Da Costa's first opportunity to do specialised work came with the formation of the reconnaissance wing of 32 Battalion. He joined up, and by the end of 1977 had moved to Omauni, the recce wing's operational base.

By 1981 he had made up his mind to join Special Forces. Since he had experience in small team work at 32 Battalion Recce Group, he wanted to apply his skills in a specialised environment. He was also under some pressure from his colleagues, because some of the 32 Battalion soldiers were already at 5 Recce, so he and three friends started to prepare. The four of them were transferred from 32 Battalion to Phalaborwa in February 1982. In April they did Special Forces selection with a group of 30 soldiers. Da Costa was one of only six who passed, and was soon transferred to 53 Commando.

At the end of 1984, when the Small Teams commando was established at 5 Recce under the command of then Captain André Diedericks, Da Costa wasted no time in applying, as he believed that, in his own words, he "was destined for greater things".

Prior to the deployment, Da Costa and I had worked out a programme for the two weeks of rehearsals: PT every morning, and then movement techniques, including patrolling, approach methods, anti-tracking and establishing hides. The PT sessions were a combination of buddy exercises and long-distance running with boots, webbing and weapons. To carry the big man was no mean feat, as he weighed at least 20 kg more than me, but I figured I'd rather get used to it for the day I needed to carry him out of Angola. The buddy-PT with combat gear also ensured that our kit was totally prepared, that there were no loose ends, and that every single item was secured with a string. It also meant that our boots would be worked in and ready for the long trek.

Over the heat of the day we'd prepare equipment – packing rucksacks, testing radios and fine-tuning our personal webbing. The afternoon would be spent planning, preparing maps and working out SOPs for the team, which we jotted down and memorised. Escape and evasion (E&E) plans were discussed and rehearsed in the finest detail.

After dinner we did night-work sessions, going through the same drills as during the morning's programme. We'd practise the same patrol techniques, but simulate various scenarios in the dark, applying immediate action drills to every contingency. Slowly but surely, Da Costa and I started to blend as a team. We complemented each other in every respect. We would often find ourselves doing the same thing, or following the same course of action, without even having consulted one another.

One morning after our PT session, the ever-pragmatic Da Costa raised the matter of our rucksacks again. If we took the bulky Small Team packs along on the mission, we would not have the immediate advantage of deception when spotted by the enemy. The lightweight "SWAPO" pack, on the other hand, would not be big enough for radios, food and water for seven days, as well as all the optical equipment required for a reconnaissance mission.

Da Costa suggested that we take the big packs and make sure we didn't move in daytime. The packs could also be cached close to the target when we started the final stalk. In the end we decided to take the Small Team pack, which I was grateful for, as the SWAPO pack didn't have a frame and could be quite uncomfortable.

When it came to our food and water, we knew that everything would have to be carried, since there was no possibility of a resupply. There would be no cooking, so the gas stoves and cylinders could be discarded. Also no tins – because of their weight. That left us with "zap"[15] meat, energy bars and peanuts. Vitamin-enriched energy drinks would round off our diet; water would make up easily 70 to 80 per cent of the total weight. Da Costa's pack weighed in at a relatively modest 80 kg when we were finally ready to deploy.

For a patrol formation during the final approach, I would take the front, with Da Costa carrying the HF radio as usual to my right and slightly back, 20 to 30 metres, depending on the undergrowth and the moon phase. Incidentally, there would be a half-moon during our deployment; this was ideal for an area reconnaissance, as the team would have moonlight for the first half of the night, and no moon during the early morning hours – just what we wanted for a penetration.

We had to make a final decision on the method of insertion. The combat force would be stationed at a UNITA base approximately 60 km from the target area. From there the reconnaissance team had to infiltrate to an area from where the final recce could be launched. It was decided that a team with three Unimogs would drop us off and return to the main force until it was time for our pick-up.

Contrary to our regular Small Teams procedures, we did not have a dedicated Tac HQ commander and signaller. The team would travel in the HQ grouping under Colonel James Hills, the

OC 5 Recce. When deployed, we would talk back to the unit's signal section at regimental HQ. This was not ideal, as it was standard procedure to have a dedicated comms system – radios, signallers, allocated frequencies and a well-rehearsed no-comms procedure – for the recce team. One certainly did not want to compete for air time when the bullets were inbound.

But Da Costa spent many hours with the HQ signallers, testing frequencies at various distances and talking them through our no-comms procedures. At the time his Afrikaans was limited to "Manne, moenie kak aanjaag nie [Guys, don't bugger up]", flavoured with exotic Portuguese swearwords that fortunately only he could understand. In the end he was satisfied, and the national service signalmen developed a grudging respect for the bulky Portuguese.

A day before the deployment, all the groupings were mustered for an initial Int and Ops briefing. The final briefing for the attack would be given at the forward base – after the reconnaissance. A massive sand model had been built under a double tent canopy. Major Dave Drew, the intelligence officer for the deployment, presented the general intelligence picture. Then he designated Captain Robbie Blake, at the time the intelligence officer for 51 Commando at Ondangwa, who had done a detailed target study of the Eastern Front HQ, to present the target briefing. The whole of 5 Recce, reinforced by a company from 101 Battalion and elements from 2 Recce, the Reserve Force element of Special Forces, gathered around the model.

The grouping leading the main attack consisted of Major Duncan Rykaart's 52 Commando – supported by the company from 101 Battalion as well as elements from 2 Recce. Major Niek du Toit and 53 Commando would be deployed as stoppers to the north of the base, while Major Buks Buys would lead 51 Commando to an escape route west of the target. A mortar platoon would deliver indirect fire support. Da Costa and I, the two Small Team operators who would do the reconnaissance, filled the last positions around the sand model.

The Eastern Front HQ was a typical guerrilla base, with an estimated strength of between 270 and 350, depending on the movement of its detachments. The defence of the camp was based on two 82-mm mortars, three 60-mm mortars, three DShK 12.7-mm anti-air machine guns that could be deployed in the ground role, and a number of SA-7 shoulder-launched missiles. Early-warning posts were deployed four kilometres to the east and south of the base.

It had been gleaned from radio intercepts, direction-finding and SWAPO prisoners of war that the base was situated next to a southward-flowing river, with a vehicle track passing east–west through the base. However, the recce team would have to pinpoint the position, determine a location for the forming-up point, decide on the direction of attack, and allocate positions for the mortar platoon as well as the cut-off groups. A tall order, I thought, considering we had only six days for infiltration, reconnaissance and exfiltration.

FAPLA's 35 Brigade was positioned at Techamutete, about 60 km northwest of the target, while tactical groups were stationed at Cassinga and Cuvelai to the west and southwest. A Cuban regiment was based at Jamba to the north (not the Jamba that served as Jonas Savimbi's headquarters). Fighter aircraft were operating from Menongue, a mere 80 km north-east of our target.

Colonel Hills presented the Ops briefing himself. The columns of vehicles would depart from Oshivelo in the early morning hours of 3 November. By first light the convoys would be south of the border west of the Cubango River, in order to cross that night. The logistics echelon, under RSM Koos Moorcroft, would follow the next night. The whole force would regroup north of the border and head along an established UNITA route to the forward base approximately 60 km east of the target area. From there the recce team would be deployed, while the attack force would remain in position until they returned.

When I caught Da Costa's eye, his faced was pulled into a grimace. I knew what he was thinking: it went against all principles to do a reconnaissance against time, especially where the success of the attack depended entirely on what the recce team reported. Moreover, we both understood that if the team was compromised it would mean certain failure, as the attack would have to be called off, or – worse – that the enemy could be ready and waiting for the attack force.

When I told Colonel Hills after the briefing that there was not enough time for a proper reconnaissance, and that we should have deployed earlier, he just said, "Vasbyt, Kosie, ek weet julle kan [Hang in there, Kosie, I know you can]." As a sign of affection, he used to call me by the diminutive form of my name, but at that moment I was in no mood to appreciate it.

"But what if we don't find the base? I mean, if it's not there and we need more time?" I persisted, because I knew every step we made would be scrutinised by everyone in the unit. I sure wasn't ready for failure.

He cut me short. "The base is there and you'll find it."

End of story. Hills was confident that the intelligence was accurate and that the "A-Team", as he used to call us, would be successful.

"If you are compromised or you don't find the base in six days, we'll move in with the whole force. Then it becomes an area operation," he said, but it was little consolation to the team. To us it was crucial that the base was located, but time was not on our side.

During our long vehicle infiltration, Da Costa and I drove in the command group, sharing a Casspir with one of the two unit chaplains, Padre Thinus Riekert, as well as some of the intelligence staff. Thinus was a deeply religious man but also an enlightened individual. We had many long, interesting conversations on the road and came close to solving the world's problems with our infinite wisdom and insight.

After four days of travelling, the whole force arrived at the UNITA forward base from where both the reconnaissance and the attack would be launched. The UNITA base commander was clearly not happy with the large force moving into his territory, as it could compromise the position of his base – especially considering that it was within 80 km of Menongue airfield, where FAPLA had a squadron of MiG-21s. But he must have received instructions to accommodate us, and to this end did his best to please the South Africans.

Da Costa and I didn't waste any time. We made a final comms check, packed our kit on one of the Unimogs and said our goodbyes. I drove with the team leader on the first vehicle and navigated on a bearing straight towards the target area. After 20 km we stopped. It was just short of last light. So far we hadn't seen any tracks. We got off and the vehicles immediately turned around and left on their tracks. We moved into the undergrowth and waited for our eyes to adjust to the coming darkness. The noise of the Unimogs died away and all was quiet.

The moon was up and we decided to make good use of the available light, knowing that we were still far from the target. We covered a good fifteen kilometres, applying anti-tracking and movement techniques as much as the relatively fast pace allowed. When the moon set, at 02:00, we got a few hours' sleep but dawn found us on the move again.

With the sun behind us, we decided to steal a few hours of daylight. We still hadn't found any spoor and the bush was untouched. By mid-morning we decided not to push our luck and went into a hide. We settled into a routine of listening and watching. In the late afternoon we were rewarded with the first sign of the enemy – a series of explosions far to the west. I took a bearing and logged it, roughly drawing the direction on the map.

Again we decided to use some daylight, but this time we had the late-afternoon sun against us. As this was very dangerous, we decided to wait until the sun had set behind the tree line. Nevertheless, we made good time and went well into the night by the bright and beautiful moon. Early the next morning we were up and moving. We soon found some old SWAPO tracks, probably from a hunting party, and decided to don our anti-track bootees. By mid-morning we were in a hide again.

Before long we again heard continuous explosions. "Mortar practice . . ." Da Costa whispered.

Again I took the bearings and logged them on the map. As long as the enemy was there, we'd certainly find them.

In the heat of the day I crawled over to Da Costa to discuss our approach. The plan was to move at an angle towards the target area, logging the sound of explosions as we approached. We would keep moving until we had passed the suspect area. Only once we had a reasonable grasp of the base's location would we turn and start moving towards it. We would start the final approach only as soon as we knew the exact location. I tried not to think of a penetration yet. That was the dangerous part – and hopefully would not be necessary.

By the third evening I was certain that we were close. We had located fresh tracks, all leading towards the suspected target area, and we occasionally heard the distinct crack of AK shots. That night we kept moving northwest on our bearing, past the area we now knew was the hot spot. In the early evening we heard vehicle movement for the first time. I duly took the bearing and logged it.

Bingo! Right direction. Right distance.

At first light the next morning we were hidden away in a thicket, backpacks camouflaged, food and water handy for the day, antenna up and the radio prepared. At any time now we could expect a security patrol or a hunting party to come by. We knew from experience that the stationary person had the advantage. In the flat savanna terrain, with its occasional thick undergrowth, a man on the move was invariably the first to be seen – exactly why an area reconnaissance in the bush was so difficult.

There was no high ground to establish an OP. Climbing a tree would be counter-productive, as you would just have tree canopy all around you – and in the process expose yourself to early-warning posts. You would be the intruder in a world the freedom fighter knew intimately. You would most likely approach from a direction *he* had determined – by the position he had chosen for his base. He would have arcs of vision (and of fire) across a chana or flood plain *he* had picked and prepared.

The fourth day passed slowly and, for me, extremely stressfully. Because of the uncertainty and the urgent need to locate the target, I found it difficult to pass the time. We slept in turns, albeit briefly and fitfully.

We had two days left to confirm the location visually, do a close-in recce and get back to the main force. I found some consolation in the big man's relaxed demeanour. He seemed unfazed. I prepared a message detailing our finds of the day. Da Costa, lying on his side next to his radio, went through the ECCM procedures and transmitted the message.

There was also a message for us – from James Hills: "UNITA getting restless. Have to move in 2 days. Skuimbolle. JH."

Literally translated, *skuimbolle* means "foam balls". It refers ostensibly to the foam produced between the buttocks of a horse when it pulls a cart. This was Hills' way of saying we should get a move on.

That night we swung from our original northwesterly bearing to a direction due west, certain that we had passed the base area. We went slowly. The moon was slightly from behind, giving us a minor advantage in case anyone might be stationary in front of us. It was painstaking work, moving from shadow to shadow, anti-tracking with every step, constantly communicating with the other. After covering about three kilometres, I was certain that the base would be directly south of us. We stopped and conferred.

Da Costa agreed. This was it; we could start the approach. "But I think we should take the backpacks," he said. "We are not close enough yet."

We decided to move with the packs until the moon had set. In the early hours of the new day we would approach with combat webbing only.

Once the moon was down, we stashed the backpacks and wiped out all signs of our presence before venturing out to locate our target. We used first light to gain a few hundred metres, encountering numerous tracks and cut-off trees, but no SWAPO. Soon we realised that there was no way we could approach the target in daylight, as the undergrowth was becoming too sparse. We went down and, after conferring quickly, decided to go back to the packs.

Back at the hide we crawled in close to the kit and covered each other up, readying ourselves for another long day. As the day dragged on we had a lot to log, again plotting everything we heard on the map. We were close – if only they didn't find us first!

During the late-afternoon sched we reported that we would be going in close that night. Again we received an urgent message that the main force had to get moving the next day. After last light we kitted up and slowly closed in on the area where we believed the base was. By now we were patrolling at a snail's pace, working our way due south. Following a technique we called caterpillaring, Da Costa patrolled a few hundred metres forward in light order, and then returned for his kit. We would then both move forward with the packs to his last position and put them down, after which I repeated the routine.

By midnight we still didn't have any sign of the base. I was becoming concerned. Had we passed it too far to the west? Or were we still on the eastern side of it?

We took in a hide and tried to work out where we'd gone wrong. "Where is the river line where they are supposed to get water?" Da Costa asked, voicing my concern. "And the road that runs through it?"

"It must be further south," I said. "They must get their logistics from somewhere . . ."

Time was running out and we did not know which way to move. I made the call to cache our packs before first light and move out in light order, firstly south and then due west. In this way we should find either the road or the river.

With the first faint light of dawn we were moving, deliberately now. Our eyes were piercing the half-light, and both of us knew that first light was a bad time to walk slap-bang into an enemy base, as soldiers tend to be exceptionally alert at this time. Sound and smell travel far . . .

We saw it simultaneously – the road running east–west in front of us. While crossing it through a thick patch of undergrowth, we noted three fresh tracks going east, probably to an early-warning post. Away from the road we swung west, and soon came upon the flood plain of a river. My heart was pumping. This was it – the junction of the river and the road, the flood plain across which their arcs of fire would be trained. I looked at Da Costa, and he indicated with a nod that he agreed.

But there was no way of crossing the open area in broad daylight. We went down and started crawling in the short grass towards the river line. Suddenly Da Costa stopped and pressed himself further down into the wet grass, the thumb of his left hand pointing downwards in the classic sign indicating enemy presence.

From the tree line across the river a SWAPO patrol of five or six men emerged, apparently not suspecting anything, as they casually started patrolling along the river line to the south.

Da Costa cupped his left hand behind his ear, indicating to me to listen. But I had already heard the commotion among the tall trees from where the patrol had appeared. I could distinctly make out laughter, a vehicle door slamming and orders being yelled. For some time we just lay there, trying to judge the size of the base by the sounds we were hearing. Occasionally we dared to sneak a peek across the open chana, but we were too low to see into the shaded tree line.

After a while I indicated to Da Costa to move back, as we could also expect a patrol on our side of the river. To get any closer, we needed to approach the target from a different direction.

Slowly we crawled back into thicker bush, making sure not to leave any drag marks on the ground that was still wet with morning dew. We backtracked the same route to our packs from where we moved out a further two kilometres to make comms.

My message was short and to the point: "Base found. Enemy. Number unknown. Need one day and night to confirm."

James Hills' voice came on the air. He obviously didn't bother typing a message: "Negative. Negative. No time. I need you here tomorrow morning. We are moving tomorrow."

Da Costa and I exchanged glances. No time for a close-in recce? Tomorrow morning? Sixty kilometres to go? Enemy all around? This was a tough one.

I tried once more, a brief message to confirm that we had found the base, but needed time for confirmation. But that was it. The colonel maintained that they couldn't wait any longer. Time was of the essence. Later he would explain his decision: they had good reason to believe that some of the UNITA elements were in contact with SWAPO, and that our intentions could become known to the Eastern Front HQ at any moment.

The call was made. We would head back and make the best of the situation. For another kilometre we remained vigilant, moving from cover to cover, constantly checking our backs, changing direction and anti-tracking. Then we increased the pace. By first light the next morning we had covered 30 km, and requested a pick-up in the same area where we'd been dropped. Just to make sure the 5 Recce guys did not confuse us with SWAPO, I took off my shirt to expose my white upper body. By mid-morning the Unimogs drove into the RV, and it was a huge relief to see their smiling faces.

In the camp we found 5 Recce preparing for war. Weapons were being cleaned and oiled, vehicles refuelled from the bunkers, camouflage nets pulled tight, food and water secured. The intelligence guys had already drafted a sand model; we just had to fill in the details.

Colonel Hills called all the commanders in for a quick debrief before issuing orders. I ran them through the events of the previous days and described the location of the base, drawing the road and the river line on the sand model. On the map I plotted a six-figure grid reference of where I estimated the centre of the base to be.

Then came the questions.

"How many are there?"

"Did you see any bunkers?"

"How big is the base?"

"What weapons do they have?"

Da Costa and I covered what we could, but in the end the information, from the attackers' perspective, was sketchy. Finally one of the commando leaders asked, "Are you sure the base is there?"

"The base is there," I said sternly, "at that grid reference. With vehicles and a lot of people."

Then one of the commanders asked Colonel Hills, "So what happens if the base is not there?"

"Then 5 Recce will have a new transport park commander," the OC joked, perhaps in an attempt to break the tension. I was quite amazed that they doubted us – after all our trouble to locate the base. We'd even been ordered to return before we could do a close-in recce.

"The base is there," I repeated. "I'd put my life on it."

Dave Drew gave a quick intelligence update, explaining the location of the base and the approximate size. Then James Hills briefed us on the attack. The plan was straightforward. That night I would lead the two stopper groups, 51 and 53 commandos, as well as the mortar platoon, in on the actual line of attack – on foot. Along the route in we would mark the axis of advance with toilet paper to ensure that the main force got to the right position. Once at the forming-up point, exactly three kilometres from the target, we would leave the mortar platoon to deploy in a clearing next to the east-west track. Then we would break away from the attack axis and navigate to a position two kilometres north of the target, where 53 Commando would deploy as a stopper group. This navigation would be by dead reckoning (DR), relying on bearing and distance, as there were no outstanding features in the flat terrain.

Once 53 Commando was in position, I would then navigate to a position three kilometres west of the target, leading the men from 51 Commando to their cut-off position along the east–west road, where we would wait in ambush for any fleeing cadres.

The assault force – regimental HQ, 52 Commando, a company from 101 Battalion, as well as elements from 2 Recce (the Reserve Force contingent that had been called up for the operation) – would follow just before first light. Da Costa would do the navigation to the forming-up point.

The assault force would form up and advance to contact. At first light, as the attackers reached the river line, the mortars would open fire to soften up the target. Then the attack would commence. It seemed straightforward enough.

Before last light that evening, we started moving out. The vehicles took us to within 20 km of the target. Then we set out on foot, found the east–west vehicle track and made good time. By 02:00 we were at the forming-up point. The mortar platoon deployed and set their weapons to fire at the six-figure grid reference I had given as the centre of the base. We marked the forming-up point and the axis of advance with toilet paper, then set out on a bearing to 53 Commando's position, circumnavigating the target area. This was pure DR navigation, as there were no features to guide us, but I was confident that I had led them to the right position.

We set off for 51 Commando's position to set up an ambush west of the target. The men were deployed in an extended-line formation next to the road, facing north, the only cover a termite heap behind which the RPG gunner lay. We waited, listening on the radio as the assault force formed up and started their advance to contact. By first light we could actually hear the vehicles, but the order never came for the mortars to open fire.

Then the voice of one of the commando OCs came on the air, "There's nothing here . . . No movement. Do you think we have a new transport park commander?"

The response, "Nothing here. It's a lemon. Sure we have a new –"

Then all hell broke loose.

A DShK 12.7 mm deployed in the ground role created havoc as it covered the eastern entrance to the base. In the opening shots of the attack one of the 52 Commando Casspir drivers, Corporal ML Mashavave, was killed. In the meantime, 53 Commando, having advanced further south because they could not detect any enemy activity, had to withdraw out of the line of fire, missing the opportunity to cut off some of the cadres who were fleeing directly north.

Luckier was 51 Commando. A peculiar-looking SWAPO command vehicle came careening down the track and erupted into a ball of flame as the RPG rocket found its target and bore down on the poor RPG gunner behind his termite mound. Literally centimetres from the frightened man's face it came to a standstill, half-suspended over the mound.

Seconds later a Gaz 66 truck followed. The RPG gunner, probably still in a state of shock, missed the target, but two operators with SKS rifle grenades planted themselves in the road and stopped it in its tracks, while the rest of the operators blasted away at the driver and passengers.

It turned out that there were a comparatively small number of enemy in the base, as the majority of the cadres were at the rehearsal area twelve kilometres further west. When the attack commenced, the SWAPO HQ and protection element, realising that the attack force was far superior, decided to flee. Thus only a limited number of cadres were killed. Later that morning, as I was sitting in the centre of the base at a bunker that appeared to have been the command centre of the so-called Eastern Front HQ, Captain Robbie Blake, the 51 Commando intelligence officer, drove up in his Casspir, got down and handed me a slip of paper.

"What's this?" I asked, wondering if there was another target.

"It's an eight-figure grid reference from the SATNAV (a satellite navigation system and forerunner of the GPS)," he said. "Looks like you were right. It's the position you gave us."

I checked my map and realised that the grid reference corresponded exactly with the position of the base I had conveyed to the OC the day before.

In the meantime 52 Commando had reorganised and driven west to engage the rehearsal area. They were ambushed by a large SWAPO force hiding in thick bush on the side of the road, but managed to swing the vehicles into combat formation and fought straight through the ambush site, killing seven enemy. Throughout the rest of that day the three commandos were engaged in follow-up operations. Numerous contacts ensued and a total of 39 SWAPO fighters were killed.

That afternoon, during an ambush laid by more than 100 SWAPO soldiers, Corporal André Renken was killed instantly when 2 Recce's Casspir was shot out with an RPG. Throughout the day a few operators from 5 Recce were wounded, mostly by shrapnel, and had to be evacuated by helicopter.

Renken and Mashavave were the only South Africans killed in the operation. Mashavave's body was flown back after the initial attack (the combat zone had to be cleared before the helicopters would approach for the pick-up), while Renken's remains were placed in a body bag and transported in our Casspir. The high spirits Thinus Riekert and I had felt on the inward journey were gone. As soon as the convoy reached an area considered to be out of the immediate threat of the MiGs from Menongue, the Pumas were called in to take the remains back to Oshakati.

The convoy took another four days to reach Oshivelo, where an extensive debriefing took place. The operational vehicles were driven back to Phalaborwa in convoy, while the commandos were trooped back by C-130.

While the reconnaissance for Operation Colosseum was one of many recce missions I participated in, for me it determined future modus operandi. The mission set the trend for a phased approach to locating an enemy base in the bush – initially through continuous reporting of noise (this while approaching the suspect area at an angle and passing it at a distance of three to four kilometres), then building a picture from visual signs, and finally from a close-in reconnaissance. Later, Da Costa and I analysed the sequence of events meticulously and compiled a textbook for specialised reconnaissance missions based on the actions taken during those few days.

In subsequent years, after the first democratic elections and the integration of erstwhile opposing forces, Da Costa, then a senior warrant officer at the Special Forces School, became instrumental in training young operators and establishing Special Forces doctrine. As a role model for aspirant operators over the years, he has exerted immeasurable influence and played a major role in shaping the lives of so many young men.

Operation Abduct I

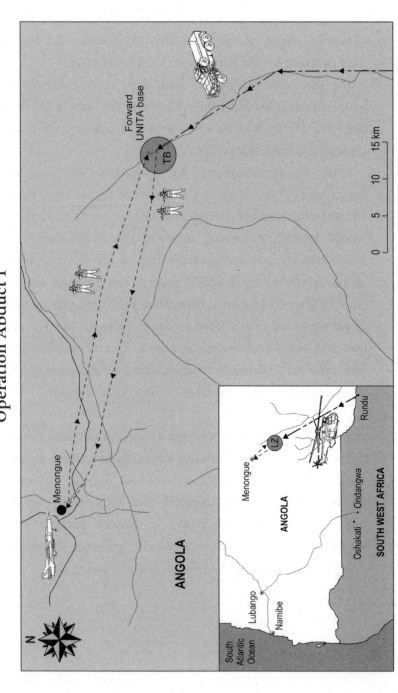

6

Operation Abduct 1
January-February 1987

---

*"One of the greatest forces in the lives of warriors
is fear, as it spurs them to learn."*

– Carlos Castaneda, *The Wheel of Time*

BY LATE 1986 the idea of destroying FAPLA MiG-21s and
-23s on the runways of the air bases at Menongue and
Lubango had been on the cards for months. Diedies was certain that he could convince the bosses to send a small team to
do the job, as it was virtually impossible for a fighting
patrol to infiltrate either of the targets. Both airfields were
exceptionally well protected, had open cultivated lands for
kilometres around them and had a spread of FAPLA, Cuban
and SWAPO deployments in the vicinity.

At that point, the MiGs ensured that FAPLA had air superiority in southern Angola. They had the advantage of
holding time, or time-over-target, as they had a mere 60 to 80
km to fly to the combat zones. The South African Mirage F1s
and Buccaneers, however, had to fly from Grootfontein; by
the time they reached their targets, they had only ten

minutes of fuel left. Hence they seldom engaged in dog-
fights, as their window of opportunity was too limited. The
Impala jets operating from Ondangwa and Rundu had neither the range nor the armament to engage the MiGs.

With Dave Drew's assistance, Diedies had been studying
the patterns at Menongue, in Cuando-Cubango province,
trying to ascertain the number of fighters, where they were
parked, how they were protected and how they could be
approached.

While the rest of 5 Recce was deployed on Operation
Colosseum, Diedies travelled to Pretoria to make presentations
to the GOC Special Forces, Major General Joep Joubert. The
idea was proposed to the Chief of the Defence Force, General
Jannie Geldenhuys, who agreed to the plan in principle but
had to clear it with the Minister of Defence.

The operation was approved, but we still had to present
the final plan and get authority for air support. This required
some powers of persuasion, as it would be considered an act of
sabotage – and a breach of international conventions – if a
South African soldier was caught placing explosives on
FAPLA aircraft. Up to that point UNITA had claimed all the
successes for downing enemy aircraft.

Menongue would be the first target, mainly because fighters were operating from there against the South African forces
deployed at Cuito Cuanavale, but also because it was considered
an "easier" target than Lubango.

It was business as usual as Diedies, Neves Matias, José da
Costa and I returned to Sawong to prepare for our next deployment. We forced ourselves to adapt to a switched routine

– working at night and resting during the day. Every night we would practise navigation, patrol tactics and stalking a target.

We spent hours stooped over maps and aerial photos, working out routes, hiding places and a final approach. A photo interpreter from the Air Force, equipped with all the latest aerial photography, state-of-the-art stereoscopes and even a scale model of the target, was there to assist us.

We also used the daylight hours to study the dimensions and vulnerable points of MiG-21 and -23 jets. Using enlarged graphics of the aircraft, we determined exactly where to position the explosives for maximum effect, the idea being that the charge would cause a secondary explosion of the fuel tanks, which in turn would damage adjacent aircraft. Our reasoning was that if a charge could be placed on every second or third aircraft, we could effectively cripple the whole airfield.

We had also tested a range of blue and grey camouflage in varying light conditions. In the end we decided to use a single type of clothing for day and night. It appeared that dark blue and olive green had similar qualities in the pitch-dark conditions we were aiming for. In better-lit areas such as dam walls and power stations, a light blue or grey colour would be suitable, but, since our target area would be fairly dark, we decided on an olive drab as best suited to both day and night conditions.

For the final stalk Diedies initially wanted us to use tracksuits made of an elasticated nylon-type material, as he thought it would be better for crawling and climbing fences. However, we soon realised this was not practical, as thorns and dry grass tended to stick to the material and it got hooked on the bushes too easily.

281

For protection, as well as for silent movement during the stalk, we exchanged the normal anti-track covers for grey sheepskin covers over the feet, knees and elbows. At some point during the rehearsals – and actually during our first deployment – we had the woollen covers stitched to the actual clothing, covering the knees and elbows, but this proved to be a nuisance when walking. Finally Whalla-whalla van Rensburg, our unit tailor, came up with a solution: woollen covers with broad elastic bands that could be pulled over the knees and elbows, with the added benefit of pulling the sleeves tight to the body. For the approach to target we could therefore use the normal canvas anti-track covers, and don the sheepskin protection once we started the actual stalk.

For the Menongue target we decided that three of us, Diedies, Neves and I, would approach the outskirts of town, and that Neves would remain on the high ground east of the target to maintain radio comms with the Tac HQ while Diedies and I did the final penetration.

The charges were specially prepared by EMLC – moulded explosives, Torpex with an aluminium base as incendiary, and a time-delay trigger device code-named Tiller that would give us enough time to move out of the area before arming itself. Tiller also incorporated a light sensor as well as a potent anti-lifting device. To conclude the package, each device had a tube with two chemicals. When squeezed, the chemicals mixed and formed a quick-drying, potent epoxy glue – the so-called Vernon Joynt glue, after its inventor, the ingenious Dr Vernon Joynt.

To carry the explosives to the target, we designed a pack containing compartments for nine charges, each of which could be reached without having to take the pack off – except the one in the centre of the pack, which could not easily be reached by hand. This pouch we stacked with one day's food and our E&E kit.

Water was another challenge. In order to be agile and flexible for the stalk, we preferred not to carry water bottles in kidney pouches on the sides of the body. Thus a full water bag was attached to the centre of the rucksack. The bag had the added advantage that the water would not make a noise, as it would in a half-filled bottle, while we were on the move.

Our preparations were put to the test when, during the last two weekends before our deployment to Rundu, we conducted full dress rehearsals at Hoedspruit. There we recreated the conditions we expected at the target – the distance to approach to the perimeter fence, a dark moon phase and the distance to cover on the hardstand to reach the aircraft.

The SAAF had been requested to provide us with all necessary support, and so one of the fortified hangars was left open, while four Mirages were parked outside. The base security squadron had been put on alert for the weekend. As far as they were concerned, the Recces would be doing an exercise against them and they would go all out to detect us.

The three-man team crossed the perimeter fence undetected. We lay up inside the base for a day, and then donned the sheepskin covers and infiltrated to the hardstand where the Mirages were parked. It was a pitch-dark night, and we found that we could stalk the "enemy" – our own Small Team colleagues and some counterintelligence personnel from HQ in Pretoria guarding the planes – to within a few metres before we were detected. We practised the stalk, fine-tuning the posture and adjusting the equipment until finally, in the early hours of the morning, both Diedies and I could stalk to within touching distance of the sentry.

The dress rehearsal at Hoedspruit gave rise to another ingenious invention: a harness we designed for the night-vision goggles. The normal neck strap was no good when you had to crawl or climb. The new harness consisted of a neck strap with the addition of an elastic band around the body, which would hold the goggles tight to the chest. In this way the operator could use both hands without having to worry about the night-vision goggles swinging loose. When he wanted to use the night vision he simply had to pull it away from the chest, while the elastic would tug it back into position once he let go. Also, to prevent the greenish glow from the night vision reflecting on the face, we had a piece of sheepskin moulded around each eyepiece.

I attended the final briefing in Pretoria with Diedies. Since approval for the mission had already been given, this briefing served to coordinate Air Force support, as well as contingencies in case of a capture or E&E situation. Diedies ran through the operational plan and then covered all the contingencies should anything go wrong. He listed the requirements for C-130 transport to Rundu, drop-off and pick-up by helicopter and procedures for telstar (comms relay). Close air support was not even mentioned, as the mission would be completely clandestine and non-traceable. UNITA would claim any credit, and the South African government would deny involvement in the event of the mission being compromised.

284

For this operation a new element was introduced to the emergency plan. Each operator drafted a personal contingency plan, dubbed "Captured Info", that contained all the actions he would execute in case he was captured and managed to survive. The content would be memorised and the document handed to the Tac HQ commander for safekeeping before the deployment. Each operator had a secret code – unobtrusive hand signals, facial expressions or blinking the eyes in a certain way – by which he would communicate should he be captured and exposed on TV.

Every possible means of communication with own forces would be considered and described in detail, while methods of receiving messages, through a Red Cross representative, a visiting family member or a lawyer, would be included. Coded messages could, for example, be hidden in the text of a magazine that the captured operator might receive through a visitor. The Captured Info plan became part of our emergency procedures; we rehearsed it before every deployment until the content was ingrained.

A few days after arriving at Rundu, mission commander Ormonde Power called us for an intelligence update from Dave Drew. While the rehearsals were reassuring, the final intelligence brief was not. According to information gleaned from UNITA, the MiGs were allegedly guarded by FAPLA troops who slept underneath them.

Just before deployment, Colonel Terence Murphy, the senior Ops officer at Special Forces HQ, flew to Rundu from Pretoria, accompanied by Eric McNelly, the counterintelligence guy, and Oom Sarel Visser, our chaplain. Colonel Murphy asked to see the team alone. When he faced the three of us – Diedies, Neves and me – behind closed doors he said, "We cannot afford to have you compromised – either killed or captured. The boss man said I must give you the option not to deploy. If they are indeed sleeping under the aircraft there is no way you can get in without being compromised."

"You see, Colonel," Diedies responded, unfazed, "if we don't go, we'll never know. Let's rather go see for ourselves. If they are indeed sleeping under the aircraft, we can't do the job. If they're not, we'll get the job done."

And that was that. No further argument.

Still, these must have been trying times for Diedies. He had become engaged, and his fiancée, Rietjie Wentzel, worked at the intelligence division of Special Forces HQ. Rietjie was close to the action in the sense that she was informed about all our missions. She would literally follow every step of the deployment and would know immediately when the team was in trouble.

Final kit inspection was done by Eric McNelly and Diedies. They went meticulously through every single piece of equipment, Eric checking for non-traceability and Diedies for functionality, camouflage and whether the item was properly secured to the webbing. Every torch, every night-vision device, every radio had to be switched on and tested. Magazines were emptied and reloaded; weapons were tested again.

Just before we deployed, Oom Sarel read from the Bible, gave a brief message and shared communion with the operators and the doctor.

Two Pumas transported us to a UNITA base approximately 80 km southeast of Menongue. Our old friend Mickey, now a

UNITA major, flew with us and acted as our liaison. It was a well-established base, and we were allocated the "guesthouse", complete with beds and mattresses made of cut branches and grass. We had to wait a while for our transport and for the right moon phase – between dark moon and first quarter – which would give us a slight moon in the early evening.

When our transport, a South African Kwêvoël truck, finally arrived, it took a day's slow driving to reach the drop-off point, as UNITA was weary of FAPLA aircraft and ground patrols. At the drop-off the UNITA soldiers established a temporary base where they would wait for our return. The doctor remained with them, while Diedies, Neves and I started the approach to the target.

Even though the Menongue airfield might have been easier to penetrate than Lubango, it was an exceptionally difficult target to reach due to the open fields surrounding the town. Furthermore, the Angolan militia, a uniformed citizen force equipped with rifles, had the nasty habit of patrolling from kraal to kraal, occasionally shooting, apparently at random and at no specific target. This was quite nerve-racking to a team hidden in the undergrowth.

Diedies and I left Neves on the high ground east of the target. He would establish comms and wait for our return. If we didn't show up after two days, he would E&E back to the UNITA forward base, from where they would launch a search.

I navigated, as DR navigation had by now become my forte. During the planning and rehearsals, Diedies and I had agreed that I would navigate to the target, while he would lead the way once inside. The standard procedure by that time was

287

that he would be in front without night-vision goggles, relying on his senses only, while I would bring up the rear with night vision. The reason for this was that the person with the night sights would be temporarily blinded every time he removed the instrument from the eyes. However, the goggles served the purpose of picking up the glow of fires, cigarettes and other light sources.

For the penetration, Diedies had his South African-made BXP (with silencer) at the ready, while I had my AMD-65 out. Should we bump into enemy soldiers we could eliminate them without making too much noise and move out before the alarm could be raised. On the actual target it might even give us the chance to finish the job. The AMD was meant for more serious business – if we had to engage in a firefight.

At first light we found ourselves on the edge of the cultivated lands. Hiding places were scarce, but we managed to crawl under a thicket, where Diedies covered me up with leaves and grass, then crawled in close for me to cover him. By then we had perfected a technique where we would lie close together on our backs, the one's head by the other's feet, weapons at the ready. This provided us with good all-round observation; as our heads were facing upwards we could detect noise and movement all around. It also gave us split-second reaction time in all directions, as one could either sit up or roll over. For drinking water, each had a tube leading from the water bag inside the kit. For nourishment we would snack on energy bars or nuts at the quietest time of day – when the sun was at its highest and sound and smell did not travel far.

The biggest challenge was waiting for the day to pass. Boredom can bring on all kinds of negative thoughts, and the fear of being compromised is an ever-present companion. That day proved to be a particularly demanding one. There was much shooting and yelling all around us, to such an extent that we thought our tracks had been discovered. By about 09:00 two youngsters made their appearance and climbed a tree overlooking our hide. The next moment they started chopping away at the higher branches and spent the whole day trimming the tree away to a stump. Most of the time one of the tree-choppers was almost directly above us.

Late that afternoon we heard considerable jet aircraft activity in the direction of our target, which made us wonder whether they had been scrambled for a mission.

It was not yet dark when we crawled out of our hiding place and started moving. Time was of the essence – we had to be on target by 01:00. We had set 02:00 as final cut-off to move out, because it would take three hours to get back to the tree line before first light. We had just started moving when we bumped into an old man returning from his fields. Diedies kept his cool and spoke to him in Portuguese, urging him to get back to his house as it was getting late. Luckily he didn't put up an argument, hurriedly turned his back and started moving back to town.

By midnight we had reached the river just east of the runway. The aerial photography had not told us how deep and marshy it was, and it took more than two hours to cross. At some point during the crossing one of my feet got stuck in the mud and my anti-track cover got left behind. Diedies wasn't too happy about this, but there was no time for tears. Fortunately, I still had my sheepskin bootees. We were already running late.

After crossing the river, we followed a road that led straight to the runway, and soon bumped into a checkpoint with some guards, complete with a boom gate and a dug-in tank in a defensive firing position. It took us an hour to skirt the position, moving extremely slowly as we did not know if there were any troops lying in trenches.

By 03:00 we reached the eastern end of the runway. It was already an hour past our cut-off time and we hadn't even seen an aircraft. We decided there and then to get out before daylight. I led the way, and we were still inside the base when the first faint light of day appeared in the east. We covered the last two kilometres to the relative safety of the tree line in broad daylight, praying that we wouldn't encounter security patrols that early in the morning.

By 06:00 we moved into dense bush and just kept going. Diedies was out of water and we had to share my half-litre. We had been going for thirty-six hours, and it was starting to take its toll. By 09:00 Diedies was severely dehydrated and I was in no position to assist him.

At last we were forced to sit down for a brief rest. As we looked back on our route, Diedies managed to say, through parched lips, "Kosie'tjie, hierdie is kak [This is a load of crap]." "Dit was laaste. Ek kruip nie weer in terr basisse rond nie. Nooit weer nie! [Never again. I'm not going to crawl around terrorist bases ever again]."

I couldn't agree more, and I told him so. Then we each popped one of the performance-enhancing amphetamines we used to carry for such emergencies, and used the induced energy to cover distance. About four hours later, as the midday heat was at its most intense and the drugs started to wear off, Diedies suddenly stopped. Clearly at the end of his tether, he sat down and called me back.

Finding it almost impossible to speak, my colleague croaked, "I've given it some thought. What if we go back tomorrow night? We are now familiar with the target and with the shortest route to it. We know where to cross the river. We know where the guard post is. We can do it."

I was flabbergasted. He was completely spent, and yet was already making plans to return to the target.

"Just think about it; they don't know about us," Diedies maintained. "We have all the advantage we need."

Such was the nature of the man. Even in the most desperate of situations he could still see an outcome. In his most exhausted moments he would look at a situation with the clearest perspective and force his mind to look beyond his physical suffering.

"Okay," I finally said, "I'll think about it, but first let's find the rest of the guys."

We both had another amphetamine pill and kept moving. By the time we found the first UNITA guys that afternoon, Diedies was leaning on me for support, barely able to walk. Neves had already moved back, not knowing whether we'd been captured or not, and was happy to see us safe.

The doctor immediately put Diedies on a drip and suggested we each take a Valium to get some decent sleep. Over a hot meal we discussed the prospect of approaching the target again the following night. Neves had, in the meantime, made comms and given the Tac HQ a brief rundown of the situation. I prepared a message on Diedies' instructions, motivating for a second penetration attempt and outlining the plan.

Before last light we again heard much aircraft activity in the direction of Menongue. It sounded like fighters taking off. I took my Valium and vaguely wondered where all the planes were going before falling into a deep and dreamless sleep.

Diedies and I were up before first light. The drip had clearly revived him, as he was in good spirits and joking: "Is jy bang, Kosie? [Are you scared, Kosie?]"

"I'm never scared," I chirped, "just careful. After all, I don't want to carry you out again . . ."

We decided to leave Neves at the temporary base, where he could maintain radio comms with the Tac HQ and, if necessary, orchestrate a search and rescue rather than sit out in the bush by himself. This time we took an HF radio with us. I discarded the improvised "bomb rucksack" and took a pack with an inner frame for the radio. The charges went in with the radio, along with extra water for both of us. We were off just after first light, and this time I wasted no time in navigating to the best position for us to penetrate.

We did much better on time, and by 20:00 that night we had skirted the marshy river area where we had wasted so much time two nights before.

Diedies took the lead after the river. As adept as I was at map and compass work, he had a knack for memorising a target and working it along the planned penetration route. This time we reached the runway by midnight. We briefly considered finding a hiding place inside the base should we not make it back to safety before first light, but both of us knew how dangerous that would be.

We kept going, maintaining a low profile on the runway. Suddenly I heard a sound behind us and pushed Diedies down firmly. It was the strangest noise, as if a light steel object was being rolled rapidly in our direction. The next moment a dog came trotting past us on the runway, not noticing us even though we were barely three metres away. The noise came from its claws hitting the tarred surface. It ran past us and disappeared, leaving two shaken but very relieved operators on the tarmac.

We reached the hardstand in front of the main terminal building. As there was some light coming from the buildings, I could see quite clearly with the night-vision goggles. But there were no jets. The only two aircraft I could see were a smallish prop job and an Mi-17 transport helicopter, nothing else.

"I see no MiGs," I said in a whisper.

"What do you mean, no MiGs? We're not looking in the right place . . ."

He brought his night vision to his face. No fighter planes. Then it hit us, right there in the dark, on the tarmac, deep in the Angolan war zone. They didn't put troops under the MiGs to guard them; they actually flew the aircraft out to a safe place every night! That was the jet activity we had heard the two previous nights.

We were devastated to realise that all our efforts were in vain – our mission would be unsuccessful. We approached the transport on the tarmac and saw that it was unserviceable. When I quietly suggested to Diedies that we should plant devices on the two aircraft, he just waved his arms; it would have been futile to give the game away at that point. All that remained was to exfiltrate quietly and rethink the whole operation.

We moved out fast. By now we knew the route well and skirted the hot spots easily. Once out of the target area, I took over and navigated us directly back to the TB. While it was a great relief to be out of danger and to see the friendly faces of our comrades, I felt very down and disappointed.

The next day we drove back to the UNITA base and were picked up by a Puma soon after our arrival. At Rundu we were met on the runway by Ormonde Power and Colonel Murphy and were sneaked off to Fort Foot in an enclosed van. We had the customary welcoming dinner with champagne and all, but for Diedies and me the evening was overshadowed by the fact that we hadn't succeeded. At the back of my mind I was already considering what we would do next.

Shortly afterwards, we received confirmation via the intelligence channel that FAPLA evacuated the fighters every afternoon from Menongue to Huambo, which was much further from the border and thus considered safer. This was excellent information, fresh and accurate, but unfortunately three weeks too late.

7

Operation Angel
August 1987

AFTER THE ANC was banned by the National Party government, in 1960, many of its leaders went into exile. The
organisation opened offices in several African countries,
including Zambia, Tanzania, Angola, Botswana, Uganda and
Zimbabwe. Umkhonto we Sizwe (MK), the ANC's armed
wing, also established a series of offices and training camps in
the frontline states from where guerrilla operations into South
Africa were launched.

The 1980s saw the ANC taking the armed struggle against
the apartheid regime to the next level, with an increase in
attacks on civilian targets and a determined attempt to make
the townships ungovernable. In 1985 the National Party government invoked the first state of emergency, and began to
employ a variety of measures, some highly controversial, to
counter the ANC.

One day late in 1986 Diedies and I were ordered to report to
Special Forces HQ where we met Frans Fourie, a highly capable

Operation Angel

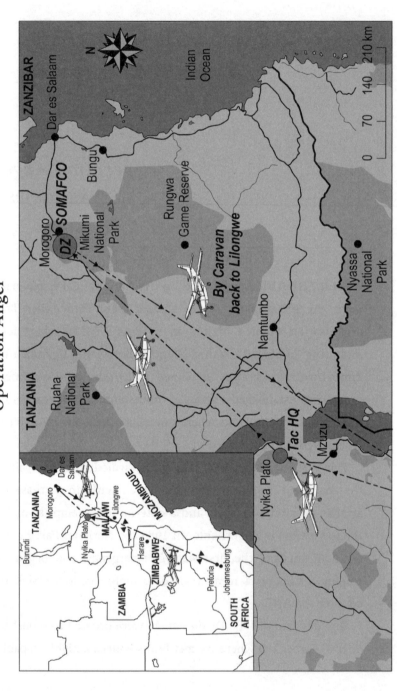

and very experienced officer from 4 Recce. A secluded intelligence meeting room had been prepared for our briefing. As a special measure to secure the venue, it was cordoned off and swept for bugs. Only once we were inside and introduced to representatives from the Department of Foreign Affairs and the National Intelligence Service did we realise the gravity of the moment. It soon turned out that we were to deploy with Frans on a highly sensitive secret mission. The operation clearly received the highest level of attention.

The meeting commenced with an intelligence overview of ANC deployments in countries neighbouring South Africa and a summary of events depicting the escalation of the threat against the state. Then the mission was conveyed to us: a raid was to be conducted in Tanzania, aimed at wiping out the entire top structure of the ANC. The operation had already been approved at the highest level and preparations had to commence immediately.

Our target was the Solomon Mahlangu Freedom College (SOMAFCO) in Mazimbu, near Morogoro in central Tanzania, where a special meeting of the ANC national executive committee would take place. The conference would be attended by all the significant leaders, including Oliver Tambo, then president of the ANC, Thabo Mbeki, Jacob Zuma and Chris Hani.

Our mission was to penetrate SOMAFCO and set explosive charges in the Hector Pieterson Conference Hall, the main venue at the facility. The plan was a rather elaborate but executable one. The team would be flown to Malawi's Blantyre International Airport, and from there to the Nyika

National Park in the northeast of the country. A secret base would be established at the Chelinda camp within the reserve for final preparation and E&E planning. It would also serve as Tac HQ and final staging point for the raid into Tanzania.

From Nyika, the team would be taken by civilian aircraft to a DZ in the Morogoro Crater. The plane would be guided in by an agent, known to us only by the code name Angel, for a parachute drop at low altitude. Angel had been recruited by Military Intelligence because of his intimate knowledge of the area and his ability to access African countries. After landing, the three-man team would meet up with Angel, who would orientate us and guide us in towards the target. Once in proximity to SOMAFCO, the agent would withdraw and the team would commence with the penetration. Charges would be planted in the main venue and the timing mechanisms set for 09:30 the next morning, when the conference was expected to be in full swing.

The team would withdraw to a remote airfield and would be picked up by fixed-wing aircraft and taken back to Malawi. If the pick-up was compromised and the team had to go into escape and evasion mode, the Tanzam railway line would be used as the escape and evacuation route, with predetermined RVs at landing strips along the line.

My first reaction was that the mission would be impossible due to the vast distances involved. My second thought was that the operation, if successful, would spark massive international criticism. But on both accounts a broad plan had already been drawn up.

With the briefings concluded, we started our planning and preparations. Hannes Venter, OC 4 Recce, was selected as the mission commander, and Dave Scales would act as Tac HQ coordinator. We worked through every available piece of information, studying maps and photos the intelligence officers managed to produce. The aerial photos were outdated but invaluable to the planning of our final penetration. We had to rely mostly on reports from secondary sources, with the result that detailed information about the target was lacking.

One thing that became clear from most sources was that the facilities were locked during the night and that we needed to establish a way of silently breaching the locked doors to the main building.

Looking back today, I realise that the information was sketchy, the aerial photography vastly inadequate and the reports from agents on the ground severely lacking. But we had a job to do and we assumed that we would be able to do a recce of the target before the penetration.

Frans and I went on a lock-picking course to master the trick of gaining access through locked doors. After five days of picking locks, I was ready to work my way into just about any vault in the country. Once we breached the perimeter, it would be my job to get us inside the conference hall, so I spent lots of time picking the locks of every door in Special Forces HQ at night.

After extensive brainstorming sessions between the team and explosives experts from EMLC, an ingenious device was designed. Explosive charges were fitted to the back of six large blocked photos of Nelson Mandela, Govan Mbeki and other high-ranking ANC leaders. The photos, which were obtained through Special Forces Intelligence, were old and grainy, but they looked authentic enough to pass casual scrutiny. The photos were glued on to a moulded frame of sheet explosives with a layer of ball bearings in front, transforming the innocent-looking posters into lethal Claymore mines. A timing device would be fitted in a gap at the back of the explosives.

Our job would be to arm the timers and glue the deadly posters to the inner walls of the conference venue. They would explode the next day when the majority of conference-goers would be in the hall.

Rehearsals were done in and around Pretoria. At Ditholo, a small military air base north of the city, we practised parachuting at low level from the aircraft, a Cessna Caravan II, which had been modified for static-line parachuting as well as to conceal our weapons and equipment. For the parachute drop, the door was refitted for easy removal. A cable was fixed to the inner starboard side for the parachute static lines to be attached to. Initially we considered freefall parachuting, but this was ruled out for a number of reasons, the most important being that we needed to approach the target area at low level to avoid detection by radar. At the time, the three of us were also too inexperienced to guarantee accurate regrouping and landing at night. In the final instance, landing a high-velocity freefall parachute on an unprepared and unmanned DZ at night was too high a risk.

OPERATION ANGEL

To accommodate the equipment, seats were removed from the centre of the aircraft and a large box fitted – more or less representing a long-range fuel tank. In it would go the HF radios for both the Tac HQ and the team, our weapons and ammunition, and all the explosive charges with their mechanisms. Special bags were also designed so we could parachute with the posters and carry them to the target.

Each of us had to memorise a cover story and received an alias passport to complement the cover. I chose to be an environmental expert from the UK who worked as game ranger in Tanzania's parks, while Diedies was a wildlife photographer and Frans a tourist. These cover stories would not stand up to close scrutiny, but would at least buy us time in an emergency.

As part of our cover, we decided to wear civilian clothing in shades of khaki and dark grey that would also help with camouflaging during the final stalk. At night, once everyone had left and the Special Forces HQ buildings were empty, we practised our stalking techniques until the small hours of the morning.

Finally, after four weeks of extensive preparation, we departed for Malawi. The pilot flew the Cessna to Blantyre and from there to the Nyika Plateau, while the operators took different commercial flights and met up with an agent from Chief of Staff Intelligence at a hotel in Blantyre. Vehicles had been arranged to transport everyone to the Nyika National Park.

By the time we arrived, Hannes Venter and Dave Scales had already set up our secret little post in a forest. For the game rangers and personnel of the park, we were a bunch of business executives breaking away on an African safari. Our HF radio antenna could be explained by claiming that Dave was a radio ham communicating with our business partners in other parts of the world. We spent a few leisurely days in the reserve making final adjustments to the plan and working through our emergency procedure with Hannes, Dave and the pilot.

Then a cold and misty D-day arrived and we donned our ops kit. The door of the Cessna was removed, seats were taken out, parachutes were prepared and the four passengers boarded – Diedies, Frans, myself and the doctor.

I have never been so hot and so cold at the same time as during that night. The pilot flew at 15 000 ft and the icy wind rushed in through the open door, but I was pressed into the side of the aircraft and lay on top of the heating system which had been turned on full blast for the flight. In front I was freezing, while my backside was being fried, quite literally leaving streaks of burnt flesh on my sides!

About 10 km from the DZ the pilot descended to 3 000 ft above ground level, trying to locate the agent's strobe. But the DZ was situated within the Morogoro Crater and was surrounded by mountains, which made it extremely dangerous to descend to 800 ft, the height from which we had to exit. After circling the area for twenty minutes, the pilot decided to withdraw.

Bogged down by parachutes and kit at the back of the aircraft, we could not communicate with the pilot and therefore had no idea what was going on. The pilot was unable to establish communications with the agent and he also could not distinguish the strobe from the numerous lights in the valley below. He had explored all alternative RVs and signals, and had concluded that Angel could not make it to the target. The pilot decided not to drop the team onto an unmanned DZ and aborted the mission.

Now another challenge faced us. Back at the Tac HQ, the fog had moved in, covering the whole Nyika Plateau and making it impossible to land. After consulting with Hannes, the pilot decided to divert to Lilongwe, hoping the mist would allow us to land there. Of course, since no flight plan had been filed, there would be questions once we landed. The parachutes were still in the aircraft and the door had been removed. The moment called for quick decisions.

On final approach to Lilongwe International at 02:00 that morning, the pilot informed the tower that we had an emergency on board and needed to land. We landed safely and the pilot taxied far down the runway, allowing the three operators to jump out with all the ops kit and withdraw into the shadows at the end of the airfield. We scaled the perimeter fence and met up with the agent from Chief of Staff Intelligence on a road adjacent to the airport.

The pilot and the doc faced a tough time having to explain the late-night arrival, but fortunately the plane was not searched, probably because there were no staff on duty. The doctor pretended to be seriously ill, fainting and gagging as the pilot assisted him into the airport building, and finally the police rushed him to hospital.

The next day we all met up at a hotel in the city. Dave Scales had driven from the Nyika Plateau to Lilongwe in the early hours of the morning and we were reunited with our luggage. After a quick debrief, we left on different flights to South Africa.

Later it transpired that Angel had indeed been in position on the ground. He had switched on the strobe and could hear the aircraft, but did not succeed in establishing communications with the pilot. The lesson I took from Operation Angel was that cooperation with agents had to be tested and rehearsed in the same level of detail as our own contingencies and that the execution of a mission could never rely on the actions of someone outside our circle of professional operators.

Looking back on the venture today, I am relieved that the operation had to be aborted. Had those ANC leaders been killed, it would have had serious ramifications for South Africa and could very likely even have disrupted the negotiations for a peaceful settlement.

8

Facing Fear

*"In a world where death is the hunter, my friend, there is
no time for regrets or doubts. There is only time for decisions."*
— Carlos Castaneda, *Journey to Ixtlan*

AFTER OUR failed operation at Menongue airfield, Diedies
and I discussed the prospects for a similar penetration of the
FAPLA airfield at Lubango, from where the bulk of FAA's
fighter aircraft operated.[16] In addition to the fighter-bomber
regiment HQ, the air base hosted a MiG-23 squadron, a MiG-
21 squadron and a variety of helicopters, including the
much-feared Mi-24 gunship. No fewer than 56 fighters were
parked in areas at both ends of the runway, some in revetments
and the majority on the apron.

A penetration of the airfield had not previously been considered feasible, since it was surrounded by enemy
deployments. Soviet-supplied air defence systems, both
radar and missiles, were positioned on the mountains to the
west and southwest, while Cuban, FAPLA and SWAPO
bases were spread around its perimeter.

However, before anything else I first had to deal with a personal crisis. It was at this point that my past experiences started to catch up with me. I had crawled around enemy bases in the dark one too many times. Too often I had been on the wrong side of an AK-47 being cocked in the clear, quiet night. Slowly but surely, my mind started telling me that the odds would turn against me.

A horrible dream started to haunt me: I would be stalking a dark and ominous house under the trees, alone, with a full moon completely blinding my vision. I knew the enemy was lying in wait, but had no choice but to crawl towards the house. Behind me I could hear movement, enemy moving in to cut off my escape, and I knew there was no way out; I just had to keep crawling towards my inevitable fate.

I told Diedies about my dream and how I repeatedly relived the tense moments during the final stalk into enemy bases. Diedies was very supportive and understood the predicament I was in, having been in that dark place before. We talked about it on numerous occasions, but in the end the dream would still be there, tangible and ever-present.

One day Diedies cut straight to the chase and asked whether I wanted to continue to operate or preferred to opt out, offering to let me stay on at Small Teams in a supporting role and act as Tac HQ commander for a while. But I had come too far in preparing myself for the ultimate in soldiering. There was no way I was giving it up because of a few bad dreams. I assured Diedies that I was set on my job, but that I needed time to work through this thing.

At the time, Johnny Koortzen, an old friend from school, was the psychologist at Special Forces HQ. I phoned him from Phalaborwa and asked whether we could meet for a chat. Johnny must have read between the lines; he immediately said he was keen to talk to me since he was doing a study on the impact of acute stress on Special Forces soldiers. I was due to take the military law course in Pretoria, which gave me an opportunity to see Johnny and, more importantly, to spend time with Zelda.

To this day I don't know whether I was wise or stupid not to talk to Zelda about my fears, but I opted not to show what I saw as my weakness. I therefore also did not tell her the real reason for my visit to Pretoria. It didn't even cross my mind that sharing my fears and uncertainties with her could have eased my burden. While I didn't want to acknowledge it, our relationship was taking strain as a result of our hectic programme and uncertain schedule.

When I walked into Johnny's office that first day, I swallowed my pride and told him about my growing sense that fate would catch up with me, and how the next time I bumped into enemy soldiers in some godforsaken guerrilla base in Africa would be my last. He listened patiently, occasionally prompting me with questions. Over several meetings, I told him about every incident since my days at 31 Battalion recce wing – every time we approached or infiltrated an enemy base, every time I had to run away to survive, every single time I had to evade an aggressive enemy on our tracks.

Just recalling all those incidents was a great relief, as the only people we ever talked to, once the debrief was done and the top-secret files had been stowed away, was the tiny inner circle of Small Teams. I had never even shared war stories with my colleagues from the commandos, as I thought it would breed animosity. And besides, talking about events from highly secret operations would have been considered a security breach.

For the first few days Johnny and I just talked about my experiences. He asked me to explain my fears and describe my recurring dream in the finest detail. Then we gradually started turning negative thoughts into positive ones, countering every weakness with a strength.

Did I believe in what I was doing?

Yes.

Did I want to do it?

Yes, I was ready to do that and much more.

How did I manage to find enemy bases out there in the bush?

Because the Int was accurate and my navigation was tip-top.

How did I get to penetrate right into the enemy base?

Because I was good at it and we were well prepared.

How did I get out of the base once we were compromised?

Because the enemy did not expect us there and we knew exactly where to go.

How have I survived all the close shaves before?

Because I was prepared.

How did I get away from an enemy that was chasing us?

Because I was extremely fit and good at anti-tracking.

How did I not get tied up in encirclement?

Because we were well rehearsed and knew the terrain. The darkness was our friend and we were exceptionally good at night work.

In time, Johnny reinforced in me the solid foundation on which our deployments were based: good intelligence, capable operators, well-rehearsed operations, emergency plans, the best equipment money could buy, a strong support system, faith . . .

Together we started building a strategy to help me manage my fear. From the beginning he made it clear that we would not try to defeat the sense of fear, but rather develop a mechanism for me to accept that it was inevitable and learn how to cope with it. It reassured me when he told me that, regardless of their bravado, every operator feared death and every one had their own way of dealing with it. He also pointed out that few operators repeatedly penetrated enemy bases alone, or with only one buddy in support. Most people found solace in numbers and did not like being alone in the bush – let alone inside enemy-infested encampments!

Johnny then worked with the concept of fear itself, and after talking about it for hours I started realising that, as a Christian, my fear was not for the actual moment of dying, but rather the uncertainty of the moment; the fear of failure or of being captured was more significant.

To counter my fear of failure, we built a strategy based on the conviction that I was better at my job than any adversary I would encounter. Not marginally better, but exceptionally so. Steadily I started to realise that every training event, every night bent over the maps and stereoscopic photos, every rehearsal was not only a skill to be mastered but also something to be ingrained in my mind as an attitude. Johnny helped me to apply a simple but effective technique in which negative thoughts and attitudes were replaced by positive ones – by giving the bad thoughts a "dirty" colour and draining them from my mind, replacing them with the bright, colourful, positive ones.

The next part of our strategy involved a mind game that I eventually became very good at, a type of positive self-talk where I not only envisaged success but also started living the euphoria of completing the job successfully – a kind of visualising oneself as a James Bond (sadly without the martinis and the girls!) and thinking of the success as being the result of your efforts. At the risk of becoming an egotistical, over-confident prick, I started applying this technique in everyday life and found it most helpful in building self-confidence.

After the course in Pretoria, I took some time off and visited my folks for a few days. While at home in Upington I received a message to call Diedies urgently.

"The big one's on," Diedies said. "I need you here."

He was, of course, talking about Lubango.

"How much time do I have?" I asked.

"Be at the HQ in a week," he said. "I'll meet you there. We'll get an Int update first."

My immediate response was to go on a three-day solo hike along the Orange River. I had to prepare myself mentally. Of course my mom couldn't understand why I came home for a holiday only to disappear into the rough on a solitary adventure.

The operation was not going to be easy. At the time Lubango was considered the best-protected airfield in Angola. The Soviet-manned radar and anti-air systems would detect any aircraft approaching from as far away as 80 km, depending on its altitude. Just to get close to it would be a challenge in itself, never mind getting past the Cuban, FAPLA and SWAPO deployments surrounding it. The penetration would require meticulous planning and pinpoint navigation – and an exceptional level of skill and determination. The mission would also take no less than three to four weeks to complete.

I hitched a ride with friends who farmed on the South West African side of the Orange River – in the same rough and rocky terrain where, years before, the International got stuck on the mountainside and I had to walk to get help. I made my way down the deep ravines to the river, and then hiked along the beautiful Orange River gorge in an easterly direction towards Augrabies Falls. It was a harsh environment, but being alone in that wide-open and unspoilt world was exhilarating. That first night I slept under an overhanging rock with the dark and ominous water of the Great Gariep rushing by just a few metres from me. The rugged edges of the mountains towered above me on both sides of the river. It was a lonely and desolate stretch of earth.

On the third day I crossed the river to the South African side, where my dad picked me up. Two days later my car was packed and I was ready to join André Diedericks for our excursion to Lubango. It would turn out to be the experience of a lifetime.

Diedies had chosen his most trusted team for the job. A three-man team was needed for the target and so José da Costa had been pulled in as the third man. Boet Swart would be the mission commander in the Tac HQ at Ondangwa, Dave Scales in charge of signals, and Dave Drew was the intelligence officer. Even the helicopter crews from 19 Squadron were the cream of the crop: two stalwarts, Commandant John Church and Captain Gees Basson, would pilot the two Pumas.

We would infiltrate by helicopter to the mountains southwest of the target, then move on foot towards Lubango along a route straddling the highest ridges. Da Costa would remain on the high ground immediately southwest of the town to maintain comms or initiate emergency procedures, while Diedies and I would penetrate the airfield. Once on the apron where the aircraft were parked, we would split up and each work our way down the two lanes of MiGs.

The intelligence presented to us in Pretoria covered everything in the greatest detail. The positions of the FAPLA, Cuban and SWAPO deployments were meticulously plotted. With the assistance of the aerial photo interpreters, we "flew" every inch of the infiltration route, utilising the fancy stereoscopes. We plotted a primary LZ and some alternatives for rappelling from the helicopters. In the end I had mind-walked a hundred times the route I was to navigate. We even mapped out most of our lying-up places. We knew the layout of the target so intimately I could almost have done the operation blindfolded.

With the experts from EMLC, we did revision of the Tiller charges, once again going through the arming procedure and safety measures.

Soon we were off to Phalaborwa to prepare and rehearse. Diedies and I jacked up our knowledge of Portuguese phrases and again spent many hours rehearsing on the runway of Hoedspruit air base in the dark hours of the night. We became such masters at the art of stalking that I was actually looking forward to the exhilarating adrenaline rush on the night of the penetration. I had not entirely overcome my fear, but at least it was more contained and I now knew how to channel it.

The operational team did final touch-ups and spent the last three days in Pretoria, mostly fattening up and briefing HQ on the final plan. I used the time to work through my "fear-control" plan with Johnny Koortzen. He made me talk through the rehearsals and describe how we had mastered the stalking techniques. I had to explain how good our equipment was and how well prepared we were. After these sessions, and once I'd worked through the "self-talk" techniques, I could imagine nothing but success. Mentally, I was as prepared for the operation as I could ever be.

The sessions with Johnny had the added advantage that they would help Small Team operators in future. I noted down all the techniques and later captured them in a staff paper that would be incorporated in Small Team training manuals. In this way I compiled a series of lessons on so-called soft issues under headings such as "Self-motivation during small team operations", "Control of fear and panic", "Compiling a diet for long-term deployments" and a range of other aspects not covered in conventional training manuals.

While I was riding the crest of the wave in my professional life, the same could not be said about my personal life. Zelda wanted a bigger commitment, but I wasn't ready for a more serious relationship. We loved spending time together, but life at 5 Recce was fast and frenetic and I wasn't ready to settle down yet. She sensed my wavering, but never challenged me with an ultimatum.

The uncertain status of our relationship was disconcerting, especially since, at that time, I needed the reassurance that things were okay back home. However, the situation was entirely the result of my own immaturity. I simply didn't have the skills to handle it.

For both of us, breaking up was an extremely emotional experience. We were at a resort outside Pretoria, enjoying each other's company and whiling away the hours. I was intent on ending the relationship, as I was about to depart on my most dangerous mission thus far. I was afraid of not coming back to her, and didn't want her to sit and wait for me.

Without my knowing, Zelda had bought me a pullover as a gift
– a sort of truce to initiate a new beginning in our relationship. However, she sensed what was about to happen and gave
me the present before I could say anything.

There was a powerful emotional connection between us,
and we felt a mutual attachment that, I had to admit, although it
came too late to rebuild the relationship, may have been love.
In the end, we parted that day without bringing the relationship to a decisive end, but both of us knew the coming
mission would be a watershed. We wanted to be close to
each other, but my decision not to commit made it impossible.

While I was trying to untangle myself from my relationship
with Zelda, Diedies was by now a married man. Of course, I
used the opportunity to give him a hard time for bending
his own rules by getting married, especially without my
consent. His wife, Rietjie, had been appointed communications officer at 5 Recce and lived in Phalaborwa. Although
she did not have direct access to the latest intelligence or the
team's movements, she still worked closely enough with the
intelligence section to have a fairly good idea of what was
happening. This of course didn't make things easier for
Diedies.

Operation Abduct 2

9

Three Crosses at Lubango:
Operation Abduct 2, November-December 1987

"Where there is much light, the shadow tends to be deep."
– Johann Wolfgang von Goethe

WE DEPARTED FOR Ondangwa on a regular scheduled SAAF flight. Although we wore standard-issue bush hats and tried to blend in with the rest of the crowd flying to the war zone, we still stood out like sore thumbs. For one thing, José da Costa's huge frame was hard to miss, and, for another, the Recces always "hid" their weapons in non-standard (but very obvious!) rifle bags. Even the bags used by Special Forces soldiers were different from the regular army's *balsak*. Special Forces soldiers often took the scheduled flights to and from Ondangwa, and so Recces were a fairly regular sight.

Oom Boet and the Tac HQ team had departed by road to Ondangwa two weeks before the deployment. On our arrival we found the Tac HQ at Fort Rev in the usual predeployment frenzy. The most important task that remained for the team was to brief the Tac HQ, as well as the pilots and the "back-up" team on the emergency procedures and E&E plan. Before this could be done, the team had to work through the emergency procedures, escape routes and rendezvous (RV) points to ensure that each one understood and memorised every single detail and, more importantly, that each procedure and each action had the same meaning for all three of us. The E&E plan the Tac HQ would implement if anything went wrong was then meticulously drawn on a map overlay.

We had decided on a landing zone (LZ) 60 km south of the Lubango airfield. The team would deploy by rappelling from the helicopters onto the highest mountain ridges, where we would establish a cache and observe the area for two days. Fighter jets would act as an escort for the helicopters. Because of the distances involved and the dangers of flying into an area where the enemy had air superiority, the fighters were also assigned the job of telstar should there be a communication breakdown or any other emergency. The back-up team, made up of Special Forces soldiers from 51 Commando, would deploy to the last known location of the team should the E&E plan be activated.

We would take the normal large Small Team pack for the infiltration, and switch to the pack designed for the explosives on the night of the penetration. During the final inspection our equipment was once again thoroughly checked and scrutinised for non-traceability. Not one single piece of equipment could be linked to South Africa. Then each operator handed his Captured Info document to Oom Boet for safekeeping, the contents securely committed to memory.

Our choice of weapons was, as always, meticulously planned: I would carry my trusted Hungarian AMD and silenced pistol; Diedies had a silenced BXP and a pistol (without silencer); and José da Costa took a normal AKM (the modernised version of the AK-47) and a Russian-origin Tokarev pistol. Since I was doing the navigation on the route in, I would be armed with a non-silenced weapon – to work in our favour during an initial engagement. We knew from experience that silenced weapons did not hold the enemy's heads down, presumably because they did not realise they were being shot at. Likewise Da Costa would have a non-silenced assault rifle for support fire. During the penetration, Diedies would lead with the silenced BXP, ready for initial contact. If I had to do a stalk on an aircraft, I would approach with the silenced pistol and keep the AMD on my back for firepower in case we needed to fight our way out.

Our lunch before the deployment was a lavish spread, and a cheerful atmosphere reigned. Boet Swart proposed a toast to the "conquering" of Lubango. He joked about the packs being bigger and heavier than the operators themselves.

"Small team, big pack, small brain . . ." he said, as so many times before. "I'll never understand the small minds of the men with the big packs. They could have all this wonderful food, a warm bed to sleep in, pretty girls, and yet here they are off into the bush again . . ."

The huge packs were loaded onto the choppers on the hardstand before start-up. Both helicopters had been prepared for rappelling, and the A-frames had been fitted in a closed hangar the night before. The system used for rappelling from the Puma at the time was a frame that fitted into the helicopter, with extension arms that contained the anchor points for the ropes. The frames were intended to prevent excessive external force on the superstructure of the aircraft. The plan was for the operators to rappel down first, after which the heavy packs and cache equipment would be lowered by a pulley system.

At 14:00 the Pumas, each with two additional ferry tanks mounted on the inside, had taxied out and waited for us in front of Fort Rev. We flew to Opuwa in the Kaokoland, where the helicopters had to refuel. I tried to sleep on the way, but was too excited.

This deployment was the one we had been living for; it was a textbook Small Team operation. To me it felt as though we had spent a lifetime preparing for Lubango. The very name of the place had a mysterious ring to it. Strangely, a deep and profound calmness had come over me, and a determination I had not quite experienced before. I visualised how we would fly back in the same helicopter a month later – having achieved success. I had a distinct vision of how we would approach the target and work our way from aircraft to aircraft.

This new feeling did not at all mean that I was not afraid. I did not have a death wish, nor was I under some wild delusion that we would rush in and show everyone how it was done. After weeks of meticulous planning and preparation, the sessions with Johnny and the few days I had spent alone along the Orange River, I felt content and at ease with what lay ahead.

While we waited for last light, Oom Sarel shared the customary communion with us under a cluster of trees. His message took me back a few years, to the moment before my very first Special Forces deployment with 53 Commando at Nkongo, when he had built mountains in the sand to explain the meaning of Psalm 125:2: "As the mountains surround Jerusalem, so the Lord surrounds His people now and forever."

He made this verse applicable to Lubango, and reminded us that, as the mountains surround the town to the south and west, the Lord is always there, with the only difference being that He completely surrounds us. Oom Sarel's message was simple and to the point and added to my sense of calmness and determination. Never before had the wine and bread had such a tangible meaning for me as on the eve of our deployment to Lubango, when I shared it with my comrades and Oom Boet.

After the short service I asked Diedies how he felt, knowing full well that his priorities had shifted now that he was a married man. But if I had forgotten the iron will and unique fibre of the man, his big smile and quick answer reminded me promptly. "Camels don't cry, Kosie," he said, referring to the motto displayed on the 52 Commando logo. I knew Da Costa was okay; he was as solid as the very mountains around Lubango.

Just before last light we received a message that the jets were airborne for their top-cover job. We flew straight from Opuwa to the border and crossed the Cunene River in the area west of Swartbooisdrift, then nap-of-the-earth towards the LZ, following the valleys and depressions of the rugged southwestern

Angolan countryside. Diedies, Da Costa and I were in the first chopper, along with the two dispatchers. The packs and the bulky cache equipment were in the second one, with two dispatchers ready to let the equipment down by pulley.

Three minutes from the LZ the doors were opened and the struts from the A-frames pushed out. We hooked up to the anchor points and got ready to swing out onto the steps. After orbiting the LZ area once, John Church, the lead pilot, approached a protruding rocky ridge and eased the aircraft into a hover. On the dispatcher's command I swung out onto the steps, with Da Costa following behind. As I was about to launch, I felt the dispatcher's hand on my arm and saw his outstretched hand in a "don't go" gesture. The next moment the helicopter lifted off and we started flying from outcrop to outcrop, looking for a smoother surface on the rugged mountaintop.

But I was in trouble. Da Costa, who was on the strut in front of me, was pushed against me by the rush of the wind. I held on to the rope for dear life, but felt it slipping slowly from my grip. I pulled the loose end around and tried to hold it down tightly against my body with both hands to improve the friction on the descending device, but slowly and steadily it slipped. Da Costa's massive weight, compounded by the wind rush, was now squarely on me, and my cramped hands couldn't hold any longer.

After what felt like an eternity, the aircraft reduced speed and slowly moved into a hover. It was not a moment too soon. Without waiting for a signal, I let go, and had to use both hands to control the rope as I descended slowly onto the rocks below.

Da Costa followed, while Diedies had already touched down after descending from the port door of the helicopter. The second helicopter, carrying the equipment, moved in. The three of us received the packs at the bottom, unhooking the karabiners as they touched down. When I received my pack, I realised its frame had broken under the weight of the kit. As prearranged, I gave the rope three fierce tugs to inform the dispatcher that we needed a spare pack. For some reason there was no response and the helicopter took off. As the aircraft moved away and the noise subsided, we informed the pilots that we needed another pack. However, since they had been circling the area considerably longer than planned, they thought it better not to return for fear of giving our position away.

This left us in quite a predicament. The frame of my pack was completely shattered, and the only alternative was to use one of the much smaller packs from the cache. I packed the explosive charges, night-vision goggles, as much water as I could force in and some of my rations. The rest of the food was shared between Diedies and Da Costa.

We used the rest of the night to cache the extra food, water, batteries and a radio. Since we were quite high on a rocky outcrop, we considered it safe to stash the kit in hollows among the rocks. After first light we sterilised the area, checking that the outcrop was free of tracks, everything was hidden and the vegetation restored to how it was before.

For the remainder of the day we remained on a nearby peak, watching the cache area and the valley below. Except for dogs barking and a cock crowing in the distance, it was quiet. We didn't see any people, nor did we hear any vehicle or aircraft movement, so we decided not to waste any time and to start moving that night. Even though I had strapped some extra water bags onto my rucksack, I was still carrying much less weight than Diedies and José. I took the lead, navigating along the mountain ridge leading north towards Lubango. It was hard, meticulous work, as I had to find the easiest route in the rugged terrain, all the time considering my two heavily laden comrades, but at the same time keeping high enough up the mountain slopes to avoid the areas where people might find our tracks.

By first light every morning we moved as high as possible up the mountainside, carefully picking our hide in thickly vegetated or rocky spots to ensure we stayed off the beaten track. After we had settled down on the slope, I would take a day pack and move to the top of the mountain ridge, from where I could keep a better lookout and at the same time plan the route ahead.

The infiltration did not go without incident. Late one afternoon while waiting for the sun to set, we watched an old man armed with a bow and arrow walking straight through our hide, not looking left or right. To this day I don't know if he saw us, but we soon packed up and anti-tracked away from the area.

Another incident took us completely by surprise. Diedies was studying his map when a huge snake appeared out of the blue and sailed right across his lap. We must have been in its territory, for it whiled away the rest of the afternoon in Diedies' company. Fortunately, our comrade was so stunned that he could not move, and just watched the snake until it eventually disappeared into a hole.

As we closed in on the target area we passed a plateau with spurs sloping down to the savanna below. Early one night we were moving past one of these ridges when all of a sudden we heard music high up on the mountain. We moved into cover, took our packs off and listened to the noise. It gradually grew louder and we soon became aware that it was the sound of a group of men singing in harmony. There was a fence line running down the mountain straight towards us, and we realised that the singing voices were moving towards us along the fence. We ducked into cover and waited.

A group of about twenty men appeared, singing a touching song about the ANC martyr Solomon Mahlangu. It was the same song I had heard during the Know Your Enemy course as part of my Special Forces training. Listening to those beautiful men's voices in the still night air, singing a song that, to me, was completely out of place deep inside Angola, was a strange and quite moving experience.

The men were passing barely ten metres from us when, suddenly, one of them jumped over the fence and ran towards the cluster of bushes where we were hiding. The singing died down, as everyone waited for their comrade, who stopped close to our hiding place. The sound of a bowel movement shattered the silence as he took a crap almost in our faces. The rest of the "choir" burst out laughing, making funny comments about the man's running stomach. We literally had to clamp our mouths shut not to join in the laughter.

Soon the stray soul rejoined the group and the singing resumed. We listened in stunned silence until the sound eventually faded away far down the mountainside. Then we finally gave in and laughed until we could no more.

That night we had yet another strange experience. We had moved down a depression into a thicket where we wanted to grab two hours' sleep before establishing an OP for the day. Just as we had taken off our packs and settled down, Da Costa jumped up with a muffled scream. Diedies and I grabbed our weapons and rolled around into cover behind our packs. I quickly realised what was happening when I felt the sting of ant bites all over my body. Unknowingly we had bedded down in the path of a colony of killer ants; by the time we realised it, they were all over us – into our kit and under our clothing.

Da Costa was dancing around like a madman, ripping his clothes off and slapping the tiny creatures from his body. Diedies and I soon joined in, but then realised that our efforts were fruitless, as we were still in the colony's killing zone! With no regard to tactics or silence, we grabbed our garb and gear and moved to "safety". After testing the ground a few times – in a very literal sense – we found an antless spot, and took our time to remove our clothes and shake out the little beasts. For days after that, right up until we reached the target area, we still discovered ants in our kit.

One evening when we were about 20 km from the target, passing through the Huila district, we decided to make up some time by moving barefoot on a sandy pathway running along our bearing. It was pitch dark – ideal for the penetration. Once again I took the lead, walking without night-vision goggles, weapon at the ready, and relying on my senses to pick up any sign of people approaching. Diedies followed with the night vision, using it intermittently to detect sources of light such as the embers of campfires. Da Costa brought up the rear, cautiously checking behind for anyone who might be catching up on us.

Smelling rather than seeing the vegetation, I realised that we were passing a built-up area with bougainvillea along its fence line. It turned out to be a Roman Catholic mission. As we passed a gate in the walled perimeter, Diedies pulled me by the sleeve and handed me the night-vision goggles, indicating that I should look at the wall. The eerie green light of the night-vision equipment revealed a larger-than-life statue of Christ. It was almost like a vision, and the three of us moved off into the night, the image clearly imprinted on our minds.

Before first light we were atop the mountain overlooking Lubango, where we had planned to spend three days watching the area and building up a picture of the target itself, the routine, best infiltration route and escape routes. But we were in for an unexpected and unpleasant surprise: the whole mountain had been stripped of undergrowth, leaving no cover for us. We also discovered smouldering moulds used by the local population for the manufacture of charcoal. What we hadn't realised from the aerial photos was that the lower brush had been removed to feed the smoking coal ovens. The tree canopy shown in the photos had suggested that it was a thickly vegetated area, but the reality on the ground was vastly different.

327

We were in trouble. We searched frantically for any kind of cover, but the mountain offered nothing. It was now broad daylight and we had nowhere to hide. Below us we could hear the buzz of the town as it awakened to the new day. In the distance we could see aircraft activity on the airfield. Finally we decided to lie down in a slight depression and wait out the long hours. We covered the kit as best we could. Diedies got up into a tree, while I made myself small between two packs. Da Costa, who had a Cuban peaked cap and FAPLA officer's insignia, would act as our deception.

Before long we could hear people coming up the mountainside, and soon groups of women and children swarmed across the open terrain in search of more vegetation to destroy. Da Costa and I made ourselves as small as possible, and managed to survive until mid-morning when two women with a string of children in tow walked straight into our hide. Da Costa had no choice but to get up and wave them away. They got such a fright that they dropped their bundles there and then and started running down the mountainside, howling.

This created a stampede, as the children tagged along screaming, not exactly knowing what the threat was. Da Costa ran after them and shouted for them to come back, trying to calm them down. But the damage was done. The whole bunch disappeared down the mountain in the direction of the FAPLA base at the bottom.

It was time for action. If we were caught in the open terrain we would be in serious trouble. We decided to withdraw deeper into the mountain and look for better cover. But first

Diedies ordered me to take pictures of the target area from the tree. I climbed the flimsy branches of the tree as high as I could and took a panorama of the airfield and the military bases below. Then we gathered our gear and moved in a westerly direction, taking care not to leave any tracks.

After about two kilometres we came unexpectedly upon a shallow valley with a thickly vegetated river line, where we found a thicket of bamboo reeds to hide in. It was isolated cover, offering no escape routes, but it was the best we could get. We carefully anti-tracked past the thicket and then dog-legged back into it. For an hour we kept vigilant watch on our track and listened for signs of a follow-up.

During the morning sched we informed the Tac HQ of our predicament. Boet Swart reacted promptly and sent a message that we should not take the risk, as the odds were clearly against us. However, he asked Diedies to make another sched in the afternoon, as he needed to consult with Pretoria before giving us a final decision.

We considered our situation and weighed up the pros and cons, contemplating whether the enemy would be on the alert and waiting for us. Our instincts told us the job was impossible: we would have to infiltrate a further seven kilometres through a populated area to the airfield, dodging numerous deployments of soldiers to get to our target, and then still penetrate the airfield defences to get to the fighter aircraft. Time would become a critical commodity.

A further challenge, now compounded by the lack of cover on the mountain, was the problem of getting out. We tried to work out a time schedule and a route from the target to the nearest cover. Now that we had seen the target area, we realised that we needed at least two hours under the cover of darkness to get to safety after laying the charges, which meant that we had to finish the job by 03:00 in the morning. This was cutting it fine, as we only intended to penetrate the perimeter by 01:00.

We discussed our options, knowing we could no longer watch the target for a few days as initially planned, because we did not know whether the women had reported us to the enemy or not. Finally we came to the conclusion that we would have to penetrate that night, against all odds. At least we had had a glimpse of the area and would be able to navigate accurately to the point of entry.

In the afternoon, during the final sched, there was a message from the GOC himself, who told Diedies to use his discretion, while reminding him that it was not worthwhile losing an operator, as it would have international consequences. This message increased the pressure on us; responsibility for failure would be placed squarely at our feet.

Finally, late in the afternoon, Diedies called us together again and said, "Hey, guys, there's only one way. We came here for a reason. What are we waiting for?"

Both Da Costa and I had also made up our minds by that time, and the job was on.

We decided to move the timeline forward to gain a few extra hours. By 16:00 Diedies and I started to prepare our penetration packs. We armed the charges and placed them in their individual pouches. Each of us had a water bag and emergency rations in the central pouch, together with the "Vernon Joynt glue" to stick the charges to the aircraft fuselages. Then we donned our penetration gear: the regular chest webbing with pistol; essential survival gear and emergency kit; Tacbe-499 radio beacons, strobe lights and infrared torches; sheepskin covers for knees and elbows; and night-vision goggles on the chest. I rounded off the picture with an Afro wig as headdress tied to my shirt.

Before last light we cached the packs in the bamboo thicket and made our way to the side of the mountain where we had ascended that morning. Da Costa moved along with a day-pack and the HF radio. The plan was that he would stay on the highest point of the mountain closest to the target. He would wait until first light the following morning and then, if he hadn't heard from us by 06:00, move back into cover. The bamboo thicket would serve as our emergency RV for a full twelve-hour period. At last light the following night Da Costa would start his exfiltration along the E&E route. If nothing had been heard from us by then, the E&E plan would be activated.

We parted quietly, shaking hands and wishing each other well. It was still light enough to maintain a steady pace down the slope. Halfway down the mountain Diedies stopped me and pointed up the mountain to the west. Against the last red light of the setting sun, on the crest of the next mountain ridge, was Christo Rei, the statue of Christ overlooking the town. It was a most striking sight, and, had it not been for the harsh reality of what we were about to do, the view might have been as if from a dream. Looking back at the experiences of that night, it was indeed a significant moment.

We made good time and reached the railway line by 20:00, and then moved along the vehicle track next to it. Once a group of soldiers passed us from the front, but Diedies exchanged some brief greetings with them and they didn't even bother to stop, obviously in a hurry to get to their destination. It was Saturday night, and we had bargained on some heavy partying among the various deployments of soldiers.

The Cubans were notorious for boozing and taking drugs, and the chances of them carousing with their FAPLA comrades were a hundred to one. Indeed, as we approached the Cuban base among the bluegum trees, we could hear loud Spanish music and drunken voices singing along. There was clearly a party on the go, and we decided to hang around and listen for a while. It was still early and we had to wait for the right time to penetrate. The merry mood continued, and we decided that the Cuban contingent posed no threat that night.

Following the railway line, we moved further east towards the target. At 23:00 we left the tracks and turned north on a bearing to the point where we wanted to cross the perimeter fence. I took the lead, as this was pure DR navigation and we needed to find the exact penetration point in the pitch dark. Furthermore, we needed to navigate accurately to the aircraft parked on the eastern apron of the runway, approximately 1 500 m north of the crossing point. Once the charges were placed, we would have to navigate back to the point of penetration.

We reached the perimeter fence by 23:30 and decided to stay put and listen for a while. Just as we had settled down, a patrol of six guards passed us on the vehicle track inside the fence line. They walked quietly, without talking, which meant that they would probably have picked us up had we started cutting the fence earlier. We gave them a few minutes to disappear and decided to cross before the next patrol came around.

During the rehearsals we had practised a technique in which Diedies would hold the fence down with his gloved hands while I did the cutting. This would prevent the taut wires from snapping with a twang that (as we knew from previous experience) could alert the whole of southern Angola. However, we soon discovered that the fence wire was not taut at all and that I could cut it alone – while covering the clipping noise with a cloth brought exactly for this purpose. Diedies moved back into the brush to listen for further patrols.

It was slow work, as each strand of cut wire had to be treated carefully. I did not want to make any noise, and the loose part of the fence had to be folded back and tied into position with the strands of cut wire to make it as inconspicuous as possible. By 00:30 the hole was ready, and we entered as quietly and as quickly as possible, careful not to leave any tracks on the ground. I folded the loose fencing back and tied it in its original position. In the dark it would pass as untouched, and we intended to use it as an escape in case of an emergency.

I navigated past some bunkers, possibly an ammunition store for the fighter aircraft ordnance, which we could not recall from the aerial photos. Once again I moved without the night-vision goggles, while Diedies scanned the night with his goggles to locate any sign of danger. I had my AMD at the ready, while Diedies moved with silenced sub-machine gun. We reached the hardstand by 01:00 without encountering any guards. Using the night vision, we could make out a MiG-21, barely 30 m away, crouched on the tarmac against the skyline, with the dark shape of another aircraft further off. We crouched down in the low bushes bordering the tarmac and quietly discussed our approach, as well as our escape route and emergency RV – which would be the hole in the fence where we had entered.

I would take the first aircraft, and then we would work our way down the line of fighters along the tarmac. We decided against the initial option of splitting up to reach more planes in the shortest possible time; in the darkness it was impossible to determine separate lines of targets for each operator.

Silently, with deliberate, slow movements, I slid my pack off and took out the first charge, together with a set of glue tubes. With practised fingers I undid the straps of the pouches and arranged the rest of the charges so they would be within easy reach. I felt strangely calm and ready for the task at hand. The overwhelming fear I had experienced in the past was absent. Instead, a sense of sheer dedication to get the job done had taken over. Deep inside I knew that I was exceptionally well prepared for this, and that the stakes were too high to fail.

Diedies positioned himself on the edge of the tarmac to listen out and warn me if anyone approached. Quietly, I slipped the charges back on and draped my AMD in a fireman's sling down the centre of my back to allow freedom of movement. Then I started the stalk towards the aircraft, silenced pistol cocked and ready in the right hand, charge in the left and night-vision goggles on my chest.

Ten metres from the aircraft I stopped to observe with the night-vision goggles. The darkness of the night was absolute, as we had hoped, but it also meant that I could not see below the fuselage. Not even with the beam of the infrared torch could the night-vision goggles penetrate the complete blackness under the belly of the MiG-21.

The night was dead silent. There was no sound from underneath the aircraft, nor could I make out any shape under the belly. I realised I needed to go lower to observe better. Slowly, and as quiet as a mouse, I eased forward to move into the blackness under the fuselage so I could look up against the ambient light of the sky.

I crouched to move in under the wing.

Then a voice pierced the silence of the night from the darkness underneath the plane. My worst fear was coming true.

"Quem são você ...?" The voice was hesitant at first, restrained with fear.

Then stronger: "Quem são você? [Who are you?]"

Then the all-too-familiar cocking of a Kalashnikov shattered the fragile night air, barely three metres away under the belly of the aircraft, cracking like a rifle shot in the darkness.

As so often before, I was confronted in the pitch dark with the penetrating, nerve-racking sound of an AK-47 being cocked in my face as I crept around in an enemy base. This time I also felt exposed against the night sky on the open tarmac. My own weapon was slung on my back; the silenced pistol in my hand was of no use if I couldn't even see my adversary.

The guard's voice now became bold and challenging: "Onde você vai? [Where are you going?]"

A second AK was cocked as if to bolster the challenge.

The long hours of rehearsals during those dark nights at Hoedspruit Air Force Base kicked in – instantly and instinctively. In a split second I had covered all the options in my mind – the shortest route to safety, the best course of action in case of white light, the most effective way to present myself as the smallest target possible. I mumbled drunkenly in Portuguese, automatically recalling the phrases we had rehearsed so often: "Companheiro, o que você faz . . .? [Comrades, what are you doing . . .?]"

At the back of my mind, I knew from previous experience that they would not open fire immediately. I knew my enemy was scared and uncertain. They could not see me clearly and had no idea who I was. I had to move now.

This was my only chance.

Keeping up my incoherent babbling, I pretended to stumble, and in the process ducked low down on the tarmac, reducing the clear target my silhouette presented against the skyline. Going low, I crawled back towards our RV, where Diedies waited anxiously. He had heard the encounter and was ready to move. We hurriedly discussed our options and waited for reaction from the guards. Although we could not see anything, we heard muffled sounds coming from the direction of the aircraft. Could we exploit their confusion and move round to the aircraft on the far side? Soon we saw movement against lighting in the distance, and then our minds were made up for us as a vehicle with a spotlight started moving along the tarmac in the direction of the hardstand.

We knew we had to get out of there. "The hole in the fence . . . We have to find the hole in the fence!" Diedies whispered.

I flicked the compass open and faced south to find the back bearing of our approach to the apron. As I fixed the compass reading and looked up at the night sky to find a suitable star, I saw the Southern Cross, or Crux. At that moment it was at the apex of its pathway through the sky, pointing vertically down and almost inviting us to follow it. We both looked up at the constellation of stars and realised it was the third cross in as many nights to make an unexpected but major impact on us.

It was strangely comforting – to follow the cross amid the commotion erupting around us. The enemy was now obviously looking for us, apparently strengthening their defences around the aircraft, as we could hear a number of vehicles moving into position. We moved quickly, following the Southern Cross and going low through the shrubs, once again avoiding the cluster of bunkers we had encountered earlier.

As we approached the perimeter, slowly and very quietly, Diedies again urged from the back: "You must find the hole, Kosie, we cannot cross over . . ."

We reached the road where the patrol had passed by earlier, but the reaction apparently hadn't reached this far. In the direction of the tarmac we could hear vehicles and voices as the enemy started coordinating their search. I brought my gaze down from the Southern Cross, and suddenly spotted the hole in the fence right in front of us, squarely on our bearing.

We wasted no time in getting through to the relative safety of the brush outside. In a matter of seconds we had passed through and soon were back at the railway line. Diedies insisted we sit down to reassess the situation. We were both immensely relieved as the realisation dawned how we had been led to a safe exit.

"What about the trains?" I whispered. "Shall we move along the railway line and blast some locomotives?"

Diedies didn't even consider it for a moment. "It's either the aircraft or nothing," he answered. "We don't want to spoil any future chances, and it wasn't the aim of the operation in any case."

For Diedies, second best would never do. The first principle of war – the maintenance of the aim – was non-negotiable. We either did the job we had come for, or we accepted failure. Much later, when we debriefed and carefully relived the operation, and once again weighed our chances of success, I realised how important was this principle. It would not have made sense to divert the focus to a lesser target with no bearing on the bigger war effort – especially in a situation where the defeat was tangible and the need to obtain some sense of achievement was overwhelming.

We moved quickly back along the tracks. With all the excitement we had not kept track of time, and we knew that we had to be out of the area before first light, as a search would certainly be launched. We once again passed the Cuban base, but this time it was dead quiet.

At the foot of the mountain we took a short rest. We scrambled up and tried to call Da Costa on the Tacbe. As we approached the point where we had left him the previous night, he suddenly answered, and we gave the "all clear" password. He appeared out of the darkness from under a tree and said he had been listening to us scramble up the mountainside, but was not sure whether it was own forces or not. After Diedies briefly filled him in on the night's events, he had the same reaction as I did: wasn't there any other target? Couldn't we stick around and find something else to destroy? Should we simply turn back empty-handed?

There wasn't any time to argue the point, and, even though it weighed heavily on our minds, we all knew withdrawal was our only option. Da Costa led the way to the bamboo thicket and we repacked our equipment after disarming the charges. He then set up the radio while we sorted out our kit. Dave Scales responded immediately when Da Costa sent the familiar clear call in Morse. He had clearly been sitting by the radio the whole night. Amazingly, despite the odd hour, we had a full signal.

Dave asked if he should "pull" us, triggering the two radios into frequency-hopping mode. Da Costa responded with a "dah-dit, dah-dah-dah" – meaning no. Dave then wanted to know if everyone was okay and whether we were together, to which Da Costa responded in the affirmative. Then came the question everyone at the Tac HQ anxiously wanted an answer to: "Successful with your enterprise?" To this our man answered with a very deliberate "dah-dit, dah-dah-dah".

After asking a few more questions Dave was satisfied that Da Costa was not communicating under duress. He understood that we were moving out and that the next sched would only be by late afternoon.

We donned our anti-track covers and moved out in a south-westerly direction, still deeper into the mountain. I set a fast pace, as we wanted to clear the immediate area where, in the morning, the enemy would likely search with helicopters. Every now and again we encountered small villages or farmsteads in the valleys, which we took care to avoid.

Where the terrain allowed, we spread out and anti-tracked as well as we could, considering the speed of our retreat. At some point we passed beneath a cluster of trees in what appeared to be some kind of an orchard. The familiar smell of fresh guavas filled my nostrils, and I reached up in the dark to touch some of the fruit. We stopped for a moment to grab a handful each. Most of the guavas were ripe and delicious. We munched down a few, and then stuffed our pockets before moving off again.

Like that time during Junior Leader training when I passed through an orange grove, it was an invigorating moment. It completely revitalised us in body and spirit. We were in high spirits after eating the guavas, in spite of our failure and the likelihood that every FAPLA and Cuban soldier in southern Angola was looking for us.

We moved on and just kept going, hour after hour. At mid-morning a shower of rain erupted. We made good use of the downpour, and were thankful that the few tracks we might have left were now obliterated. Only late that afternoon, when the rain had subsided and our clothes started to dry on our bodies, did we stop for a cup of coffee and something warm to eat. Far off to the northeast we could hear aircraft and helicopter movement, but, except for a few MiGs passing high overhead, no aircraft came any closer.

We travelled through most of that night, but were too tired to keep up the pace and slept for a few hours before daybreak. We found good cover on a rocky outcrop, and carefully listened throughout that day for any reaction. We knew the enemy would search further from their base, and would likely apply the tactic – which all three of us had encountered before – of dropping off soldiers to patrol dry river beds or set up OPs in areas where they could dominate the terrain.

On the third morning we reached the pick-up point, having walked more than 60 km in the rough terrain. We used the whole day to watch the LZ area, as we didn't want our helicopters to run into trouble. Our pick-up arrived just before last light and the three of us jumped into the first helicopter, as we were much lighter than during the infiltration. The pilot told us that Oom Boet Swart was on board the second helicopter and conveyed his greetings. We then settled into the job of watching out for enemy aircraft. I got a fright when I suddenly saw a fighter against the skyline, but the crew reassured us that they were our own Impalas escorting the helicopters.

Once we crossed the border into South West Africa, we veered left and headed for Ruacana, while the second helicopter had to go back to Opuwa to pick up the forward Tac HQ established for the pick-up. We refuelled at Ruacana and then flew back to Ondangwa where a feast awaited us at Fort Rev.

We sat down to our meal as the second helicopter came in, and waited for Oom Boet to make his grand entry. But then someone came rushing in to say there had been an accident – Boet Swart had been run over by a helicopter. We rushed out to the apron and found Oom Boet in a pool of blood on the tarmac. The doors had been opened while the aircraft was still moving and Boet, recognising the familiar lights of Fort Rev in front of him, thought they had come to a standstill. He descended the steps and fell – directly in front of the aircraft's wheel. Gees Basson, fortunately a very experienced pilot, pulled up immediately when he felt the obstacle, not realising it was Oom Boet. This ensured that Oom Boet was not crushed by the full weight of the helicopter.

Late that night, while standing with the other Small Teams operators around Oom Boet's bed in the sickbay at Ondangwa, I once again realised what an extraordinary individual he was. He had just undergone emergency surgery and was about to be evacuated to 1 Military Hospital in Pretoria. He was practically on his deathbed. We were called in to say our farewells, and stood with tears in our eyes, when Oom Boet suddenly spoke, in a faint but clear voice.

"Small brains, what are you doing here around my bed?"

Diedies replied that we had come to greet him, and he asked mischievously, "So where are you all going, then?"

During the extensive debriefing process back at Special Forces Headquarters, we spent many hours inventing and analysing ways of engaging enemy aircraft guarded by troops sleeping underneath them. Various devices that could be set up at a distance of 30 or 40 metres from the target were evaluated, but in the end the authorities decided there would not be a third Operation Abduct, as it was evident that the enemy were expecting us to attack their fighters, and the risk of penetrating an enemy airfield was now considered too high.

Operation Abduct might not have been a success, at least not in terms of its strategic aim, but for each of us – the three operators who had prepared for months, spent countless nights rehearsing and finally executed that mission – it was a personal success. In all aspects it was a classic Small Team deployment that tested our skills, endurance and dedication to the limit. In the end it turned out to be the life-changing experience I had expected it to be. I knew that in future I would prepare the charge and stalk that aircraft with the same dedication, any time, every time.

Epilogue

OOM BOET SWART, warrior extraordinaire, was flown back to South Africa and survived the ordeal. After numerous operations and a long recuperation process, he took up his post as second-in-command of 5 Recce once again. Exactly one year after the night of the accident, he was awarded the "Chopper-Stopper" trophy by Gees Basson and the chopper boys from 19 Squadron – a mounted scale model of the yellow wheel blocks used to immobilise a stationary helicopter.

Having spent every possible moment of his time on Small Team operations and training over the years, Diedies was, in his own words, "a grossly under-qualified major by Infantry Corps standards" and had some serious catching up to do. Thus, for almost the whole of 1988 he was on a course at the Army College in Pretoria while I took command of 54 Commando.

The Border War was not over yet. During the latter part of 1987 and throughout 1988 South African forces were tied up in operations Moduler, Hooper and Packer at Cuito Cuanavale in eastern Angola. In the west of the country, Cuban and FAPLA forces advanced steadily towards Ruacana in a concerted effort to exert pressure on Pretoria. Special Forces reconnaissance teams were in great demand, but due to an unforeseen setback I would be out of action for the rest of the war.

In 1988 a number of new Small Team candidates were recruited from the Special Forces training cycle. In the past, an operator had to have at least two years' experience with an operational commando before he could join Small Teams, but an exception was made to train newly qualified operators in an effort to bolster the strategic reconnaissance capability. We presented the reconnaissance course at 5 Recce, utilising the Small Team guys as instructors. One morning during PT I took the students up a rocky outcrop outside the base to give them an orientation of the terrain. When jumping from one cliff to the next, I lost my balance and fell. One of the students tried to catch me, but I took him down with me. Together we took a ten-metre fall down the cliff face.

Both the student and I sustained injuries that put us out of commission for months. Fortunately, there was a strong element of Small Team operators who could finish the training and take the newly qualified teams through their paces. After a few weeks in hospital and subsequent physiotherapy treatment, I joined the new teams on their first deployment. In June 1988 Dave Scales and I established a Tac HQ at Fort Rev, from where a number of deployments would be launched.

For me, this last Small Team deployment of the war turned out to be a most rewarding experience, since I had a "bird's-eye view" from the Tac HQ and could watch a perfectly planned and expertly executed recce mission unfold. A large Cuban deployment, which would serve as a staging point for an expected advance on Calueque, had allegedly been established at Techipa, west of the Cunene River. A Small Team consisting of Menno Uys and Mike Mushayi was tasked with determining the position and strength of the base.

The team was inserted by helicopter, and over the next two weeks executed a classic recce mission of the Cuban forward deployment. In the Tac HQ I had the opportunity to see Dave Scales in action as he guided the team along, sometimes encouraging, sometimes coaching, always remaining calm and collected, always in complete control. After every sched I plotted information from the team's message on the map, systematically piecing together the intelligence picture until we had a six-figure grid reference and details of vehicles and strengths. The team withdrew without the enemy becoming aware of their presence. The mission was a resounding success that embedded Small Team tactics, at least for me, as a tried-and-tested modus operandi.

At the end of 1988 Diedies left for 1 Recce in Durban. He was promoted to the rank of commandant and offered the position of OC 1.2 Commando, the Special Forces training unit on the Bluff. I was sad to see my friend and close colleague leave, but realised that times were changing and that one had to adapt. Although this move heralded the end of an era, it was not the end of our friendship, and over subsequent years we would still have great times together.

André Diedericks left an immeasurable impression on my life. He departed on his final solo mission in 2005 when he died of cancer. Diedies left behind his wife, Rietjie, and two beautiful daughters, as well as a close circle of Small Team comrades who will never forget him. The little honour I bring him in this book will never do justice to the unique character of my team mate and friend.

José da Costa remained with 5 Recce and played a major role in the selection and training of young operators, exerting extraordinary influence and shaping the lives of numerous Special Forces soldiers. In later years he was transferred to senior warrant officer positions outside Special Forces to gain broader experience, but was eventually brought back to the Special Forces School to apply his vast knowledge and experience there.

The Border War came to an end and so did the era of specialised deep penetrations behind enemy lines. But my own career in Special Forces was far from over. At the end of 1989 I was also transferred to the Special Forces School at 1 Recce in Durban, where I took command of the Special Techniques Branch. With a capable team of operators, I taught the skills I had accumulated over the years. We presented the reconnaissance course, sniper training, basic and advanced photography, and climbing techniques in both mountainous and urban environments.

As a runner-up prize for my excursions into all kinds of exotic places, I was awarded the Honoris Crux Bronze for bravery. Although I am not particularly boastful about this, as I have always known my fears and have never considered myself as an extraordinarily brave man, I treasure it because the citation was compiled and submitted by the man who to me was the personification of the ultimate warrior – my team buddy and mentor, André Diedericks.

In 1991 I took over command of the Training Commando from Diedies, a job I thoroughly enjoyed. Boet Swart had in the meanwhile retired and moved to Pietermaritzburg with his new wife, Sophia, a military historian and former lecturer at the Military Academy at Saldanha. One evening, while visiting them at their home, I paged through a photo album lying on a coffee table and noticed a photo of a very beautiful blonde girl who used to be a student of Sophia's.

I was intrigued, and inquired about her. Sophia told me her name was Karien and that she was still studying at the Military Academy. Even though she was a thousand kilometres away, I wasn't deterred. I drafted a letter, which Sophia offered to deliver. Before long Karien came to visit, and within one week of our first meeting we decided to get married – and have been so ever since!

In 1994 I was transferred to the HQ in Pretoria to oversee all Special Forces training. In 1999 and 2000 I did a brief stint at 4 Recce in Langebaan as second-in-command, but soon had to move back north as I was appointed Senior Staff Officer (SSO) Operations back at Special Forces HQ.

In 2003, after the closure of 1 Special Forces Regiment in Durban, it was decided to establish the Special Forces School as an independent and fully fledged unit at Murray Hill, north of Pretoria. I took command of the newly founded unit and established it as a nationally recognised training provider, of course with the help of a highly capable team. During that period, the Special Forces Training Cycle was accredited as a formal qualification, one of the very first in the new outcomes-based dispensation in the military.

In 2007 I was posted to the South African embassy in Saudi Arabia as Defence Attaché, an opportunity I still consider the culmination of a wonderful career, and in a sense a reward for the odd bit of hardship I had to endure in my 26-year Special Forces career!

But my small team story would not be complete if I didn't conclude with a "final mission". In 2010, while still stationed in Saudi Arabia, I decided to do a 200-km solo hike through the Rub' al-Khali, the "Empty Quarter" of the Arabian Peninsula – the largest sand desert and one of the most barren areas on earth. I wanted to retrace the steps of the great adventurers of yesteryear, the likes of Wilfred Thesiger and Harry St John Philby. This time, however, it would be done on foot with the old Small Team pack.

By this time I was married and the father of five-year-old twins, so I agreed, at Karien's prompting, to build in safety measures to increase my survival stakes. One week before the trip we drove deep into the desert and established a water cache at the halfway mark – at a place where some dilapidated infrastructure indicated that people had once lived there. At the time there was a real threat of religious fundamentalists targeting Westerners, but I took the risk of venturing alone into the desert.

On the way back from a 4X4 tour in the desert, I was dropped off with a 60-kg pack and set out on a bearing in the direction of Riyadh. I was carrying 40 kg of water, as the searing heat made one consume more than eight litres a day. To save water, I only hiked at night and in the very early hours of the morning, covering 28 km a day. On the first day I barely rested, because I soon realised that once I had put the heavy pack down I couldn't get up again. The terrain was flat, with no vegetation, and there was nothing I could use to pull myself up. So I just stayed on my feet and rested by bending over with the pack and leaning on my hiking stick.

Later on, once I hit dune country, it became easier to stand up by taking advantage of the slope of the dune. The disadvantage of the dunes was that I couldn't get the heavy pack up the steep incline of the leeway, the side of the dune sheltered from the wind. This was a problem especially at night, as I could not see the lay of the land and invariable found myself at the bottom of a dune I could not get across. I would then have to move back along the base of the dune to where the incline allowed me to cross.

It was tough and challenging, but in a sense the most rewarding experience of my life, as I again felt the exhilaration of mastering my old fears and becoming one with the desert around me. During the hike I relived every Small Team deployment, recalling both the hardships and joys, and buried the last of my fears in the sands.

Notes

1   The AMD-65 (in Hungarian: Automata Módosított Deszant 1965) was the upgraded paratrooper version (with folding stock) of the Russian AKM assault rifle.

2   On 19 December the US Senate passed a bill, known as the Clark Amendment, to force the White House to terminate its support of both UNITA and the FNLA. The senators were clearly not eager to be trapped on the side of the apartheid regime. See Scholtz, L, *The SADF and the Border War*. Tafelberg Publishers: Cape Town, 2013.

3   Sector 10 covered Kaokoland and Ovamboland; Sector 20 covered Kavango and Western Caprivi; and Sector 70 covered Eastern Caprivi.

4   Later, when the Zambians closed the door on SWAPO and demanded that they evacuate their training bases in the west of the country, the reconnaissance teams started operating exclusively within Sector 10's area of responsibility in Ovamboland.

5   Ultra-high frequency (UHF) was generally used for communications with jet fighters, while VHF was used with choppers and slower fixed wings.

6   FAPLA, or People's Armed Forces for the Liberation of Angola, originally the armed wing of the MPLA, was the Angolan regular army.

7   The Ratel, a six-wheeled infantry fighting vehicle (IFV), is still used by the SANDF.

8   The Buffel was a mine-protected infantry mobility vehicle (or troop carrier) that could carry a section of ten men.

9   EMLC, the Afrikaans acronym for "electrical, mechanical, agricultural and chemical engineering consultants" (Elektriese,

Meganiese, Landboukundige en Chemiese ingenieurskonsultante), became highly controversial due to its link with the Civil Cooperation Bureau (CCB) and allegations that it had manufactured different kinds of deadly devices to support the apartheid regime.

10 The PKM 7.62-mm general-purpose machine gun, developed in the Soviet Union in 1961, is still in wide use today.

11 Mine-protected infantry mobility vehicle originally developed by the CSIR.

12 Sawong was an acronym for "Suid-Afrikaanse Weermag Operasionele Navorsingsgebied", or South African Defence Force Operational Research Area.

13 The Heckler & Koch MP5 9-mm submachine gun is widely used by special operations and specialised law-enforcement units worldwide.

14 The Syncal 30 HF radio, as well as the base station radios, were equipped with "hopping mode", a function whereby the two (or more) radios would use the same code to synchronise and then run ("hop") through different frequencies while communicating. This was applied as an electronic counter-countermeasure (ECCM) to disrupt enemy listening-in or direction-finding devices.

15 Food that was pre-cooked, vacuum-packed and then irradiated at Pelindaba to last for months.

16 FAA, or Força Aérea Angolana, is the Angolan Air Force.